Vehicle for God
The Metaphorical Theology of Eberhard Jüngel

Vehicle for God

The
Metaphorical
Theology
of Eberhard Jüngel

by Roland Daniel Zimany

Mercer University Press

ISBN 0-86554-444-1

BX
4827
.J86
Z56
1994

MUP/H353

Vehicle for God.
The Metaphorical Theology of Eberhard Jüngel.
Copyright ©1994
Mercer University Press, Macon, Georgia 31207

✝✝✝

✝✝✝

Library of Congress Cataloging-in-Publication Data

Zimany, Roland Daniel, 1936–
Vehicle for God : the metaphorical theology of Eberhard Jüngel /
by Roland Daniel Zimany.
x+180 pp.   6x9" (15x23cm.).
Includes bibliographical references (pp. 149-72) and index.
ISBN 0-86554-444-1 (alk. paper).
1. Jüngel, Eberhard.
2. God—History of doctrines—20th century.
3. Metaphor—religious aspects—Christianity.
I. Title.
BX4827.J86Z56   1994
230'.044'092—dc20   93-47161

CIP

Contents

Preface

A new star has arisen on the horizon of Christian theology—Eberhard
Jüngel in Germany. Although in continental Europe Jüngel is regarded as
highly as such other Protestant theologians as Wolfhart Pannenberg and
Jürgen Moltmann, his works are only beginning to be discovered in En-
glish-speaking countries. One purpose of this book is to make his ideas
more widely known.

Fundamentally, Jüngel's theology combines the thought of Karl Barth
and Martin Heidegger. It does so by uniting Heidegger's approach to language and thought with the content of Barth's theology; and it is able to
do so because Jüngel has found that many of Heidegger's assumptions
are implicit in Barth's own thinking. As a result, Jüngel has advanced
beyond the New Hermeneutic of Gerhard Ebeling and Ernst Fuchs. In the
process, he has practically brought to a close the half-century-old debate
between the dialectical (Barthian) and existentialist (Bultmannian/early
Heideggerian) poles of kerygmatic theology, by incorporating both of
them into his own perspective.

Jüngel's synthesis is made possible by a surprising affinity between
Barth and Heidegger with regard to epistemology, hermeneutics, the role
of language, ontology, and the relation between philosophy and theology.
Both Barth and Heidegger appreciate the guiding principle of phenomenology and of the doctrine of revelation, namely, that only when the
object of our consideration makes itself known to us do we know it
correctly. Consequently, both have similar hermeneutical stances. Just as
Heidegger expects Being to make itself known through poetic language,
so Barth understands God to use the words of the Bible as vehicles for
Self-revelation in the present. And just as Heidegger denies that Being
can be encapsulated in objective language, so Barth argues that even
when the language of analogy is used to speak of God, it cannot be an
analogy that compares objects but only one that compares relations. With
regard to ontology, each man considers the nature of the ultimate
"object" of his study (God for Barth, Being for Heidegger) to be dynamic
and concrete, rather than static and abstract. Both men also agree that

human development does not follow the path of realizing a predetermined essence but that people form their individual human realities through existential involvement (although Barth finds the general contours of full humanity in Jesus Christ, whereas Heidegger accepts no such standard). Finally, both consider theology to be a phenomenological study, and both agree that theology should not be limited to any particular philosophical framework.

Jüngel's use of these concepts has caused him to claim that all theological language is, in a sense he will define, metaphorical, thereby setting the stage for God to make God's own truth known when God is spoken about. Jüngel understands the analogy of relation to serve as a vehicle for such revelatory movement (paralleling Heidegger's concept that Being moves toward thought, rather than vice versa), because he conceives of that form of analogy in such a way that when it is used, God can come to us directly. (In such an encounter, Jüngel considers God to be more similar to us than dissimilar.) Indeed, God's very Being is in coming (in movement within the Trinity and in revelatory word-events) and therefore is not to be found in the static conditions that natural theology examines. In coming as Word and through language, God destroys the distinction between transcendence and immanence, since language and its meanings include both. But then God is present while also being absent, since neither language nor action can capture reality fully.

Because God, as Love, relates to us and thereby originates love, God is reflected also in human love. Based on a study of human love, coupled with a phenomenology of the biblical account of the Cross and Resurrection, Jüngel develops a doctrine of the Trinity. The Father's abandonment of the Son to death, while the two remain united in the Spirit, requires a Trinitarian formulation of God, because of the multiplicity of "Persons" involved. Human love implies that God, as Love, is not selfless without being self-related and therefore that God's Being includes the conditions for internal relationship. The Cross also shows that Nothingness (a reality of particular interest to existentialism) is within God and that God can properly be expected to be found in the transitory. Indeed, in the light of the Resurrection, God is seen to be the unity of death and life for the sake of life.

Jüngel applies these concepts to the Barth-Bultmann debate by claiming that we *can* speak objectively about God (contra Bultmann) by speaking of corporate and individual experience of God (pro Bultmann), because in that experience God's relational Being is present among us. Against Barth, Jüngel approves of bringing to biblical interpretation perspectives from outside the Bible, but, pro Barth, he subordinates those perspectives to God's own use of them and to the Bible's self-understanding. By viewing the Bible metaphorically, Jüngel combines Bultmann's recognition that we necessarily bring presuppositions to our interpretation of a text with Barth's injunction that we trust God to appear as we immerse ourselves in the text.

In this present study, I do not attempt to explain Jüngel's more arcane pronouncements. Nor do I try to explore every profound or insightful chain of thought that Jüngel has pursued. Rather, I examine the basic categories of his thinking, the highlights of his theological concerns, and the major proposals that he has offered to date.

This report is based not only on Jüngel's published works but also on his lectures and seminars that I attended in Tübingen during the 1976–1977 school year. In addition, I am grateful to Professor Jüngel for the many opportunities he provided for consultation with him at that time and for subsequent correspondence.

This entire project had *its* roots in the efforts of Frederick Herzog, my dissertation advisor at Duke University, who called my attention to Jüngel in the first place and who paved the way for my initial meeting with him. For that assistance and other guidance, I am forever in his debt.

At the other end of the chronology of this project, I want to express my appreciation to Gregory J. Meyer, chaplain of Blackburn College, who read the manuscript and made suggestions that have enhanced the lucidity of this effort.

Abbreviations in the Notes

Titles of many works of course appear in shortened form following their first citation. Focal works frequently cited are subsequently identified by the following abbreviations. (See also the bibliography, below.)

BT   Heidegger, *Being and Time*
CD   Barth, *Church Dogmatics*
ET   English translation
Ger   (Original) German text
GGW   Jüngel, *Gott als Geheimnis der Welt*
GMW   Jüngel, *God as the Mystery of the World* (ET of GGW)
MW   Jüngel, "Metaphorische Wahrheit"
PJ   Jüngel, *Paulus und Jesus*
PT   Heidegger, *The Piety of Thinking*
T   Jüngel, *The Doctrine of the Trinity*
WF   Ebeling, *Word and Faith*
WM   Heidegger, "What Is Metaphysics?"

Chapter 1

Jüngel's Theological Development

During the third decade of the twentieth century, two thinkers, Karl Barth (1886–1968) and Martin Heidegger (1889–1976), irrupted onto the stage of theology and philosophy with such force that they have continued even to the present day to exert enormous influence on Christian theology— and not only within the German-speaking world from which they sprang. Although their thought holds several features in common, it laid the foundation for considerably divergent avenues of theological endeavor, due especially to the work of Heidegger's initial representative in the theological realm, Rudolf Bultmann (1884–1976).

Eberhard Jüngel sits on the shoulders of those giants. Instead of deserting the rich veins of thought they provided, he has continued to mine them, and in so doing, he has seen ways of bringing harmony to viewpoints that they had treated as incompatible, thereby strengthening the final product even further. The intellectual force and the creativity of both Barth and Heidegger/Bultmann are clearly evident in Jüngel's own theology.

The debate between Barth and Bultmann provided the dominant polarity of thought during Jüngel's formative years, and Jüngel's theology cannot be fully appreciated apart from an understanding of the issues involved. This book begins, therefore, by reviewing the highlights of that debate, while paying special attention to those features that contributed most fundamentally to Jüngel's own theological synthesis.

Before highlighting the debate, however, a brief summary of Jüngel's life and work will provide an introduction to the man himself.

An Academic Biography

Eberhard Jüngel was born on 5 December 1934 in Magdeburg, Germany, where Martin Luther went to school for a year as a young teenager. Jüngel's university studies took place primarily in Berlin with one of Bultmann's students, Ernst Fuchs (1903–1983), who influenced Jüngel's approach to the question of the historical Jesus, and whose hermeneutic of the New Testament stimulated his interest in the broader question of the function of language.[1] Jüngel was content to glean individual insights form Fuchs, rather than a systematic body of thought. Later, Jüngel also had discussions with Barth in Basel and with Heidegger in Freiburg and vicinity, while—at least for part of the time—he was an assistant to Gerhard Ebeling (b. 1912) in Zurich.

Jüngel received his doctorate in theology in 1961. From that time until 1966 he was an instructor (*Dozent*) in New Testament at the Kirchliche Hochschule (church seminary) in East Berlin.[2] He was ordained in 1963. He left what was East Germany in 1966 to become professor of Systematic Theology at the University of Zurich. Since 1969 he has been professor of Systematic Theology and Philosophy of Religion at the University of Tübingen.

His doctoral dissertation, entitled "The Relation of the Pauline Doctrine of Justification to the Teaching of Jesus," was published in 1962 as *Paulus und Jesus*. The subtitle calls it "An Endeavor to Make the Question of the Origin of Christology More Precise." In it Jüngel argues that the Kingdom of God (= the reign of God = God) can be present only in parables. He thereby preserves the difference between God and the world, and he also thereby indicates that the goal of human existence lies out-

---

[1]Although Fuchs claims that his own approach to language is not bound to the later Heidegger (Robert W. Funk, *Language, Hermeneutic, and Word of God: The Problem of Language in the New Testament and Contemporary Theology* [New York: Harper & Row, 1966] 49n.16), Jüngel reports that Fuchs pursued his hermeneutical studies in "conversation" with Heidegger and that those studies were essential for Jüngel's understanding of Barth. Eberhard Jüngel, "Der Schritt zurück: Eine Auseinandersetzung mit der Heidegger-Deutung Heinrich Otts," *Zeitschrift für Theologie und Kirche* 58 (1961): 122n.8.

[2]Berlin-Zehlendorf

side ourselves. Jesus, he says, enabled us to speak definitively about God's reign. We can do so because Jesus was determined by the kingdom of God: in him history and the eschaton were together; that is why Jesus can be called "the Christ" and can be the basis of faith. Moreover, his own behavior served to interpret his parables, so there is more than a minimal basis for relying on his disciples' understanding of them.[3] Jüngel also argues that Paul's doctrine of justification was derived from Jesus' life and teaching, which Paul interpreted to be one of preaching and bringing the eschaton, and that the teachings of both men were eschatological, in that both pointed to a new Being from outside oneself.[4]

Jüngel's postdoctoral work (*Habilitationsschrift*) was *On the Origination of Analogy in Parmenides and Heraclitus*.[5]

Among more than 175 books, articles, and book reviews that he has published to date, three others offer the most significant indication of the direction of his thought. The first of these, *The Doctrine of the Trinity: God's Being Is in Becoming*, was published originally in German under the title that serves as the subtitle in the English translation. It was presented as responsible discourse on the Being of God, in accordance with the views of Karl Barth. It is an insightful paraphrase of Barth's doctrine of the Trinity, in which Jüngel joins Barth in claiming that since we know God from God's revelation in Jesus Christ, what we see in Jesus has implications for God's own Being, because revelation is God's Self-interpretation. Since revelation is an event, God's Being also is not static but is event and therefore is in motion.[6] And since revelation shows that God enters into relations with human beings, God's own Being must be

---

[3]Eberhard Jüngel, *Paulus und Jesus: Eine Untersuchung zur Präzisirung der Frage nach dem Ursprung der Christologie*, Hermeneutische Untersuchungen zur Theologie 2, 4th ed. (Tübingen: J. C. B. Mohr [Paul Siebeck], 1972) 135-39, 279-83. Hereafter cited as PJ.

[4]PJ, 266-67.

[5]Eberhard Jüngel, *Zum Ursprung der Analogie bei Parmenides und Heraklit* (Berlin: Walter de Gruyter & Co., 1964).

[6]Here is Barth's contribution to the compatibility that Jüngel finds between Barth and Heidegger. Barth's hermeneutic of subjective revelation via the Word of God, Bultmann's "Word of address," the New Hermeneutic's "word-event," and Heidegger's notion of language speaking Being all depend upon a dynamic concept of ultimate reality, which all parties share.

in relation and, thereby, in Self-interpretation. But if (contrary to process theology) the sovereign God is not to be made dependent on people, as a result of the relation that God is in, then the relation that applies to God's Being must be essentially a relation within the divine life itself. This relation is asserted in the Trinitarian doctrine of God's three modes of being, a doctrine of a relationship in which God affirms Godself. And since a relationship is not static but is always becoming, it can be said that God's Being is in becoming, a becoming that is also a hermeneutic, that is, a Self-interpretation.[7]

Jüngel's most detailed work on language and its application to theology appears in an article published in 1974 and translated as "Metaphorical Truth: Reflections on Theological Metaphor as a Contribution to a Hermeneutics of Narrative Theology." In it he stresses the imaginative use of language, presents his claim that "the language of faith is metaphorical through and through," and uses principles from the later Heidegger and the New Hermeneutic (see below) to explain how God can address people through language, especially language pertaining to Jesus Christ, in whom God once came to expression.[8]

To date, Jüngel's most complex book is *God as the Mystery of the World: On the Foundation of the Theology of the Crucified One in the Dispute between Theism and Atheism*. In this book Jüngel deals with a wide range of interrelated topics. He explains the "Death of God" movement as the logical outcome of Descartes reducing God to a principle

---

[7]God's becoming and Self-interpretation occur within a double relation: first within God and then, self-consistently (and in that sense unchangingly), in a relation with the changing world. Eberhard Jüngel, *Gottes Sein ist im Werden: Verantworliche Rede vom Sein Gottes bei Karl Barth: Eine Paraphrase*, 3rd ed. (Tübingen: Mohr [Siebeck], 1976). ET (from 2nd ed.): *The Doctrine of the Trinity: God's Being Is in Becoming*, Monograph Supplements to the Scottish Journal of Theology (Grand Rapids: Eerdmans, 1976).

[8]Eberhard Jüngel, "Metaphorische Wahreit: Erwägungen zur theologischen Relevanz der Metapher als Beitrag zur Hermeneutik einer narrativen Theologie," in Paul Ricoeur and Eberhard Jüngel, *Metapher: Zur Hermeneutik religiöser Sprache*, Evangelische Theologie: Sonderheft (Munich: Chr. Kaiser Verlag, 1974) 110, 116. Hereafter cited as MW. Trans. J. B. Webster, in Eberhard Jüngel, *Theological Essays* (Edinburgh: T.&T. Clark, 1989) 58, 64.

"needed" in order to assure the continuity of the thinking human self.[9] He suggests that the possibility of acknowledging God at all is grounded in the fact that God addresses us through the language of the Bible. And he presents an interpretation of the phrase "God is love," by a careful examination of human love and by arguing that God's love is present in human love.

In human love, self-relatedness and selflessness are not contradictory, since a lover gets a new self (the result of a relationship with a beloved) only by self-giving. Therefore love, when it is strong because it has overcome the death of not-loving and the risk of being rejected, can confidently stream forth to encounter the world and draw it into the lovers' relationship. So, too, God's Being (as Trinitarian internal and external relation) is love, in that it gives itself by entering the transitoriness of the world and, especially as depicted in the Cross and Resurrection, conquers Nothingness for others, thereby letting those others participate in the new possibilities of God's life. The mystery of the world, which God is, is the history of God's acts of love for the world. These topics will be treated at length in subsequent chapters.

Jüngel's Theological Roots

The contours of the debate between Barth and the theological adapters of Heidegger are generally well known.[10] They deal chiefly with three issues: (1) the starting point of theology (divine revelation versus human experience and existentialist philosophy) and consequent hermeneutical

---

[9]Eberhard Jüngel, *Gott als Geheimnis der Welt: Zur Begründung der Theologie des Gekreuzigten im Streit zwischen Theismus und Atheismus* (Tübingen: Mohr [Siebeck], 1977) 146-203. Hereafter cited as GGW. ET: *God as the Mystery of the World*, trans. Darrel L. Guder (Grand Rapids: Eerdmans, 1983) 111-52. Hereafter cited as GMW.

[10]As a selection from the extensive secondary literature, treatment of the main issues may be found in William E. Hordern, *A Layman's Guide to Protestant Theology*, rev. ed. (New York: Macmillan, 1968); James C. Livingston, *Modern Christian Thought: From the Enlightenment to Vatican II* (New York: Macmillan, 1971); James D. Smart, *The Divided Mind of Modern Theology: Karl Barth and Rudolf Bultmann, 1908–1933* (Philadelphia: Westminster, 1967); and James M. Robinson and John B. Cobb, Jr., eds., *The New Hermeneutic*, New Frontiers in Theology 2 (New York: Harper & Row, 1964).

considerations; (2) the appropriate role of the historical-critical method; and (3) the question of what can be learned reliably from the Bible about God's will and the historical Jesus. Central features of Heidegger's thought both contributed to the debate and also affected Jüngel's thinking directly.

A review of all of these elements sheds light not only on the similarities between Jüngel and his predecessors but also on the differences between them. We shall consider those predecessors in discrete sections. The way in which Jüngel appropriates each thinker is summarized at the end of the section devoted to that individual.

Barth

Jüngel's theology generally is so compatible with Barth's that a summary of Barth's approach to theology can serve practically as introduction to Jüngel. That compatibility, which is discussed at the end of this section, resides in similar handling of how God can be known, of God's nature, and of the centrality of Jesus Christ for Christian theology.

In the second edition of Barth's commentary on the Epistle to the Romans, published in 1922, Barth issued a resounding "No!" to the liberal theology of the nineteenth century. Contrary to the conviction that knowledge of God could be pieced together from objective study of the Bible, of nature, of ourselves, or of other religions, he proclaimed that an absolute contrast exists between humanity and God. Søren Kierkegaard's phrase "infinite qualitative distinction" undoubtedly was in Barth's mind when he wrote, "The Gospel proclaims a God utterly distinct from men," who are "incapable of knowing Him."[11] God cannot be found either within nature or within ourselves.

Barth took the traditional doctrine of sin seriously and asserted that, as a consequence, human knowledge of God is always colored by self-interest and therefore is distorted and misleading. Accordingly, human beings cannot be the arbiters of the truth of God. Human conceptions of God "produced out of the treasury of the human mind" or "deduced from its deficiency" are bound to be wrong.[12] Yet as a sure sign of the pres-

---

[11]Karl Barth, *The Epistle to the Romans*, trans. Edwyn C. Hoskyns (London: Oxford, 1933) 28.
[12]Karl Barth, *Church Dogmatics* III/1, trans. J. W. Edwards, O. Bussey, and Harold Knight (Edinburgh: T.&T. Clark, 1958) 358. Hereafter cited as CD.

ence of sin, we insist on constructing a concept of God that limits God to the world that we comprehend, even though we accord to God the highest place in that world. "In so doing," Barth pointed out, "we place [God] fundamentally on one line with ourselves and with things. . . . Secretly we are ourselves the masters in this relationship."[13] In our arrogance, we assume that we must have the capacity to generate knowledge of God.

It is precisely this Cartesian self-certainty that Barth challenged. Blinded by sin, people do not understand even themselves. On what foundation, then, can they build an objective view of God?

Barth's answer was that God is present only in God's revelation. God's Being is in God's act. Accordingly, God is not an object in our world for us to study or to speculate about. For that reason, Barth set himself against all attempts by metaphysics to depict God's reality in a comprehensive system.[14]

Because God is a *revealing* God, Barth's doctrine of God was, from the outset of his *Church Dogmatics*, a doctrine of the Trinity. Only the Trinity could provide adequate conceptualization of God's reality as revelatory, because it provided for a dynamism of relationship within God with potential for "spilling over" into revelation. The Trinity also explained how revelation could be revelation of God's own Self, because it claimed that the same modes of Being that were present to human perception—namely, the Absolute seen in Jesus Christ in the convicting

---

[13]Barth, *Romans*, 44.

[14]Karl Barth, *Church Dogmatics* II/1, trans. T. H. L. Parker et al. (New York: Scribner's, 1957) 73; *Church Dogmatics* III/3, trans. G. W. Bromiley and R. J. Ehrlich (Edinburgh: T.&T. Clark, 1960) 389. Barth claimed to be opposed even to a metaphysical system based on the Bible (*Church Dogmatics* I/1, trans. G. T. Thomson [Edinburgh: T.&T. Clark, 1936] 156-58). There is some question, which Jüngel shares ("Womit steht und fällt heute der christliche Glaube? Elementare Verantwortung gegenwärtigen Glaubens," in *Spricht Gott in der Geschichte?* [Freiburg: Herder, 1972] 168), as to whether Barth himself was fully successful in avoiding metaphysical constructions. To this charge Barth probably would have replied that he was merely "spelling out" the content of God's revelation in Jesus Christ as he perceived it and that, in any case, whatever truth his writings contained about God would be dependent upon God to make clear to the reader.

power of the Holy Spirit—were the very same modes of God's very own Being.

Barth's faith that God is self-revealed centered on Jesus Christ. Consequently, the person of Jesus became the focal point of Barth's theology. Barth's thought moved not from timeless truths or from the general to the particular, but from the concrete person and work of Jesus Christ, and especially from his crucifixion and resurrection, which Barth understood as the restoration of the covenant between God and humankind. This Christocentrism led Barth eventually to speak of "the humanity of God," rather than of God as "the Wholly Other." He spoke of God's eternal will to be involved with humanity, to be with us while remaining distinct from us, and to express true Godness through the true humanity of Jesus.

History, therefore, was primarily the history of God's covenant of grace, made with Israel, frequently broken by Israel, and finally fulfilled in Jesus Christ. Using the covenant as an important hermeneutical too, Barth replaced the notion of a sacred history (*Heilsgeschichte*), recorded at face value in the Bible, by what he called "primal history" (*Urgeschichte*), that is, events within world history that both create and express the significance of history but that are seen only by faith.[15] Those "hidden" events are what Barth considered to be most important, because they contained the history of God's "dealings" with the world, a history that continues, as long as the ways of the world are not the ways of God. This view of the eschatological dimension in history enables Barth's theology to give serious attention to the recorded revelation of the Bible, while simultaneously directing its gaze forward to the new work that, in accordance with that already final revelation, the Holy Spirit continues to engage in.

Jüngel's writings show his theology to be in general agreement with Barth, while taking issue with him on occasional minor points. Jüngel is pointedly opposed to natural theology as the basis for Christian theology, and he accepts Barth's views on the need for God's Self-revelation. He, too, is careful to maintain a distinction between God and the world, while nevertheless claiming that God is involved with the world. He agrees that God *is* only when God acts, and he accepts the importance that Barth places on the doctrine of the Trinity as a means of conceptualizing that

---

[15]Smart, *Divided Mind*, 114-15.

understanding of God's dynamic reality. With Barth, he bases his theology on God's revelation in Jesus Christ, even to the point of finding God's godness in God's becoming human in Jesus. He also does not expect any future revelation to contradict or vary from the revelation that God has already provided in Jesus Christ. For Jüngel, too, theology seeks a pure understanding of God's reality and will. For him, too, theology is intended primarily for use within the Church.

Where Jüngel differs from Barth is in his willingness to consider what philosophy and linguistics can teach, either analogously or directly, and how they can be applied, especially as catalysts, to provide insight for theological understanding. This difference is significant enough to allow him to feel at home on Heideggerian soil; yet it is not so great as to estrange him from Barth's own theological interests.

Early Heidegger

Like Barth, Heidegger also challenged some of the assumptions of his day. Specifically, he charged that science and philosophy were based on unexamined presuppositions regarding the Being of their subject matter and regarding Being in general.[16] Ever since Plato, Western philosophy and science have been concerned with beings, he said, and have lost sight of Being itself—that is, they have failed to consider the question of what Being is.[17] And in their study of "whatness" (for example, Aristotle's *ousia*), of individual beings, they have mistaken their own objectivizations for Being itself, with the result that their notion of Being is one of a static presence.[18]

---

[16]Martin Heidegger, *Being and Time*, trans. John Macquarrie and Edward Robinson (New York: Harper & Row, 1962) 71-77. Hereafter cited as BT.

[17]BT, 268. Martin Heidegger, *Was ist Metaphysik?*, 11th ed. (Frankfurt-on-Main: Vittorio Klostermann, 1975) 25; ET: "What Is Metaphysics?" trans. R. F. C. Hull and Alan Crick in *Existence and Being*, ed. Werner Brock (London: Vision Press, 1949) 356-57; hereafter cited as WM. Idem., "Nietzsches Wort: Gott ist Tot," *Holzwege* (Frankfurt-on-Main: Vittorio Klostermann, 1950) 195-96. Idem., *What Is Philosophy?*, trans. William Kluback and Jean T. Wilde (New York: Twayne, 1958), 54.

[18]BT, 414; WM, 380-85, Ger. 43-46. Heidegger even charged his fellow existentialist, Jean-Paul Sartre, with adopting a metaphysical viewpoint and forgetting Being itself. Sartre said that existence precedes essence, but he

Heidegger called for a reopening of the question of what "Being" means.[19] Finding that Kant's transcendental logic "is an a priori logic for the subject matter [only] of that area of Being called 'Nature',"[20] he undertook, in his major work, *Being and Time* (1927; ET 1962), a more comprehensive approach to understanding Being. Because people are the only beings who know that they exist and who can raise questions about what Being is, he made a phenomenological study of *Dasein*, the Being peculiar to persons. He claimed that *Dasein* understands both its own Being and the Being of all other entities as well.[21]

Although we may always have an intuitive, prereflective understanding of Being, Heidegger contended, we truly become conscious of Being, for the first time, in the experience of a profound anxiety or dread (*Angst*) that does not have any apparent cause. It is then that we see that the entities within the world have no importance, either for supporting us or for threatening us.[22] Our existence is seen to be grounded beyond them, in Nothing; and only when we stop trying to ground ourselves in something else do we come to realize what Being is. The awareness of Nothing also drives home the fact that there is Being at all.

Since Heidegger's answer to the metaphysical question of the ground of human existence was "Nothing," he considered metaphysics to be ultimately useless. Metaphysics seeks to establish a foundation for human beings in an essence or in some other specific "something," and since Heidegger believed that that was not possible, he worked to develop a way of thinking that would overcome metaphysics.[23]

---

understood those words in terms of the metaphysical assumption that there is a clear distinction between them and that meaningful chronological priority can be given to one or the other. As Heidegger pointed out, however, "the reversal of a metaphysical phrase remains a metaphysical phrase." *Platons Lehre von der Wahrheit. Mit einem Brief über den "Humanismus"* (Bern: Verlag A. Francke AG., 1947) 72; ET: "Letter on Humanism," trans. Edgar Lohner in *Philosophy in the Twentieth Century*, ed. William Barrett and H. D. Aiken II (New York: Random, 1962) 280.

[19]BT, 1, 21-35.
[20]BT, 31.
[21]BT, 32, 362-63, 488, 34, 102.
[22]BT, 231-32.
[23]WM, 375, 380, Ger. 38, 43. "Die Überwindung der Metaphysik," *Vorträge*

Another aspect of traditional philosophy that Heidegger wanted to overcome was the chief contribution of René Descartes. In Heidegger's thought, the *Dasein* does not possess the self-certainty of Descartes's "I," because *Dasein* is projected into Nothing.[24] Although the early Heidegger looked to *Dasein*'s own resoluteness to effect its authentic existence, he nevertheless did not believe that *Dasein*'s Being stems from an individual's own decision. Rather, a person's Being precedes that person's thinking about Being.[25]

Moreover, Heidegger denied that there was such a thing as "an isolated 'I' without Others."[26] A subject is always in relationship with others, he said. It would not be the same subject if it were not in relationship. As a result, it cannot make a decisive distinction between its own, particular self and the others with whom it is in relation.[27] Heidegger saw *Dasein* as being related to all beings in such a primordial way that he could say, "Dasein in itself is essentially Being-with."[28] *Dasein*'s way of being includes, already, the things outside its decision-making capacity. *Dasein* automatically includes the world around a person.

Heidegger also taught that people are not to be understood in the same way as things are understood. A person is not a "what" or an enduring substance. A person does not have a predetermined essence. Rather, a person is a process of being related to everyone and everything that combine to constitute the person's inner and outer world. A person has possibilities, rather than properties, and those possibilities exist in time, are modified over time, and, indeed, are the origin of *Dasein*'s awareness of time (through the process of the potential becoming actual). Accordingly, people are not complete but are always forming their Being.

By being with others, however, we often are influenced by the common viewpoint of the masses of people, to the point that we are absorbed in their way of being and thus lose our own individuality and become in-

---

und Aufsätze (Pfullingen: Günther Neske, 1954).

[24]WM, 370, Ger. 35. *Dasein* also is always less than its full potential and unaware of it (BT, 330). That, too, keeps it from being fully certain of itself.

[25]BT, 32. *Dasein* is pre-*cogito* and thus is "pre-ontological," prior to thought (*logos*) about Being (*on, ontos*).

[26]BT, 152.

[27]BT, 143, 155.

[28]BT, 156; see also 33, 82, 92, 155, 160-61.

authentic. Heidegger called this condition "fallenness." In contrast to the Christian use of that term, however, he suggested that what we are fallen from is our own distinctiveness.[29]

Instead of acceding to the standards of others, not deciding for our own possibilities, and letting circumstances mold us, we can choose our own authentic possibilities, remain open to change in the future, and accept the risk of following the unique features of our own instincts and decisions. Such freedom occurs in resolute behavior, as resoluteness brings this "moment of vision" to the present by orienting *Dasein* according to the potential of its own interests and according to the truth in its past. Resolute behavior becomes possible under three different circumstances, namely, in the face of anxiety, in anticipation of literal or figurative death, and in response to conscience.[30] When resolute behavior occurs, we become aware of who we really are.

From Heidegger, Jüngel gets his appreciation of phenomenology. He also takes seriously Heidegger's insistence on the reality of Nothingness. He accepts, in addition, the "Being-with" nature of human being, along with the changing and developing character of existence. But he warns against "a theological usurpation" of Heidegger's thought.[31] Often he is content with adding a Christian meaning to the conclusion reached by a Heideggerian train of thought, thereby showing a relationship between the two points of view, while, at the same time, not deriving one from the other.

Jüngel does not endorse Heidegger at every point, however. He interprets the early Heidegger to hold that existence is performance, and with that characterization he disagrees. He understands Heidegger's concept of *Dasein* to pertain to a person drawing existence from the world and its Being alone, with no reference to God. In that view, there is no difference between human being (even when it is open to others) and nature. As far as Jüngel is concerned, such a *Dasein* can do no more than ask itself the question about Being. He also shares Bultmann's objections to Heidegger's early thought, which are discussed in the next section.

---

[29]BT, 68, 164-66, 220, 225, 264.
[30]BT, 387, 232, 343, 369, 394, 307-308, 353, 333.
[31]Eberhard Jüngel, "Vor Gott schweigen? Theologie in der Nachbarschaft des Denkens von Martin Heidegger," *Frankfurter Allgemeine Zeitung*, 25 May 1977, 25. (The title Jüngel submitted to the editor was "Vo*n* Gott schweigen?")

Bultmann

Heidegger's philosophy was brought into Christian theology by Bultmann, a biblical scholar whose methods of interpreting the Bible inevitably had theological implications, many of which brought him into conflict with Barth. Bultmann's position in the debate influenced Jüngel both directly and indirectly. Jüngel accepts some of Bultmann's theology directly and has, as a consequence, been stimulated to attempt to resolve the traditional conflict that it generated with Barth. Indirectly, some of the positions of Jüngel's closest teacher were developed as alternatives to specific theological steps taken by Bultmann.

Demythologizing and the Historical Jesus. Bultmann denied that the "modern mind" was capable of grasping God as an object of study. He also saw a need to translate the Christian message in a fashion compatible with the contemporary view of the world. And since the New Testament was replete with an outmoded, mythological view of the structure of the universe and of pivotal events of the world's past and future, he offered his now-famous program of "demythologizing," to arrive at the message hidden in the husk of the first-century worldview. In the words of his initial proposal,

> We are . . . bound to ask whether, when we preach the Gospel today, we expect our converts to accept not only the Gospel message, but also the mythical view of the world in which it is set. If not, does the New Testament embody a truth which is quite independent of its mythical setting? If it does, theology must undertake the task of stripping the Kerygma from its mythical framework, of "demythologizing" it.[32]

---

[32]Rudolf Bultmann, *Kerygma and Myth: A Theological Debate*, vol. 1, ed. Hans Werner Bartsch, trans. Reginald H. Fuller (New York: Harper & Row / Harper Torchbooks, 1961) 3. See also *Jesus Christ and Mythology* (New York: Scribner's, 1958) 36. The preached message (*kerygma*) of the primitive Christian church was a mythological mixture of Jewish Messiah-King, Son of man, and two aeons; of a savior-god who dies and rises again; and of the Gnostic redeemer who descends from the realm of pure spirit and reascends. Such imagery, understood literally, has no meaning to the modern, educated mind. If it were to make sense at all, its truth would have to be found behind its figurative or mythological forms. Mythological language was not objectionable in itself, however, so long as it was not interpreted as conveying literal information about God and the world.

Bultmann believed that God deals with the world paradoxically and not as part of an objectifiable "history of salvation" (*Heilsgeschichte*) or of a routine interaction between a natural and a supernatural order of things. That belief provided additional grounds for demythologizing the Bible.

Bultmann's understanding of the paradoxical nature of God's presence derived from his career as an originator and perfector of scholarly tools for studying the New Testament. From that work, he concluded that is was erroneous to read the Bible as a history of salvation, because to do so would be to understand literally what was really transcendent and therefore not objectifiable. He distinguished between the everyday realm of human culture and the realm of religious faith, and he said that the objective, positivistic historian, who is interested in what "actually" happened, is limited to working with data from the realm of culture only. But data from that realm do not include the transcendent. Consequently, he considered history as recorded in the Bible to be superfluous to faith.

The New Testament writers had placed Jesus within *Heilsgeschichte* and its *kerygma*, with the result that the historical Jesus has been totally obscured by them. From that standpoint, Bultmann contended that we must never expect to learn what the flesh-and-blood Jesus was actually like.[33] Any attempts to do so would be just to read our own predilections into the texts, as Albert Schweitzer had shown that the authors of the liberal nineteenth-century books about Jesus' life had done.[34] Moreover, God was not imparting Godself in the events of Jesus' life; nor does the New Testament provide a picture of the authentic nature of human beings.[35] Consequently, learning about the historical Jesus was not important. For Bultmann, the possibilities of human existence derived not from the *content* of Jesus' life but from faith *that* God had revealed authentic existence in the death and resurrection of Jesus Christ: not from the "what" but from the "that" of Jesus Christ.

---

[33]Rudolf Bultmann, "Jesus and Paul," in *Existence and Faith: Shorter Writings of Rudolf Bultmann*, ed. and trans. Schubert M. Ogden (Cleveland and New York: World Publishing / Meridian Books / Living Age Books, 1960) 184-96.

[34]Albert Schweitzer, *The Quest of the Historical Jesus: A Critical Study of Its Progress from Reimarus to Wrede*, trans. William Montgomery (repr.: New York: Macmillan, 1961 =1910).

[35]Bultmann, *Kerygma and Myth*, 1:27.

An Existentialist Hermeneutic. Drawing on Heidegger's position that every problem is approached from a particular perspective related to the specific situation to which an investigator or inquirer is tied,[36] Bultmann argued that all biblical interpretations are determined by the interests that the reader brings to the text and are based on principles and conceptions that are presupposed.[37]

Bultmann believed that the right question to ask the Bible was "the question of human existence" and of human anxiety, and Heidegger's existentialist philosophy provided the language with which to raise the question.[38] He suggested that the Christian notion of not having an abiding city here on earth was simply being restated in more modern terms by Heidegger's claim that *Angst* reveals that we are "not at home" in the everyday world. Indeed, he said that

> Heidegger's existentialist analysis of the ontological structure of being would seem to be no more than a secularized, philosophical version of the New Testament view of human life. For him the chief characteristic of man's Being in history is anxiety. Man exists in a permanent tension between the past and the future. At every moment he is confronted with an alternative. Either he must immerse himself in the concrete world of nature, and thus inevitably lose his individuality, or he must abandon all security and commit himself unreservedly to the future, and thus alone achieve his authentic Being. Is not that exactly the New Testament understanding of human life?[39]

From that perspective, Bultmann claimed that God can be found only when existence brings a crisis in meaning, as a result of which one decides for one's true self by a leap of faith.[40] For him, authentic life is based on faith in the grace and forgiveness of God. This faith can result

---

[36]BT, 191, 265, 359-63.

[37]Rudolf Bultmann, *Essays: Philosophical and Theological*, trans. C. G. Grieg (New York: Macmillan, 1955) 240ff., 252ff.; *History and Eschatology* (Edinburgh: University Press, 1957) 113ff.; *Jesus Christ and Mythology*, 46-52.

[38]Bultmann, *Kerygma and Myth*, 1:192; *Jesus Christ and Mythology*, 55.

[39]Bultmann, *Kerygma and Myth*, 1:18, 24-25.

[40]Rudolf Bultmann, *Jesus and the Word*, trans. Louise Pettibone Smith and Erminie Huntress Lantero, new ed. (New York: Scribner's, 1958) 87, 89, 102-103, 154; *History and Eschatology*, 152, 155; *Theology of the New Testament*, trans. Kendrick Grobel, 2 vols. (New York: Scribner's, 1951, 1955) 1:9, 21-22.

in our opening ourselves freely to the future as a gift from God, rather than trying to create our own security by clinging to tangible realities or to the judgments of others. We are to trust in God alone. Such faith frees us from anxiety.

Bultmann's existentialist focus on the individual person led to a train of thought that resulted in the claim, contrary to Barth, that nothing could be said objectively about God. We can speak only subjectively about what God does in creating faith and a new self-understanding for the individual. Whereas Barth's theology focused on the Word to which faith responds, Bultmann focused on the other side of the (same) coin, namely, on the fact of faith that responds to the Word. Bultmann taught that doctrines are not true in the abstract, but only when they are experienced existentially.[41] Similarly, God does not act in events that a person can view objectively. Rather, God acts only when a person is drawn into an event in such a way that that person comes to believe God has acted.[42] In an important sense, therefore, "theological thoughts are the explication of man's understanding of himself."[43]

Deviation from Heidegger. Bultmann deviated from Heidegger in at least three related ways. First, Bultmann claimed that analysis of the human predicament does not fully reveal all human possibilities. Second, there are paradoxical, surprising, or at least not-self-evident characteristics of what it means to be fully human that Christian faith understands to be "given." Third, people are not rulers over their own Being. Therefore, they cannot save themselves. Although a person's "authentic nature is not an endowment of creation," neither is it "a possession at his own disposal."[44] Since all people are blinded by sin, they do not have the power to question themselves objectively. Consequently, they cannot identify their authentic selves and radically change what needs to be changed. People are in need of being set free from this blindness, because the faith to "see" is not part of their natural disposition.

This setting free is and must be the work of God, who alone can question us, our authority, and our understanding of ourselves. God does this questioning primarily through the *kerygma*, the preaching of Christ

---

[41]Bultmann, *Kerygma and Myth,* 1:76-77.
[42]Bultmann, *Jesus Christ and Mythology,* 68.
[43]Bultmann, *Theology of the N.T.,* 2:249.
[44]Bultmann, *Kerygma and Myth,* 1:29; see also *Theology of the N.T.,* 1:232

crucified and risen. Jesus' entire life was only a preparation for the revelation of God in the Church's preaching of the Cross. God confronts us also in the biblical text, so that what is normally taken to be the object (namely, the text) assumes the role of questioning us, the subject. The Bible not only shows me a new way of understanding my existence; it also addresses me. In his later years, Bultmann tended to expand the sources of our contact with God, so that he could say that "the revelation of God is realized . . . in the concrete events of life,"[45] and not only in the Bible and in the preaching of the Church.

All of these points of contact become eschatological moments, in which we experience the intangible reality of God's forgiveness and grace and in which we come to know the demand of the Ultimate. Through them we see ourselves differently: Authentic existence is revealed: We get a new self-understanding.[46]

Comparison with Jüngel. Unlike Barth, Jüngel can understand Bultmann's claim that to talk about God is to talk about human being, because Jüngel believes that "confrontation with the truth of one's own being is the place of theologically responsible talk of God."[47] Theology is not the study of one's own being; but it also is not a formulation of God-in-the-abstract. It occurs responsibly, says Jüngel, only when it derives existentially from one's own encounter with God. Jüngel does not limit that encounter to the matter of one's individuality or authenticity, however.

Also like Bultmann, Jüngel makes full use of scholarly tools for studying the Bible, in order to establish the setting from which the text can speak metaphorically. Jüngel's interest in metaphor also allows him

---

[45]Bultmann, *Jesus Christ and Mythology*, 58. Recall, also, what was said about our seeing God acting in events, albeit only by faith.

[46]Even if Bultmann followed only Heidegger's view of *Dasein*—to say nothing of the Christian view—a new self-understanding would not be limited to the *cogito*, since *Dasein* includes its environing context of nature and people, and since the way in which *Dasein* sees *its* world is the way in which it sees the world at large. Accordingly, to understand oneself differently would also imply understanding one's world at large differently, attended by different behavior toward the world at large, as well.

[47]Eberhard Jüngel, "Redliche von Gott reden: Bemerkungen zur Klarheit der Theologie Rudolf Bultmanns," *Evangelische Kommentare* 7 (August 1974): 475.

to acknowledge the presuppositions that Bultmann said everyone brings to the interpretation of Scripture, because metaphor requires the active engagement of the reader's imagination, thereby providing a means of both engaging and transcending presuppositions.

Unlike Bultmann, Jüngel considers the text of the entire Bible—Old Testament and New Testament—to be capable of speaking to us today, metaphorically. Also unlike Bultmann, he is willing to look for traces of the historical Jesus in the New Testament, in order to find clues to the Kingdom of God, which he considers to have been present in Jesus in parabolic form. Jüngel's God is *always* potentially present, not only at the point of human decision for authenticity; but the time and place of God's more "substantial" presence lies in the mystery of God's freedom. Bultmann had said, "We cannot speak of what God is in Himself but only of what he is doing to us and with us."[48] Jüngel, like Barth, is willing to speak about God, because he claims, along with Barth, that speech about God can be true, because God can reveal its meaning.

Later Heidegger

Heidegger may have been impressed by Bultmann's refusal to declare that people are fully the captains of their souls. In any case, not many years after the publication of *Being and Time*, a different theme and tone began to appear in his writings.[49] He stopped emphasizing determination

---

[48]Bultmann, *Jesus Christ and Mythology*, 73.

[49]It is not easy to identify when Heidegger's turn in thought began, because some of his earlier writings were reworked before they were published, and some of his collected works contain essays that were written at various times prior to their publication date. Signs of the change occur in the 1930s, however, in *What Is Metaphysics?*, *On the Essence of Truth*, and "Hölderlin and the Essence of Poetry." It has been suggested that Hitler's manner of taking charge of reality may have induced Heidegger to modify his original orientation (James M. Robinson, "The German Discussion of the Later Heidegger," in *The Later Heidegger and Theology*, ed. James M. Robinson and John B. Cobb, Jr., New Frontiers in Theology 1 [New York: Harper & Row, 1963] 8-9n.26). Some scholars insist that Heidegger's *Kehre* (turn) was a radical departure from the position he took in BT. (For discussions of this debate, see *The Later Heidegger*, 13-16, and John Macquarrie, *Thinking about God* [New York: Harper & Row, 1975] 191-93.) It does seem that his later viewpoint was not what he had in mind when writing parts of his earlier works. While that may be true, Heidegger insisted that

to be oneself by resolutely taking hold of that existence that lies before one. Instead, his focus shifted to a more passive orientation in *Dasein*, to openness to Being, to the receptive "letting be" of what is. Although in *Being and Time* he had already acknowledged that Being was beyond the categories of thought, it was only in his later writings that he drew the conclusion that, since Being is not an existing thing that can answer straightforwardly the question of *what* Being is, it can only be evoked and experienced. His later work looked to poetry and mystical language as ways of expressing the truth about Being—or better, as ways of letting Being express the truth about itself. Meaning was to be given to us rather than obtained by us.

But while he no longer depicted the human being as resolutely standing in Nothing's place, *Dasein*'s role was by no means one of complete passivity, either. Heidegger characterized *Dasein*'s new status with the following words: "man is not the master of beings. Man is the shepherd of Being."[50] "Care" had become care for Being itself, not simply for *Dasein*'s own concernful purposes. And a distinction was drawn between that of master, who imposes control, and that of shepherd, who responds attentively and who guides or cultivates what is found (sheep, Being), in accordance with its own inner dynamic.[51] Being may be given, but only by sensitive and active human involvement is its potential brought to realization.

Heidegger's concern with responsive shepherding of Being—rather than with mastery of beings—was accompanied by his opposition to the notion that truth can be under the control of human judgment (*adaequatio*

---

his change was, in any case, a logical consequence of his earlier thinking and that his later work could be understood only by way of his earlier work. (William J. Richardson, *Heidegger: Through Phenomenology to Thought* [The Hague: Martinus Nijhoff, 1963] xxii. Heidegger, "Humanism," 280, Ger. 72.) Other scholars, including Jüngel and Macquarrie, endorse Heidegger's claim. (Jüngel says that BT does not offer an interpretation of human existence but is really about what the word "Being" has to say. "Nicht nur eine geographische Bestimmung," *Evangelische Kommentare* 1 [August 1968]: 468.)

[50]Heidegger, "Humanism" 281, 288, Ger. 75, 90.

[51]This interpretation of "shepherding" is based on two of Heidegger's essays in *Vörtrage und Aufsatze*, viz., "Das Ding" (185) and "Bauen, Wohnen, Denken" (147-51).

intellectus et rei) in a universally demonstrable way. As an alternative, he said that *"the essence of truth is freedom,"* which "reveals itself as the 'letting be' of what-is," so that what-is can make itself known.[52] This is the direct opposite of imposing presuppositions onto what-is. It is also the direct opposite of a static concept of truth as universally evident. Instead, it provides for a concept of truth as event, according to which something is true only when a person discovers or recognizes it to be true. Heidegger then correlated letting-be with concealment, because the act of revealing, which can occur when something is "let be" (that is, permitted to make itself known, apart from the presuppositions that the human intellect brings to it), also conceals other things. It conceals them by directing our attention away from them or by merging them into what is revealed, so that they do not stand out (in our perception) in their own right. Heidegger concluded that truth includes a mystery that hides.[53]

Despite *Dasein*'s continuing role, Heidegger's new emphasis was on Being as ultimately the master of the situation in which people find themselves. Within their situation, people feel "tossed about." Hence, Being is prior to our action. It is the context of our activity and the momentum that is already present, conditioning that activity.

Given the priority of Being, a change had to be made in the relation between language, thought, and Being. Instead of starting with words that have specific meanings, using those words to form thoughts, and then following those thoughts to an understanding of Being—which understanding would be predetermined by the meanings we gave to the words with which we started—Heidegger called for a reversal of that sequence. In that reversal, Being is the foundation of our thought, which then responds by forming words that reflect the stark reality of that Being. The point of the reversal is to free ourselves from traditional ways of thinking, in order to enable our minds to develop words that will give us new perspectives on reality or (what is the same thing) will bring new "dimensions" of being to our attention. As Heidegger said, thinking seeks the word in which Being can "become language" and thereby be communicated.[54]

---

[52]Heidegger, *Existence and Being*, 330, 332-33.
[53]Ibid., 350.
[54]WM, 389-91, Ger. 49-50.

Another of Heidegger's claims, therefore, was that language can "speak Being" or can make us aware of reality in fundamentally new ways. But in making that claim, he was not referring to everyday thought and language, but to those occasions when new words, phrases, or metaphors are coined, or when conventional language is treated figuratively. The language he selected as most revelatory of being was poetry, which is characterized by the absence of fixed meanings and by an appeal to the imagination. Such—and similar—language interprets its own meaning, he claimed (as did Ebeling and Jüngel after him), when the Being that it bespeaks "resonates" with the hearer's own experience of Being, or is incorporated meaningfully into the hearer's worldview, or generates new insight or awareness.

From the later Heidegger, Jüngel has derived his understanding of truth as the dynamic revelation of and "letting-be" of what-is. More importantly, from Heidegger Jüngel also gets his understanding of the value of language for revealing the Ultimate. When Jüngel claims that the parables reflect Jesus' own (God-determined) Being, he is applying Heidegger's explanation of how Being expresses itself in language. When considering how *God* addresses us through language, however, Jüngel applies that reasoning only analogously. He argues, simply, that the fact that language can open us to spheres of understanding and meaning that the language had hitherto neither denoted nor connoted—that is, the fact that language can reveal Being—suggests that it is also possible for God's reality to come to our awareness through language. Language, therefore, can be a vehicle of direct divine revelation. As a theologian, Jüngel does talk about God, whereas Heidegger generally does not.

The New Hermeneutic

Whether or not Heidegger had learned from Bultmann, it was clear that Bultmann was affected little by Heidegger's turn in thought. Bultmann continued to depict God as being real only in the call for decision. He also continued to understand the Bible only within the framework of existentialism and to view a person's particular historical context as having no theological significance. It was left to Bultmann's students, therefore, to modify what they regarded as extremes in his position. They did this, in part, by reexamining the nature of language, along the lines that Heidegger had come to suggest. Fuchs and Ebeling took the lead in this connection. To a considerable extent, Jüngel followed in their path.

After noting some of the similarities in their thought to that of Bultmann, similarities that Jüngel shares, I shall consider the directions in which they moved.

Comparison with Bultmann. One characteristic Fuchs and Ebeling have in common with Bultmann—and with Barth and Jüngel, for that matter—is that they are all "Word of God" theologians. The foundation of their theology lies not in metaphysics or in nature but in God's Self-revelation by means of "the Word." While Bultmann said that Jesus rose into the *kerygma*, Fuchs and Ebeling say that Jesus inaugurated a word-event that happens in the Church's proclamation. Knowledge of God comes not from words about God but from God's own speaking to us. Past revelation is true only when it becomes true through personal encounter with God as the Word, speaking through—and sometimes in spite of—the preaching of the Church.[55] Fuchs adds that God chooses to be as word: God is not static, God addresses us—a notion that, from a human perspective, is not very different from Barth's claim that God's Being is in act. But the scope of what Fuchs means by "language" extends beyond talking to action, as well, since even a simple movement expresses something.[56]

For Fuchs and Ebeling, however, the Word does more than simply call us to a decision. That call is the sole function that Bultmann ascribed to the Word, as they interpret him. In contrast to Bultmann, Fuchs says that the word in which Jesus meets us not only criticizes our existence but also supports it. Then both he and Ebeling make a point of claiming that God's call *enables* us to do what it calls us to do.[57] God's Word of address is an *empowering* word. Not only does it speak, but it enables its hearer to speak of God, as well. Fuchs characterizes the faith that it generates as "freedom in and for the Word" (*Freiheit zum Wort*), an expression that Jüngel borrows occasionally.

---

[55]Gerhard Ebeling, *Word and Faith*, trans. James W. Leitch (Philadelphia: Fortress, 1963) 352, 193, 313, 36. Hereafter cited as WF.

[56]Ernst Fuchs, *Hermeneutik*, 4th ed. (Tübingen: Mohr [Siebeck], 1970) 71, 131.

[57]WF, 29. In view of the fact that Bultmann considered the response to God's Word (the event of faith) to be an eschatological event, i.e., a gift of God, it is questionable whether Fuchs and Ebeling advance beyond him at this point.

What the Bible Provides. Fuchs and Ebeling agree with Bultmann that if the Bible is seen only as information about God's revelation, then the ongoing character of revelation within history is misunderstood. Indeed, the very nature of revelation is denied. They agree, too, that people do not have the power to escape the present, "fallen" grounding of their existence. And they agree, consequently, that the biblical text does not exist primarily for us to interpret. Instead, its value lies in its address to us in our time and situation, an address that interprets *us* and our understanding of ourselves, calling us radically into question. But both of them have gone beyond Bultmann—in the direction of Barth—in teaching that the biblical text also *provides* us with a new understanding of ourselves.

Hence, Fuchs teaches that we can have some idea of what Jesus' way of life was and is, because Jesus' behavior during his earthly life was a model of faith, which was reflected in his teachings and which generated similar teachings on the part of his disciples. It does not matter, therefore, whether we can certify a particular teaching as coming from Jesus' lips. To the extent that a consistent model of faith and behavior can be found in the Gospels, there is at least a reasonable presumption that it is based on the historical Jesus, whose reality is presupposed in the extant accounts of his teachings and acts.[58] Accordingly, not only is the historical Jesus interpreted *by* the *kerygma*, but there are enough vestiges of the historical Jesus in the New Testament for *us* to be able to use them, in turn, to interpret the *kerygma*.[59]

Fuchs appreciates Bultmann's program of demythologizing as an effort to liberate talk of revelation from all forms of speculative, metaphysical worldviews, so that revelation can be understood as God's address to us. Finally, however, Fuchs approves of mythological language, saying that the New Testament used it to get to the depths of the historical revelation, and suggesting that the actuality of the founding event of Christian existence can bring itself to expression through such language. For that reason, the mythological language of the New Testament itself demythol-

---

[58]Ernst Fuchs, "The New Testament and the Hermeneutical Problem," in *The New Hermeneutic*, ed. Robinson and Cobb, 123.

[59]Ernst Fuchs, *Studies of the Historical Jesus*, trans. Andrew Scobie, Studies in Biblical Theology 42 (London: SCM; Naperville IL: Allenson, 1964) 28, 30-31.

ogizes the Bible, by evoking a truth that can speak to us directly and specifically at a particular moment and that therefore is more profound than the conventionally understood timeless truth of myth.[60]

New Approach to Interpretation. The new approach to interpreting the Bible that Fuchs and Ebeling developed is based on the view that human beings are conditioned by language and could not develop without it. The reality that a person perceives is colored by the traditional meanings of the language and culture in which that person lives. That language has been in the world, helping to shape it, taking on meanings, and expressing the mystery of reality, long before any particular person was born. As a result, it can impose meanings on us. It also permits understanding. At the same time, the way we understand a language is also determined by the experiences that we have as individuals.[61]

In view of the pervasive influence of language, one does not have to move behind language to find the specific piece of existence that is objectified in language. Rather, existence itself is conveyed, formed, and embodied in language itself, as the language is being used. As Ebeling has said, the basic form of understanding is not understanding *of* language, but understanding *through* (or by means of) language. Words are not the primary things needing to be understood. Rather, it is the situation that is obscure and that needs illumination, and that illumination comes by verbal statement. Words can remove hindrances to understanding and can bring something to our comprehension. Therefore, *"the word itself has a hermeneutic function,"*[62] namely, to stimulate a meaning. A word has both content and power (as will be explained below, in chapter 3); and ultimately, the meaning of a word and what it effects are identical. "We do not get at the nature of words by asking what they contain, but by asking what they effect, what they set going, what future they dis-

[60]Fuchs, *Hermeneutik*, 166-76.

[61]Gerhard Ebeling, *Introduction to a Theological Theory of Language*, trans. R. A. Wilson (London: Collins, 1973) 92. WF, 248. Fuchs, *Hermeneutik*, 63, 69-70, 131, 135-36. Idem., *Studies*, 209-12.

[62]WF, 318. See also *Theological Theory of Language*, 126.

close," what they call forth.[63] Jüngel's emphasis on the value of metaphor reflects his appreciation of these functions of language.

Word-Event.[64] The objective of the New Hermeneutic is what is called the "word-event" as such.[65] A word-event evokes an interpretation that is determined by a specific situation at a particular moment. In connection with reading a text, the term "word-event" is meant to describe the experience of the text speaking to us in a way we did not expect, in contrast to the experience of our figuring out what the text means. Because word-events occur, *words* are seen by the New Hermeneutic as having primacy over the *text*.

Ebeling points to the principle that undergirds word-events when he says that reality (*Wirklichkeit*) is effective (*wirksam*), active, and mighty, with the capacity to impress as real and to gain recognition. This gaining of recognition is accomplished through language, either oral or acted out. In a word-event, language brings an encounter with its subject, reality. As a result, Being happens. Being finds concrete expression. Not only does a type of Being (for example, love) find expression in a word initially, but when that word is spoken subsequently, that type of Being can be made present or be revived for us.

---

[63]Gerhard Ebeling, *The Nature of Faith*, trans. Ronald Gregor Smith (Philadelphia: Fortress, 1961) 187.

In this sense it can be said that language enables Being to express itself to us, as Heidegger might have phrased the matter. Fuchs goes even further and says, "Being emerges from language, when language directs us into the dimension of our existence determinative for our life" (which dimension is the meaning of the word "God"). (*Zum hermeneutischen Problem in der Theologie: Die existentiale Interpretation*, Gesamelte Aufsätze 1, 2nd ed. rev. [Tübingen: Mohr (Siebeck), 1965] 115. ET: in *New Hermeneutic*, trans. Robinson, 55.) Again, Fuchs has said that the only kind of Being that is true is Being that comes to speech or is expressed (*Hermeneutik*, 275). And Ebeling talks of life itself seeking utterance through language (*Theological Theory of Language*, 177).

[64]"Word-event" (*Wortgeschehen*) is Ebeling's phrase. Fuchs uses "language-event" or "speech-event" (*Sprachereignis*). They have the same meaning.

[65]WF, 318-20. It is important to note that a word-event does not occur every time a word is spoken, just as, for Heidegger, language does not always express Being.

As much as Ebeling and Fuchs place value on the event as such, neither of them treats it as a private affair involving just a person and a word.[66] Both of them have a greater appreciation for history and for the value of community. Fuchs has pointed out, for example, that a person encounters God's demands as much *in* history as in freedom from it. And both of them require a community in which the understanding of the word-event can be tested. Both of them teach that understanding is verified by relating to other people. For Fuchs, meaning depends upon *how* we understand, and that way of understanding entails how we exist with one another. Bultmann had called for a decision that is not grounded in the self, but where the "other" was God alone. Fuchs calls for a new self-understanding from outside ourselves—but among our neighbors. Accordingly, Fuchs replaces Bultmann's "eschatological existence" with human "unity in love."[67]

Comparison with Jüngel. The New Hermeneutic, including its notion of word-event, has had a significant impact on Jüngel, and it shares a similarity with the later Heidegger's views on language. Jüngel moves beyond the New Hermeneutic, however, on two fronts. First, he examines language more carefully and identifies metaphor as the type of language whose function most closely coincides with the experience of a word-event. He therefore can specify more clearly the nature of theological language, as it behaves in accordance with the New Hermeneutic. And since metaphor is a form of analogy, he finds a basis for compatibility between Barth's use of analogy and Heidegger's view of language. Second, he

---

[66]Their influence is evident in Jüngel, who says, e.g., that to be open to God means to know God not only as *pro me* but also as *pro te*, i.e., that faith is not structured individualistically. Accordingly, he says, openness to God is completed as openness to other people. Here lies Jüngel's criterion for political community, which provides the framework for the love-dimension of faith. Pure faith includes the present as a time of joy; but joy can be made concrete only near other people, and joy requires mediation through institutions ("Womit steht," 176-77). Elsewhere he says that we can die in peace only if we live in peace with others and are concerned for what causes their anxiety (*Death: The Riddle and the Mystery*, trans. Iain Nicol and Ute Nicol [Philadelphia: Westminster, 1974] 129-30; see also GMW, 354; GGW, 485).

[67]Fuchs, *Hermeneutik*, 248.

makes use of phenomenology to discover new depth of meaning in some biblical nouns.

From Fuchs, the teacher with whom he had most direct contact, Jüngel developed his appreciation of the text as a vehicle of God's address to the reader. He also shares most of Fuchs' approach to the historical Jesus and the value that Fuchs places on the "other" in community.

* * *

The preceding summary of the positions and movement of the theological debate since the views of Barth and Heidegger first came to prominence shows a tendency toward convergence, thanks to the shift in Heidegger's own interest which some of Bultmann's students picked up. I have considered the strands that Jüngel uses from each of these thinkers. The strands have in common an interest in the functioning of language, especially as it serves as a channel for God to come into our midst. Next I examine the way that same interest affects Jüngel's view of the role of theology and of its relation to philosophy.

Chapter 2

Theology and Philosophy

The history of Jüngel's theological roots implies that his fundamental theology places a strong emphasis on the need for divine revelation, both historically, as attested in the Bible, and currently, with the claim that the Ultimate makes itself known in the present. That starting point has implications for what Jüngel thinks theology is and for what he thinks theology's limits must be. It also provides a framework within which he wrestles with the relationship between philosophy and theology, a matter on which he formulates his position by drawing from Barth and Heidegger. This chapter deals with these topics.

Weaknesses of Natural Theology

Jüngel sets himself against all efforts to ground our understanding of God in something other than God, no matter whether that something be the universe, the human psyche, history, a metaphysical system, a principle, or an ideology. His objections to natural theology are extensive and are almost coterminus with those of Barth.

Jüngel deplores all forms of natural theology that are independent of faith or that claim the ability to critique all religions, including the truth-claims of Christianity. He points out that natural theology evolved from a time when believers sought to develop their understanding by enlisting the aid of what they could learn from nature. That step led many theologians to base their reasoning on only that which was generally applicable in nature. And that appeal to general applicability culminated in limiting one's trust to the even more general and higher authority of reason. The problem with this development, he says, is that those theologians do not expect "light" to come from a totally different direction or "dimension." At best, the "Other Dimension" simply adds greater depth to what we already comprehend, or it corrects flaws in our reasoning. As a result, instead of letting God's revelation raise questions about us, natural theology simply uses the data of revelation to construct answers to its *own* questions. As an additional consequence, God's revelation through grace loses its significance and its power, because it is viewed as only one alternative among others. People simply add it to their repertoire of approaches to God.

Contrary to natural theology, Jüngel believes that divinely generated faith provides its own evidence and does not require additional evidence of its truth, based on presumably stronger grounds. He also believes that knowledge of God is not possible apart from the revealing spirit of Christ and that the revelation of God in Jesus Christ applies universally. Furthermore, since natural theology does not provide for the Cross, it does not give adequate testimony to God's uniqueness.

Jüngel teaches, following Luther, not only that nature does not reveal God, but also that it is only by an experience of grace that one knows what nature itself truly is. He suggests that this view is the complete opposite of that of the natural theology of Thomas Aquinas, for whom grace presupposes nature. In Aquinas's view, one begins with nature, and then grace is added to improve it. By a similar logic, faith is placed in a position where it must presuppose reason.[1]

Jüngel quips seriously that natural theology cannot distinguish between God and the Devil, since it places God in partnership with the world, where the Devil is, also.

God may be considered to be the creator, but God does not testify to Godself as creator apart from revelation in Jesus Christ.[2] Consequently,

---

[1] Eberhard Jüngel, "Das Dilemma der natürlichen Theologie und die Wahrheit ihres Problems: Überlegungen für eine Gesprach mit Wolfhart Pannenberg," in *Denken im Schatten des Nihilismus*, ed. Alexander Schwan (Darstadt: Wissenschaftliche Buchgesellschaft, 1975) 426, 429.

[2] Emil Brunner represented the tradition of natural theology when he argued that the spirit of a creator is recognizable in every work that the creator makes. Since the world is God's creation, it, too, must show God's imprint. Accordingly, the world serves as a general revelation of God, and we can learn about God from nature.

Barth's first response was to deny the imprint. He said that the cosmos answers every question concerning its origin with only the mute fact of its existence. The cosmos would have to be more than a creature to give a more

the "God" known through creation is only the creature of human phantasy. As Jüngel has stated the matter, the only way to see God is to look God in the eye, that is, to return God's gaze, to respond to God's direct revelation. The trouble with natural theology is that it is always trying to take a look at God while God's back is turned.

Moreover, knowledge of God is not mere intellectual knowledge or possession of facts. Knowledge of God is salvation itself. Studying nature does not bring salvation. Only Christ does. Therefore, nature does not reveal God.

It has been argued that people have a point of contact with God, because they were created in God's image, which distinguished them, as human beings, from the animals. Even with a doctrine of the Fall, the fact that people are still human implies that they must still possess some of that image and its contact with God. But Barth has asked, What make us think that peoples' behavior can be characterized as fully human? To the extent that it cannot be (because, for example, we do not love fully and do not trust God basically and are not completely sensitive to the needs of others and do not live up to the highest ideals of humanity), there is the intimation that we have lost any reliable, inherent contact with God. He argues, further, that the image of God is not within a person but is in the I-Thou relationship, which is common both to the Trinity and to a human being. Accordingly, the *imago dei* is not a quality that a person possesses but a relationship, including the relationship with God, which people have lost. It follows, Jüngel notes, that God is not found through a person's built-in point of contact with God. God is therefore not self-evident to us.

Barth and Jüngel add that a person has no innate capacity whatsoever to be reached by revelation and to comprehend the Word when it is

---

satisfactory answer to such questions. As it is, however, it never reveals itself without concealment, pointing to a Wherefore that it declares only by being separate from it (*Church Dogmatics* IV/3, trans. G. W. Bromiley [Edinburgh: T.&T. Clark, 1961] 169). The cosmos is the opposite of God's revelatory Word, because "the Word of God is uncreated reality, identical with God Himself, therefore not universally present and fixable, nor possibly so" (CD 1/1, 180). But even if there were clues to divine reality existing in nature, human sin would keep people from finding them or from interpreting them properly (CD II/1, 103-104).

uttered. Faith, when it does develop, is itself the work of God the Holy Spirit. It is precisely in the fact that people are not open to grace and its revelation that natural theology finds its roots.[3]

---

[3]CD II/1, 183. From a slightly different angle, Barth says that if it is possible for people to be doers of the Word, that possibility is a divine possibility and is not inherent in human nature. "If we base ourselves upon what is possible to us," he continues, "we shall always believe in these our possibilities and always have to believe in them" ("No!" in *Natural Theology*, ed. John Baillie, trans. Peter Fraenkel [London: Geoffrey Bles, 1946] 117). Any discussion with unbelievers that appeals to or implies a "natural" readiness for God in them only leaves the believing in their own power, a power that even could renounce both their own position and theology's position (CD II/1, 88-94).

Another reason that people have no innate capacity to encounter God is that "freedom to know the true God is a miracle . . . not one of our freedoms" ("No!" 117). "To become free for God we must be convinced that we are not already free," Barth says. But "the Word of God excludes every other freedom except its own. Therefore even the freedom to convince ourselves of our own freedom . . . is quite untenable." He continues:

> The fact that we are compelled to try to secure at least this freedom for God, the freedom to deny our freedom, is the proof that in practice we cannot attain that renunciation which the hearing of God's Word demands of us.
>
> There is a way of asserting the *servum arbitrium* [bondage of the will] and discoursing against the doctrines of the *liberum arbitrium* [freedom of the will] . . . which is too triumphant not to betray that the renunciation is still not made. It is the idea of a *liberum arbitrium*, of a man's pride in his own decision, which triumphs in the very assertion of its opposite. That pride may only too well and gladly assume the form of a publican's Pharisaism. And even if we perceive this, our own last word will still be one form of that pride in decision.
>
> What we concede to the Word of God will always be an attempt to make good a claim to our own freedom, to go on believing in our possibilities.

Church Dogmatics, I/2, trans. G. T. Thompson and Harold Knight (New York: Scribner's, 1956) 258-59.

Barth's view that divine truth is in need of no human support is summarized well by the following analogy, written in 1886 by Eduard Boehl, whom Barth quotes:

> It is but an appearance that the rainbow stands on the earth; in reality it is vaulted over the earth. True, it lets itself down to earth, but is perceived only from there. So it is with the divine truth; the same needs no human support, as little as the rainbow needs the earth. True, it illumines man and he notices it. Still it is never dependent on man. It withdraws and man remains in darkness; it returns and man walks in the

In general, Barth teaches that our knowledge of God cannot be based on our establishing the conditions through which God can be comprehended, since that would presume that we know the way to God and are, at least to that degree, in control of God's revelatory process. Revelation can be grace only if God is in control. The mistake of at least some types of natural theology is that they want to demonstrate methodologically, as the prelude on which their theology is based, the process that God's revelation must follow, without considering the way in which that revelation has already occurred. Jüngel says that that is like wanting to prove one's own existence, based solely on the fact that there are other people who can be distinguished from other forms of life, but without taking one's own self into account.[4]

Barth insists that if we do not base theology on revelation from the outset, we cannot appeal to it later, because by then we will have already introduced human assumptions and understandings.[5] Jüngel elaborates by saying that what is objectionable about natural theology is that it insists that a concept of God or a framework for understanding God must be created first, and that only then, within it, can genuine theological statements be made. But with every concept of God we must ask, What right do we have to say that? We cannot be certain that any such concept is correct, because those concepts come from another source, not from God.

---

light. But man is not its assistant; he cannot produce the light; likewise he cannot hoard it up! (CD I/1, 255)

As evidence of the compatibility that Jüngel finds between Barth and Heidegger, it is worth noting that Heidegger, too, does not require that human effort construct the truth. "Truth is . . . revelation of what-is," he says (Heidegger, *Existence and Being*, 336). In a related way, Jüngel says that truth is its own criterion.

Even with regard to God, about whom Heidegger spoke in his last public interview, Heidegger says that God—some God other than the technical state, philosophy, and "all merely human aspirations and study"—must come to us of God's own accord (Martin Heidegger, "Nur noch ein Gott kann uns retten," *Der Speigel*, 31 May 1976, 209; interview with Rudolf Augustein and Georg Wolff on 23 September 1966), because even though God is "the most worthy object of thought. . . . that's where language breaks down" (Eberhard Jüngel, "Toward the Heart of the Matter," *Christian Century* 108 [27 February 1991]: 231).

[4]Jüngel, "Dilemma," 439.
[5]CD I/2, 296.

We attained them not by asking God but by asking ourselves. We simply
fail to see that even human reason is creaturely, and that, as Luther
taught, the particularity of revelation cannot be subsumed under the gen-
erality of available reason. Openness to God's revelation, on the other
hand, and to a new understanding of the world and of oneself in light of
that revelation makes it possible for God's true reality to break through
to us and does not decide in advance what is possible.[6]

Moreover, belief in God is primarily a *relationship* characterized by
trust and dependence. The point of the doctrine of the Fall is that all
people are incapable of the kind of trust that is appropriate to that relationship. Natural theology moves in a direction that is completely contrary to the very essence of the relationship, therefore, when it claims that
people have control over the preliminary grounds of the relationship,
which God then brings to completion. Such a claim reinforces the very
source of the brokenness in the relationship, namely, lack of trust.

Pannenberg agrees with Jüngel that faith should be grounded in a
truth outside oneself, but Pannenberg tries to ground faith in historical
facts and to decide what kind of facts would provide adequate grounding.
Jüngel does not agree that faith should be based on a knowledge given
to it beforehand. Jüngel adds that to understand, as Pannenberg does, that
God creates faith directly is only half of the truth, "which needs to be
expanded by the insight that it is precisely *faith* that God produces,
because *only* faith does justice to God, because faith *alone* lets God be
God and therefore *apprehends* God as God." Why must God first be
understood by reason as an existing X? It is "not that we should be able
to believe *without* our own reason and strength," Jüngel continues, but
that, "even with all of our own reason and strength, without faith we
cannot apprehend the ground of faith." That is what the "logic of faith"
requires. Otherwise, if we were to require that we first have irrefutable
facts or complete certainty before we believe, it would be like refusing
to eat, until we know how eating functions and what the chemical content
of our food is. If what grounds the content or object of faith is not faith,

[6]Jüngel, "Dilemma," 425, 437, 439. A weakness in natural theology's claim
that God is generally available is that talk about God becomes abstract and un-
specific. In that case, Jüngel says, God is expressed better through silence.
"Gott—um seiner selbst willen interessant: Plädoyer für eine natürlichere Theologie," *Neue Zürcher Zeitung*, 20-21 September 1975, 57.

the object loses its quality as an object of *faith*. And the object is not *grounded* in faith, if we *begin* with verifiable facts.[7]

In agreement with Pannenberg against Bultmann, Jüngel says that the *decision* of faith does not provide one with certainty of the content of faith. He then asks why that content (namely, God) itself could not ground both the decision and the certainty of the content and in *that* way keep faith from being mere superstition. He adds that faith simply cannot be grounded, if the content of faith is separated from the believing that accompanies or perceives the content.[8]

The approach of natural theology is applauded by people who are unsure of their faith, Jüngel says, but it does not convince the thinkers who are not willing to rely on faith. Yet those are the people with whom an argument by reason alone *should* have the greatest chance of success. Natural theology implies that atheism is impossible for anyone who is reasonable. Consequently, nonbelievers who are willing to confront the issue of God's reality should not exist.[9]

Natural theology does not succeed in its appropriate and well-intentioned effort to show that God is generally and uniquely interesting, because it does not allow God's *own* uniqueness to make God interesting for "His" own sake. Yet if we are willing to attribute this ability to human beings, we should not deny it to God. Jüngel suggests that attributing this ability to God is done best by a theology that behaves as naturally as possible toward the nature of the actual relationship between God and humanity, which is that God's Word addresses us humanly and is interested in us for our own sake. Therefore, he concludes, a theology of the Word of God is a more natural theology than natural theology.[10]

While Barth denies that natural theology has anything significant to offer, however, Jüngel can find a function for it. Barth concedes that natural theology and secular words can be "parables of the Kingdom." But they cannot be so, simply as the pure result of human reason. They can be parables only as God enables them to point to Jesus' truth. But they

---

[7]Pannenberg's interest in beginning with the "fact" of the Resurrection leads to what Jüngel calls the "grotesque paradox" that we must *believe* that the Resurrection is a *historical fact* that *grounds faith*. "Womit steht," 169.

[8]Jüngel, "Dilemma," 433-47.

[9]Ibid., 420, 436.

[10]Jüngel, "Gott—um seiner selbst willen interessant."

are not comparable to the Word spoken directly by God, namely, Jesus Christ, the Second Person of the Trinity. Consequently, the authority of other words is determined by fidelity to the one Word, which reveals exhaustively what God wills for us and how we are related to God. At most, then, natural theology can complement knowledge of God from the Scriptures, for the person whose eyes have been opened already by Christ.[11]

Jüngel, on the other hand, speaks of "the necessary business of natural theology."[12] He says that that business is to accompany all of dogmatics as a "moment" of revealed theology, although not as the basis for it. His own use of phenomenology suggests how he understands natural theology as a moment of revealed theology. He understands it as a technique for focusing on God's revelation and for thinking imaginatively about it, thereby creating additional avenues by which God can illumine that revelation. He also provides for testing the demands of the Gospel through dialogue with the humanities and with other theologies, but he warns against grounding those demands in the substantive features of those dialogue-partners.[13]

Revelation

Natural theology would make sense if God were speechless, that is, if the Ultimate did not periodically make Itself known. But the Christian claim that God is Self-revealing would seem to make it both futile and inappropriate to seek God in any place other than God's present and past revelation.

For Barth and Jüngel, therefore, the Subject of revelation cannot be identified with a universal reality over which people have cognitive control. On the contrary, says Barth, "Just as the reality of the Creator differs from all other reality in that it alone is self-existent and therefore original, so its self-disclosure differs from that of all other beings and every creaturely mind in that it alone is able to reveal its existence with authenticity, truth and effectiveness, and in this revelation to affirm the reality

---

[11]CD II/1, 190; IV/3, 97-99, 110-11, 116-18, 122-23, 126-29; "No!" 97-98.
[12]Jüngel, "Dilemma," 439.
[13]Jüngel, "Gott—um seiner selbst willen interessant."

of its being."[14] As Jüngel has said, "Only the speaking God himself can say what the word 'God' should provide us to think about. Theology comprehends this whole subject with the category of revelation."[15]

One approach that Jüngel takes to explicate the need for revelation is to argue that genuine knowledge and true humanity must have their origin in God and can occur only when our correspondence or contentment with ourselves is interrupted. (All new knowledge is gained through a deathlike interruption, he says.) Revelation is just such an interruption; and since it comes from God, it is the basis for claiming that God is the truth of life and the source of genuine humanity.[16]

Revelation as interruption is not unlike Bultmann's Word as eschatological event. Both of them make what should be self-evident (for example, the way of true life) become self-evident. The value of talk about God, in other words, is that it rouses the self-evident from the commonality of the all-too-self-evident. Here Jüngel sees value in Bultmann's call for decision, as an effort to get people to experience godly love in the concrete world, in such a way that the "evident" is seen in a new way. This understanding explains, for Jüngel, Bultmann's insistence not only on "ontological structures" of human being but also on the desecularizing function of the "eschatological event." This event creates an inward divorce from the dominating pressures of society and frees people from suffocating under a view of the world that does not take proper account of God.[17] Here, too, Jüngel implies that God is to be understood not as being distinct from the world but as being hidden from all who are out of harmony with God.

He teaches, therefore, that revelation is not primarily an instance of ontic, intellectual knowledge. Rather, it is the event of being given part in the Being that reveals itself. It has an ontological function as catalyst

---

[14]CD III/1, 348.

[15]GMW, 13; GGW, 14. See also GMW, viii, 34, 157-58, 177, 191, 223, 260, 295, 300, 378-79, 386-87; GGW, x, 43, 210-11, 238, 258, 303, 355, 404, 410-11, 518-19, 530.

[16]Eberhard Jüngel, "The Truth of Life: Observations on Truth as the Interruption of the Continuity of Life," in *Creation, Christ, and Culture: Studies in Honor of T. F. Torrance*, ed. Richard W. A. McKinney (Edinburgh: T.&T. Clark, 1976) 232-33, 235.

[17]Jüngel, "Redlich," 477.

for the shaping of Being. It is experienced as a new ability to be a different way.[18]

He adds that knowledge of God is lost when one distinguishes between natural and supernatural knowledge or between natural and supernatural revelation, because both are attained only by faith, which combines both polarities simultaneously.[19]

Finally, it is important to recognize that we cannot fix, even retrospectively, what God and God's Word are. Accordingly, Jüngel says that we cannot identify the Bible with the Word of God, because that Word resides only *"in the event* of the Word of God."[20] When revelation comes, it does not stay with us. Revelation is not a revealed state.[21] In Bultmann's words, with which Jüngel agrees, "Christian faith is not a knowledge possessed once for all; it is not a general Worldview. It can be realized only here and now. It can be a living faith only when the believer is always asking what God is telling him here and now."[22]

Jüngel's Concept of Theology

In view of the limits that Jüngel and his teachers have placed on human ability to comprehend God, what can theology be?

One way to begin to answer this question is to consider what theology is not. It is not the Word of God. Barth and Jüngel agree that since God's Word (that is, God, since God is fully present when addressing us) is not a concept requiring definition, theology does not consist of a set of doctrinal propositions understood as revealed truths. In other words, says Jüngel, theology cannot be absolute. Nor can it be a system of thought about God, since the continuous and consistent guidance essential

---

[18]GMW, 228; GGW, 309-10.

[19]Jüngel, "Dilemma," 429-30. Bultmann deals with this matter in the same way when he says, "Faith insists not on the direct identity of God's action with worldly events, but . . . on the paradoxical identity which can be believed only here and now against the appearance of nonidentity" (*Jesus Christ and Mythology,* 62); see also CD I/1, 188.

[20]Eberhard Jüngel, *Die Freiheit der Theologie: Vortrag für den vom Rat der Evangelischen Kirche in Deutschland berufenen theologischen Ausschuss "Schrift und Verkündigung,"* Theologische Studien 88 (Zurich: EVZ-Verlag, 1967) 9.

[21]CD I/2, 118, 267-68; I/1, 44, 127, 147-49, 243, 333-34.

[22]Bultmann, *Jesus Christ and Mythology,* 64.

to constructing an accurate system about God would have to come from God, Who is not at our disposal.[23]

For Jüngel, theology exists to serve the internal needs of the believing community, whose faith is a response to the Word of God. It is not the primary purpose of Christian theology, therefore, to make Christian faith comprehensible to nonbelievers.

What is the subject matter of theology? Jüngel makes Barth even more radical by saying that the subject matter of theology is not simply human words of proclamation, as Barth had said, but what can result from them, namely, the event of the Word of God, "for only as event can this word lay claim to be *God's* Word."[24] The content of that event is what theology strives to be in harmony with.

The significance of that event is determined subjectively. The event may be as close to God's reality as human beings can come, but Jüngel does not advocate that theology study individual experiences of revelation or of faith. He makes a point of distinguishing between God and the faith that responds to God.[25]

While the event of the Word of God, that is, God's own Self, must be theology's ultimate standard of evaluation, the appropriate *tangible* object and norm of theology is the Bible, because the Bible's language was determined by a human reality determined by God. Hence, the Bible is more likely than other objects of study to be a vehicle for putting people in touch with the Ultimate in the present. Jüngel is fond of calling theology "consistent exegesis." He says that theology is faith trying, through responsible thought and unlimited reason, to conform to the Word of God through human words, on the basis of the biblical texts.[26]

---

[23]Jüngel, *Freiheit*, 8, 28 (#3.43); CD I/1, 155-56, 311; I/2, 483. Even Heidegger supports this contention, when he says that Christian theology does not have the job of combining many different loci of faith-content into a comprehensive system, because if it were to do that, it would become a slave of that system. *The Piety of Thinking: Essays by Martin Heidegger*, trans. and ed. James G. Hart and John C. Maraldo (Bloomington: Indiana University Press, 1976) 13-14; hereafter cited as PT. Trans. from *Phänomenologie und Theologie* (Frankfurt-on-Main: Vittorio Klostermann, 1970) 23-34.

[24]Jüngel, *Freiheit*, 6.

[25]Ibid., 20-21, 29 (#4.3).

[26]Ibid., 8-10, 15, 28 (#3.41), 31 (#5.54), 32 (#6.3). Elsewhere he describes

Theology is found already in the Bible, of course, because the faith of the original believing communities could not continue to exist without theology. Faith must say what it believes, and when it expresses its thoughts conceptually, it is engaged in theological interpretation. Accordingly, Jüngel finds the task of theology to be to analyze consistently, by means of the historical-critical method, the theology already given in the Bible and then, in the light of this historical understanding, to make it speak to us today, by relating it to the present.[27]

Jüngel wants theology to speak to the present day, without, at the same time, getting caught up simply in faddism. Hence he says that theology does its job properly when it is appropriate to both its object and its time in history, simultaneously. This means that at every point in time, theology begins again with its subject matter. It is always *in via*. Jüngel warns that concern with the past can put theology so much under tutelage that it no longer comes to us simply *from* its tradition but *as* tradition, thereby ceasing to inquire into the truth for the present, to which is must be related. At the same time, however, theology also should not speak so exclusively about the present that nothing extraordinary can confront the present. He says that time not only determines, it also wants to *be* determined: God also wants to determine it.[28]

For reasons that will be evident in the next section, no law can be written to determine which of several theologies is correct. Jüngel says that theology, as he does it, is certain only of its origin (the Word of God) and its goal (to evoke an event of the Word of God).

But such an evocation means that the theology serves as a vehicle for God, letting God speak directly to provide people with understanding, since people cannot understand God unless God enables them to do so. For that reason, there is a freedom connected with theological endeavor, when theologians realize that, ultimately, they can do no more than hope

---

Christian theology, in a related way, as "explication and self-criticism of faith in Jesus of Nazareth." GMW, 155; GGW, 207.

[27]Heidegger gives his full endorsement to this approach when he says that, as in any science, the job of theology is to look behind the given organization, classifications, and concepts to see how far they conform to the object that determines the science and that, in this case, is grounded in the New Testament. PT, 13-14, Ger. 23-24.

[28]Jüngel, *Freiheit*, 5, 15-16, 26 (##0.2, 0.7). GMW, 167; GGW, 225.

for the work of the Holy Spirit. Jüngel sees theology as offering what is likely to be only an oblique angle of vision, which is not an end in itself but which, at its best, serves as a channel for God's direct communication, in the presence of which the theology pales into insignificance.[29]

Relation of Philosophy to Theology

The concepts with which theology works will inevitably fall into one philosophical system or another. They also inevitably will be unable to do justice to God, because no system devised by the finite or the tarnished is likely to fathom the infinite or perfection. Concepts will be used, of course, as a way of stating our understanding of the Word of God that came in the past and will come again. But theological concepts are not the fullness of the Word of God. They can only point to it. Theology intends the concepts that it uses to bespeak a reality unknown outside Christian faith.[30] Fortunately, in a moment of grace God can use any

---

[29]Jüngel, *Freiheit*, 22, 27 (#2.6), 4, 10, 13-14, 26, 29 (#3.9).

[30]Jüngel, *Death*, 85. MW, 118. Heidegger, too, assumes that "all *theological* concepts of existence which are centered on faith intend a specific transition of existence, in which pre-Christian and Christian existence are united in a unique way." PT, 171n.9, Ger. 29n.1. Emphasis added.

James G. Hart and John C. Maraldo, eds. of PT, apparently overlook Heidegger's footnote when they conclude that the views of Heidegger and Barth on the relation of philosophy to theology are incompatible. They argue that since Heidegger says that "all theological concepts necessarily contain that understanding of Being which is constitutive of human Dasein" (18, Ger. 29), "then the theological concepts will be able to be explicated only insofar as the theologian does philosophy. But how can theology still be considered to be a positive science when it essentially must do philosophy," especially since Heidegger says, in their words, that "the ontological elucidation codirects and corrects the science of faith" (111-12)? The answer is that theology must do philosophy only to understand the pre-Christian meanings of its concepts correctly. Heidegger says that philosophy formally points out and is the ontological corrective of *only* "*the ontic and, in particular, the pre-Christian content of basic theological concepts*" (20, Ger. 32). The ontic concepts used in theology automatically fit into some philosophical ontology and therefore can be corrected and honed by it, so as to be understood properly *in terms of that ontology*. But Heidegger concedes that theology ultimately breaks out of the common human understanding of existence. In so doing, he refuses to limit theology to his own or any other ontology. He there-

language and philosophy as a channel for Self-communication. Different
people will be attracted to different perspectives, and all of those perspectives can direct people toward the ultimate, at points where the perspectives come close to coinciding with ultimacy or where God addresses us
through them in spite of their content.[31]

Jüngel suggests that the way to protect faith from being reduced
simply to the truths of reason is for faith to understand itself better—with
the help of reason. When a metaphysics uses a particular ontology to
"spell out" divine reality, for example, Jüngel turns for protection to strict
attention to ontological terminology in theology and to Heidegger's
understanding of ontology, which he considers to be more profound than
that of the metaphysicians.[32] He comments that much can be learned from
Heidegger's way of confronting metaphysics.[33]

Yet he does not want the theologian to be held accountable to philosophy, especially if that accountability would impose a scheme of prior
understanding for elucidating the Word of God. Since that Word is continually given afresh by grace, it can be neither fully explained nor antici-
pated by any presupposed metaphysics or ontology. The role of philosophy must be neither that of a second source of revelation nor that of the
criterion of truth about God.[34] It follows even more strongly that theology

---

by preserves theology as a positive science, responsible only to its own object
of study.

[31]CD I/1, 200, 159-60; I/2, 731.

[32]Jüngel, "Womit steht," 157-58. "Vorwärts durch Annäherung?" *Theologische Literaturzeitung* 91 (May 1966) col. 335.

[33]GMW, 153n.1; GGW, 204n.1. Heidegger seeks "the essence of metaphysics," i.e., the larger unity that underlies metaphysics. He wants to overcome
metaphysics in the sense of bringing it back to its own limits and then to move
behind it to something more profound, perhaps to the "divine God" of Whom
metaphysics tries to speak. He took only two steps in that direction, however,
viz., his investigations of *Dasein* and of Being. He foresaw additional steps, as
well. Yet while Jüngel is quite willing to learn from Heidegger—and from many
others—it should be noted that he does not consider himself to be in the camp
of Heideggerian philosophy.

[34]Heidegger concurs: "Only epochs which no longer fully believe in the true
greatness of the task of theology arrive at the disastrous notion that philosophy
can help to provide a refurbished theology if not a substitute for theology."
Martin Heidegger, *An Introduction to Metaphysics*, trans. Ralph Manheim (New

should not limit itself to the thought of any one philosophy—although Jüngel is not as doctrinaire about this matter as Barth was.[35] Unlike Barth, however, Jüngel does not avoid making judicious use of philosophy, because it appears to him that even when theology and philosophy consider the same problem, they consider it in totally different ways and they work with different premises. He definitely believes that theology can learn about method from philosophy. He personally has learned from the general approach of phenomenology. In that discipline, one attempts to limit one's attention to what an object presents to one's immediate consciousness, and to limit that attention in such a way that what one becomes aware of, with regard to that object, comes only from the object itself and therefore represents the true Being of the object. He also has learned from Heidegger's related mode of questioning, which follows the lead of the questions that one's study-object itself suggests, without adding inferences or additional data based on general knowledge, in order to be led to the true reality behind the appearance of the object.

The phenomenological principle that the reality of the thing shines forth from itself provides the philosophical basis for Jüngel's focus on the Bible. If one is most likely to learn about God by directing one's attention to the objects most directly associated with God, then the Bible is the book to study phenomenologically, since the Bible is the deposit of the primal human phenomena resulting from "the divine initiative," culminating in the full revelation of God in Jesus Christ. Phenomenology is compatible with theology, because it does not impose a point of view on its subject matter.

Haven: Yale University Press, 1959) 7. See also PT, 21, Ger. 32.

[35]Jüngel appreciates Barth's question: "How can we bind ourselves to one philosophy as the only philosophy, and ascribe to it a universal necessity, without actually positing it as something absolute, as the *necessary* partner of the Word of God?" CD I/2, 733. Nevertheless, he is willing to take a more nuanced position, which enables him to justify Bultmann's use of existentialism, for example, by claiming that Bultmann uses the concepts of philosophy for different purposes than philosophy uses them and to answer different questions. Jüngel, "Der Schritt zurück," 114. Reflecting his considerable knowledge of the Greek classics, Jüngel notes that such diverse usage is contrary to Plato (*Cratylus*, ch. 10), who claims that underlying the common use of concepts is a common search.

Jüngel also looks at phenomena outside the Bible, such as human love. He looks outside the Bible to amplify a literal understanding of the Bible's imagery, so as to provide for more fruitful use of the imagination when viewing the text metaphorically. He does not restrict the Bible's meaning, however, to what he finds outside the Bible.

It is important to observe, also, that he does not begin with natural phenomena. He begins with the Bible and takes his cues from it when deciding what worldly phenomena may be worthy of investigation because of the promise that they offer of shedding light on our understanding of God and God's will. The new angles of vision that these phenomena might provide would still require divine illumination, however, in order for them to provide accurate knowledge of God. But Jüngel does not propose to begin with a phenomenological study of the structures of Being in the world, as a foundation for language about revelation and God. His primary orientation is to follow the lead of what Christianity believes to be God's revelation in Jesus Christ.

Chapter 3

Jüngel's Conceptual Tools

How does Jüngel know that Jesus is God's revelation? Indeed, what conceptual tools does he use to enable him to claim that he knows anything at all about God? These questions lead to his epistemology, which can be understood best by examining the function that he finds in language. But in order to understand his views about why language works the way it does and why it has the significance that it has, one must begin by understanding his concept of Being and its proper relation to thinking and to language. This chapter does just that, while also showing how that relation bears upon appropriate thought about God.

Concepts of Being, Thought, and Language

Being

One does not have to read much of Jüngel's writings before encountering a reference to "Being." Such a reference bespeaks an interest in ontology that Jüngel gets neither from the Bible nor from Barth but from the Heideggerian strand in his background. Following Heidegger, he regards Being as active, potential-filled, purposeful interaction between and among people and things over time. There are no static essences. Although he often treats Being abstractly, it is important to see that he considers it to be firmly rooted in history, that is, in actual events of daily existence. In his view, Being is formed through action: It is constituted by interaction. He writes that it is free; it is revelatory; it is event; and it has potential. Let us consider each of these characteristics separately.

As far as people are aware of it, Being is free because (again following Heidegger) it cannot be conceived and established objectively as an entity, with fixed parameters.

Since no definition provides adequate knowledge of Being, anything that takes place is an unveiling of Being. The mere event of bringing something to our awareness can be regarded as revelatory. Being is revelatory in that it is created freely and given anew in the process of each interaction. It is not simply what is present.

Rather, Being is event. It occurs through events.[1] Consequently, "the alternatives of 'act and Being' become irrelevant."[2] Being is when Being transpires in action. Indeed, Being is best characterized not as a noun but as a gerund, namely, the process of being.

Being also includes potential. Being is not only what is occurring already but also what is incipient. Thus it also transcends our experience of it: It is both present and absent.

Thought

"Thinking after." The dynamic, potential-laden interaction between everything that exists can generate thoughts that extend beyond what has already been established in conventional understanding, thereby bringing new aspects of Being to the fore. Such thinking can occur when, accepting the later Heidegger's revolutionary epistemological sequence, we are open to new meanings and not intent on imposing traditional meanings on the reality that we encounter and engage in. That type of thinking follows Being, and the same principle is at work in divine revelation. The resulting thought then produces words, which are intended to be reflections of the Being (mundane or divine) that has already impressed itself on the speaker's thought.

---

[1] GMW, 28, 114, 358, 374; GGW, 35, 150-51, 491, 513.

[2] Eberhard Jüngel, "Die Möglichkeit theologischer Anthropologie auf dem Grund der Analogie: Eine Untersuchung zum Analogieverständnis Karl Barths," *Evangelische Theologie* 22 (1962): 552n.44; "Vorwärts durch Annäherung?" col. 335.

The Being of an entity within the world is its involvement, says Heidegger, which "is ontologically definitive" for it. (BT, 115-16, 120). Jüngel demonstrates his acceptance of this position when he writes that when people relate to themselves and to others, they effect their ontology and are not engaged in merely ontic actions. "Möglichkeit," 542n.7; cf. BT, 32-35.

Jüngel refers to such thinking as "thinking after" Being. "Thought believes nothing," he says. "It thinks after."[3] He observes that what we think is always a result of what has already happened. Nevertheless, "thinking after" still requires us to distinguish ourselves from the object of our thought, to relate to that object critically, and to form concepts about it—concepts that will be influenced by the context of our own experience.[4] That is where faith comes in.

Thinking with Faith. The notion of "thinking after," that is, of letting one's thoughts be formed by or be responsive to an antecedent reality, applies to thoughts about God, too. Those thoughts may be affected by faith. They will be affected properly by faith when faith, too, is a response to antecedent ultimacy.

Jüngel teaches that only God can be the origin of an adequate concept of God and therefore of appropriate thought and language about God. It is only natural, therefore, that when one bases one's own thinking about God on one's own capacity, one shall either misunderstand God or find God to be inconceivable. As an example of what not to do, Jüngel cites Friedrich Nietzsche, who identified God metaphysically with infinity and then concluded that thought about God was impossible because infinity is beyond our ken. Nietzsche also taught that since one can think only about what one can create, and since one does not have the capacity to create the true God, one cannot think properly about God.[5]

Jüngel's approach to the process of thinking of God is expressed in two ways, one of which we consider now. In both instances, he claims that true thinking of God must be sparked by an encounter with God. His reliance on revelation is clear. In the first instance, God addresses us; we respond in faith; and then we generate thoughts about God.[6]

---

[3]GMW, 163 (literal translation); GGW, 219.

[4]GMW, 166-69; GGW, 223-25.

[5]GMW, 148; GGW, 196-97.

[6]Jüngel summarizes his approach by taking issue with the early Heidegger on the matter of human comprehension. Says Jüngel (beginning with a quotation from Heidegger): "'*Dasein* hears, because it understands.' By contrast, theology understands hearing on the basis of the event of being addressed, out of which understanding then emerges. *Dasein* understands because it hears. And it hears because it exists as one who is addressed." GMW, 173n.3 (translation modified); GGW, 232n.2. See also GMW, 155; GGW, 208.

God encounters us as Word. For Jüngel this encounter means that we have an ecstatic experience of the Being of God.[7] In that event, "God *makes* Himself objective," so that we *can* conceive of God.[8] And since, in that event, our own selves transcend the mundane present, we are placed into a better-than-normal position to conceive of God properly.

We are able to think of God, therefore, because of our experiences of God. But Jüngel warns that concepts formed from our experiences must always be evaluated by Scripture and by the Risen Word, God's present self-attestation.

Experiences are not perceived to be experiences of *God*, however, apart from faith. A person conceives of God properly only *after* faith experiences God's reality.[9] Significantly, therefore, faith is not subordinate to thought. To believe in the true God, we do not first develop a concept of God and then believe in it. In the cases of both faith in and thought about the true God, the existence and action of God come first. Nevertheless, even the nonbeliever can comprehend how Christians think of God, because, according to Jüngel, "one can certainly follow . . . the

---

[7]"Word of God," Jüngel explains, is an abbreviated way of saying that "God addresses us to [*auf*] Himself and thus to ourselves." He elaborates as follows:

> In that man is addressed by God to God, there is a *total removal* of the I from its being merely in the here-and-now and, accordingly, a *completely new qualification of its presence*, which one could call *eschatological spiritual presence*.

GMW, 174 (my trans.); GGW, 234-35. See also GMW, 182 (GGW, 246), where Jüngel writes of God putting us outside ourselves and being present only to the ego that is outside itself, in the ecstatic structure that might be termed "being ourselves outside ourselves."

[8]T, 45. See also 61.

[9]GMW, 154, 163-64, 191-92, 199; GGW, 206, 218-20, 259-60, 270; "Womit steht," 165. A contemporary word of endorsement comes from T. R. Martland, who writes that "it is a category mistake to look for religious objects independently of religion's sustaining light. For example, it is a mistake . . . to try to prove or disprove God's existence independently . . . from faith." God is related to faith as an object is related to the eyes that see it. "An Analysis of the Religious Use of the Implausible, or More Particularly the Incredible," *Journal of the American Academy of Religion* 46 (December 1978): 573.

movement of faith without believing—just as one can understand joy while being sad."[10]

The need to be addressed by God and to respond to God in faith, in order to think responsibly about God, establishes definite parameters on the ability of thought to deal with God. In place of a thinking that determines for itself how the Being of God is to be understood, Jüngel calls for a thinking that conforms to the Being of God: He calls for a "thinking after" God.[11] "In theology," he writes, "thinking means to attempt to conform to God with the capacity of human reason. God goes *his* way. Thought will not touch God if it goes other ways."[12] To think of God properly, one's thoughts must follow the previously given Word of God. Responsible thinking and talking about God, therefore, is an expression of God's own movement toward the believer.

Nature of Language

It is essential to understand Jüngel's view of how language functions, if one is to understand what he thinks theology can accomplish. The following survey shows that he thinks language cannot make the world around us objective. Rather, all language, in its essence, is metaphorical, although most of it is used only in its conventional, literal sense. Because of its metaphorical nature, however, it has the capacity to bring new insights, and that is the way Jüngel hopes it will work in his theological writings.

---

[10]GMW, 165n.18; GGW, 221n.17. One can *know* God (in contrast to *reasoning about* God) only through faith, however. "God is always known somehow in the event of faith," Jüngel says, and God is known in a way that is "totally obvious to faith." (GMW, 228; GGW, 310; see also T, 46). Faith's knowledge is different from conventional knowing, because only in the *event* of faith is the object of faith perspicuous. Jüngel explains that the meaning of the event of faith lies in its pointing away from itself to another, the cause of one's believing. We designate this other very formally with the word "God," he says ("Womit steht," 164-65).

[11]GMW, 153-55, 157-60, 166; GGW, 204, 206-207, 210-11, 213-14, 223. Barth says something similar when he speaks of our letting our thought be "carried along by the Word of God" (CD I/2, 734).

[12]GMW, 160; GGW, 214.

Language Is Nonobjectifying. Returning to the Heideggerian epistemological sequence that Jüngel follows, in the final step thought that
follows Being evokes language. But putting Being or reality into words
is not the same as objectifying it, because while the formation of a word
makes some part of reality clear, it obscures other aspects of reality. (One
cannot say everything at once.) In that way, however, language is true to
what Being is like, namely, both evident and hidden, explicit and tacit.
It also is true of what God is like, as the next chapter will describe.

Jüngel joins Heidegger and the deconstructionists in opposing the
Western world's traditional understanding of language, according to
which language is a system of signs (words), each of which represents
something with a fixed meaning (or cluster of meanings) based on conventional use and tied to judgments as to truth or falsehood according to
the correspondence theory of truth (namely, truth is agreement between
our perception and objective reality).[13] Words within that system give to
thought the specific content of the thing that they designate. As a result,
Being and thinking are separated, in that thinking is limited to the
restricted meanings of language and is therefore not open to input from
the greater fluidity of Being. Language is thereby made part of the
subject-object split, that is, the Cartesian assumption that the nature or
reality of everything outside a person is fixed and can neither be known
directly by the person nor influenced by the person's interpretation of it.
(The split would not be present if thinking were permitted to invent other
appropriate meanings for a given word in a particular context, rather than
being limited to fixed meanings.)

In contrast, Heidegger denied that words (when they are subjects and
predicates) must refer only to specific objects and definitions. We think
that all thinking and speaking is objectifying, he said, because we think
that when we say that something "is," we solidify the flowing "stream of
life" and make it an object that can be held in the present. We thereby
deceive ourselves and falsify reality.[14] Instead, words can only hold a

---

[13]But normal human judgments lack sensitivity precisely to those "dimensions" that can be present to a person with faith, Jüngel suggests. MW, 72.

[14]According to Heidegger, thinking and speaking are objectifying *only* in the
field of natural science and in technical matters, because the form of perceiving
in those fields establishes its subject in advance as a calculable, causally explic-
able object in Kant's sense (PT, 25, 27-28, Ger. 40, 43-44). He volunteered that,

place for the spirit, because a word is only a label and not the thing in itself.[15]

Accordingly, Jüngel affirms that words function as more than fixed signs of something else.[16] A word is not a *signum* that brings meaning. Rather, meanings bring words.[17] Consequently, there is no one right language or one right way of understanding—a claim that many natural theologies would contest. Language has a multiplicity of meanings, tied to the instance of its use. Jüngel comments that, by means of a statement, the abundant possibilities of a word are momentarily fixed; but they are fixed only until that word is used again in another conversation, since then the address-character of language (which is very important for Jüngel and about which more will be said shortly) will once again unleash the power of the possible against the "real" as previously "pinned down." Accordingly, for one to utter a true statement, that statement must be the free response of one's addressed existence and must not be limited to predetermined word meanings.[18] Such an approach to truth reflects a

---

since "theology is not a natural science," it should not be expected to use objectifying language (PT, 30, Ger. 46).

Heidegger argued that nonobjectifying thinking is "more rigorous than conceptual thought," because everything that is calculable belongs to a larger whole and eventually to the incalculable, and thought that can reflect the incalculable is the more rigorous ("Humanism," Ger. 41). It so happens, he claimed, that "the incalculable" can sometimes put a person in touch with a thinking and a truth that logic cannot grasp and that generates the freedom to sacrifice one's present understanding of everything, so that Being can take on as yet untried forms and meanings (WM, 388-89, Ger. 48-49).

[15]Fuchs, *Hermeneutik*, 208. PJ, 5.

[16]GMW, 4, 7, 9, 161; GGW, 3, 6, 9, 216. Generally, he agrees with Ludwig Wittgenstein that "the meaning of a word is its use in the language" (*Philosophical Investigations*, #43).

[17]As far back as the writing of BT, Heidegger had said, "To significations, words accrue." It isn't that words, as things, "get supplied with significations" (BT, 204). If we do not acknowledge that language stems, essentially, from Being, we shall never reach prelinguistic Being and thereby be enabled to understand Being in a genuinely new way.

[18]MW, 101, 103-104, 108n.99; ET, 48, 51, 56n.100. This is the essence of Jüngel's response to Pannenberg's plaint that Heidegger and Hans-Georg Gadamer are reluctant "to allow the [objectifying] statement form fundamental impor-

thinking that is based not on concepts but on existence, which eludes full conceptualization. Jüngel is wary of fixed conceptions, because in conceptualization a thing loses its verbal character and its freedom of movement: It becomes locked within the boundaries of conceptual thinking and is no longer a form of address that brings its own conception to the fore at the moment and in the context of the address.[19] He has qualified this position, however, by saying that although concepts cannot be substituted for the experience of reality, conceptual language is needed as a control for the building of metaphors.[20]

Language as Metaphorical. Jüngel has a distinctive way of relating language's function and freedom to the basic epistemological question of what counts as knowledge of the world and to the related question of how one understands oneself. He says that people understand themselves only as they see their self reflected in the external world. What they see or choose to see in the things of the *world* are things that they understand as symbols or reflections of aspects of themselves. Conversely, they understand their *own* qualities by identifying them with qualities in the external world. For example, because a man is tough and persevering in dangerous situations, he calls himself a "rock." Jüngel suggests, in summary, that people understand themselves cosmomorphically and the world anthropomorphically.[21]

---

tance in human language." Wolfhart Pannenberg, *Theology and the Philosophy of Science*, trans. Francis McDonagh (Philadelphia: Westminster, 1976) 176.

[19]PJ, 251. He believes that Jesus used "Son of Man," e.g., in this "nonconceptual" way. "The concepts of the Son of Man may not be ends in themselves," he says. "They must be *used* (*chrasthai*) as concepts that bring the nature of the Son of Man to expression" and that therefore can oppose already existing concepts of the Son of Man, with the present use being appropriate for the context of the moment.

He speaks out against Descartes's attempt to find certainty by means of concepts in GMW, 177-80 (GGW, 239-42).

[20]MW, 121, #17; ET, 70. How conceptual or literal language and metaphorical language interrelate is discussed below, on 56-58.

[21]MW, 84, 108, 120 (##11, 12), 121 (##12.4, 13); ET, 31, 56, 69-70. Jüngel adds that this interchange explains how truth as letting-itself-be-discovered works. But because of this inseparable relationship between human beings and the world, he questions the value of the designation "anthropomorphic." GMW, 259n.33; GGW, 354n.33. MW, 105; ET, 52.

He considers this two-way orientation of the use of language—to one's environment and from one's environment—to be a fundamental principle for the functioning of language. He speaks of people finding their way to themselves through language based on the world. When a person does that, "he always brings more into that process than he himself is." As a result, the self cannot be regarded as isolated from the world, as a thinker without a body.[22]

People take charge of their sense impressions and make a world out of them by using their imagination. This self-created world is what their words express. But although people use their experience and language to measure all things, they themselves have been determined by factors in the world outside themselves. Consequently, they have no independent status that enables them to measure the world objectively.

All language, therefore, according to Jüngel, is essentially metaphorical, in that it is derived from our relation with the world, and its meanings and connotations vary with each individual's personal experiences. No words can have fixed meanings. With Nietzsche, Jüngel argues that we cannot hold the Being of a thing in our consciousness. We know only our experience of it. For these reasons and others, a word belongs only to the immanence of the subjectivity of the ego, contrary to Aristotle's teaching: The words that we use mean to us only what we understand them to mean—and that applies to everybody. Since our sense impressions do not provide us with what Aristotle might have called the "objective essence" of a thing, a word can express only our *relation* to the thing—by functioning as metaphor. Because human language is thus structured thoroughly metaphorically, the world around us can come to our attention in a new way, as nonobjective language encourages us to understand it from different perspectives. The fact that much language does not serve that function but merely designates what we already know—that fact means that much of our language has become "dead" metaphor rather than remaining "live" metaphor.[23]

---

[22]GMW, 259; GGW, 353.

[23]Literal meanings may simply be "dead" metaphors. "Foot of the bed," for example, once was probably a "live" metaphor, as a clever way of designating that end of the bed where one's feet lie. Now it is a "dead" metaphor: It simply states a fact. See MW, 74-76, 88, 100-101; ET, 20-21, 35, 47-48. Throughout this book, the assumption is made that "metaphor" refers to a word functioning

The metaphorical character of language has the capacity to convey truth, because truth is occurrence. (God's Being is in act, as Barth has said. Jüngel locates truth in event, rather than in its conventional locus among linguistic analysts, namely, sentences.) And truth occurs in the insight sparked by metaphor.

Language as Bearer of Reality. This insight "speaks Being," that is, it makes people aware of some aspect of reality that they had not been aware of. Figurative language does not try to represent reality; rather, it "bears" reality: it brings reality to us.

Jüngel's way of expressing this Heideggerian view of the symbiotic relationship between word and Being is to say that some words function like a sacrament (defined as "a sign of the presence of the thing"). They both designate the thing and bring it.[24] Consequently, although a word is neither true nor false, a word such as "God" can be invoked in a context in which it functions like a sacrament, thereby making the accompanying sentence about God true. So what the word "God" means is found when the word has an impact as a result of God becoming evident, when the Ultimate brings itself to our attention, as in a revelation or insight. To say that a statement about God is true when God makes it true is to say that it *can* be true but does not always have to be true (while not thereby becoming false).[25]

Similarly, Jüngel sees value in narrative, because it enables the subject matter of a story to engage us existentially, as the story is being told. He writes, "In narrative, the new explicates itself in relation to the old so that it really becomes understandable as the new." "To narrate history means," he continues, "returning to its *past* . . . [and] to its *future* possibilities. . . . [N]arrative is a powerful kind of talk which should result in past history liberating its most authentic possibilities anew."[26]

---

as a live metaphor (e.g., a sad painting).

[24]Accordingly, he says that "the story of Jesus Christ, through the word which emerges from it and tells it, becomes a 'sacrament' (to speak along the lines of Augustine and Luther) before it can function as an 'example'." GMW, 309; GGW, 422.

[25]The sentence "God forgives your sins" may not be false, but it is not particularly meaningful except to a person burdened with guilt. Under those circumstances, however, its truth-value can be experienced as being quite high.

[26]GMW, 303n.11, 305; GGW, 414n.11, 417. The thrust of Jüngel's remark

Language-Events

Having noted the general features of language which Jüngel empha-
sizes, we turn now to those linguistic forms that can release the dynamism and power of words, through what the New Hermeneutic calls "language-events." In a language-event, words serve as channels for effecting
reality, for bringing new meanings, and for expressing and hence revealing God's presence. Such an event unlocks understanding, in the way in
which the Hebrews understood a word to function, which was that a
word's meaning was identical to the impact that it had on its hearer.

Understood in that way, words can function as vehicles of address.[27]
And "the essence of the addressing word is *approach through interruption*."[28] Jüngel explains what he means in his essay "The Truth of Life,"[29]
in which he argues that our knowledge of the world around us advances
only when the truth of the world succeeds in interrupting the status quo
of our contentment with ourselves. Language at its most meaningful
confronts us in a way that requires us to readjust our view of the world.

Certain language-events take place because some things cannot occur
without words, and they are what they are only when words are spoken,
as when a judge renders a decision (for example, "Not guilty!") or when
a priest tells believers that they are absolved. Jüngel suggests that "the
person addressed in such a case is pulled into the word-event." "It is
possible [also], that what a poem is *talking* about *happens* when a poem
is read." The words "speak for themselves," as we say. As another
example, Jüngel points out that curse words hurt a person and are

---

is similar to the following one by Paul Ricoeur: "The sense of a text is not
behind the text, but in front of it. . . . What has to be understood is not the initial
situation of discourse, but what points towards a possible world, thanks to the
nonostensive reference of the text." *Interpretation Theory: Discourse and the
Surplus of Meaning* (Fort Worth: Texas Christian University Press, 1976) 87.
Jüngel adds that through language, *past* history progresses as newly *occurring*
history. GMW, 306; GGW, 418.

[27]Fundamental to Jüngel's understanding of the capacity of language to
address us is his more general understanding that people are capable of being
addressed by God. GMW, 155; GGW, 208.

[28]GMW, 165; GGW, 221.

[29]Jüngel, "The Truth of Life."

intended to do so. They are not merely erroneous designations, but they draw us into their meaning.[30]

The three types of language that Jüngel associates most with language-events, however, are metaphor, analogy, and parable. Parable is discussed in the next chapter, in the section entitled "Parables of the Kingdom."

Metaphor

Barth said that when the Bible appears to present God objectively, that "objectivity" is only a *representation* of God's Being. Jüngel understands such a statement to be a call for a metaphorical use of biblical imagery.

In the past and especially in natural theology, use of analogy has been the primary means of talking about God. In place of the logic of analogy, Jüngel often prefers to use a nonlogical form, metaphor, as the most appropriate means of talking about God, because of its event-character. Traditionally, analogy has assumed that it has something to teach and that its subject matter can be grasped by a logical process of comparison. Metaphor, on the other hand, is much less clear about what it has to say, but it is clear about wanting to assert the presence of a reality that we are not accustomed to. It acts as a catalyst for that reality to make itself known, by establishing an initially unbearable tension between conventional relationships, until the new relationship or perception that the metaphor wants to present is accepted. Usually when analogy is used, objective language is presupposed, so that the role of the speaker and hearer is secondary. (What is of primary importance is the objective meaning of the language.) In metaphor, the imagination and experiences of the speaker and hearer play an essential part in the success of the communication.

Metaphor traditionally has been considered an unreal, merely figurative mode of expression, replacing the true, conventionally agreed-upon

---

[30]GMW, 10-11 (my trans.), 171-72; GGW, 10-11, 231. Cf. J. L. Austin's notion of performative utterances or "speech acts," such as illocutionary acts, in which the speaker performs or accomplishes something *in* the act of saying something, and perlocutionary acts, comparable to Jüngel's curse words. *How to Do Things with Words* (New York: Oxford University Press, 1962) 99-131, 145-63.

meaning of a word with a changed meaning, but one that bears some similarity to the original. Aristotle, for example, taught that what is said metaphorically can also be said literally.[31] Yet because there are many cases where only a metaphor can express what one wants to say, the entire traditional theory of metaphor is called into question. Indeed, recent work has shown that metaphor, parable, and analogy are special forms of proper or true speech.[32]

What is metaphoric is not an unusual word but a predication with the help of a word used in an uncommon way. (For example, in "The ship plowed the sea," "ship" and "plowed" are not uncommon words, but they are brought together in a manner which causes the hearer to think differently about a ship in the sea.) A successful metaphor makes one aware of dimensions of reality that have not been encompassed by the ways in which words with objective meanings are related to one another in conventional sentences. That is because a metaphor is a catalyst, a medium, or a vehicle for a direct application of reality, for a first-order experience rather than a second-order reflection, for a happening rather than for a detached and impersonal, objective statement. By means of the images that it juxtaposes, it catches the truth by allowing a lie. The strangeness of that juxtaposition opens a new dimension of existence to us. In metaphor, reality is surpassed by a new possibility of reality.

Jüngel speaks of a successful metaphor as an occurrence which brings existing things into language, thereby making people aware of them, to the extent that "that which is" lets itself be discovered. Thus, a metaphor is what it brings into our minds and into our language. But since what it brings is perceived as a discovery, it says more about ordinary reality than is found in ordinary reality. At the very least, it mediates a perception of the similarity of the dissimilar. Borrowing from Fuchs, Jüngel suggests that metaphor distances us from the world as we normally experience it so that we can experience what is greater than it.

---

[31]Aristotle, *Rhetorica* 1406^{b}20-22, 1407^{a}11-18, 1410^{b}18-19, and *De poetica* 1457^{b}1-8, 1458^{a}29, ^{b}17-18, in *The Works of Aristotle*, ed. W. D. Ross, vol. 11 (Oxford: Clarendon Press, 1924).

[32]Jüngel refers to the work of Ernst Lohmeyer, Ernst Fuchs, Eugen Biser, Georg Eichholz, Erhardt Güttgemanns, Dan O. Via, Walter Magass, Karl Bülher, Bruno Snell, Karl Löwith, Beda Allemann, Hans Blumenberg, Paul Ricoeur, and Amos Wilder.

Consequently, metaphor is an event that yields Being and, with it, a gain in knowledge.[33]

Since new perceptions mediated by metaphor come to us suddenly and unexpectedly, we experience them as though they were addressing us. The address occurs when the new perception comes to our awareness as the metaphor is used. In light of that process, Jüngel calls metaphor an experience of direct learning. On that basis he says that metaphor is not indirect discourse but, instead, a language form that provides for "a higher degree of directness."[34]

A person learns directly from metaphor, however, only when that person understands the metaphor. And for that understanding to take place, the addressee also must understand the literal meaning of the words used in the metaphor, just as one must understand the literal meaning or the normal situation that a joke deals with, before one can understand a joke. Accordingly, metaphorical usage cannot be interpreted without presuppositions. Metaphor and parable also require imaginative involvement for the generation of new conceptual relationships and new linguistic meanings.[35]

Jüngel considers a metaphorical language to be essential for theology, because metaphor does not allow itself to be directed by mundane reality.[36] Since God is not part of the conventional, mundane, fallen Crea-

---

[33]MW, 94-97, 107-108, 119; ET, 41-44, 54-56, 67-68. Fuchs, *Hermeneutik*, 174. Bultmann, *Theology*, 1:25.

[34]MW, 119, #6; ET, 68. GMW, 292; GGW, 399.

[35]GMW, 290-91; GGW, 396, 398. MW, 78, 97; ET, 24, 44. PJ, 130.

[36]Jüngel's own words offer a partial explanation of his concern with the function of language in theology: "Man must apparently first be *liberated* from the pressure to concentrate on himself. It is for that reason that man first becomes a '*hearer* of the word,' who cannot do anything at all as long as he is listening, and then on the basis of his hearing he can act out of the *newly gained freedom* so that his action, precisely as activity, remains a doing of the *word*" (GMW, 309; GGW, 422). The "newly gained freedom" comes from the spark of liberation and understanding generated by language when it functions as event. Jüngel's position is not incongruent with that of Barth, who quotes Luther approvingly: "Christ's kingdom is a hearing kingdom, not a seeing kingdom. For the eyes lead and guide us not thither where we find Christ and get to know Him, but the ears must do that" (CD I/1, 153). This imagery may be regarded as distinguishing between an oral/aural and a visual model of reality, which may be

tion, God can be discussed adequately only in language that opens us to the unconventional and the extraordinary. "God is a meaningful word only in the context of metaphorical discourse."[37] Metaphor provides a vehicle both for holding fast to God's revelation and for expressing it. Metaphor neither overlooks the mundanely real nor violates it but "goes behind" it and thereby enhances it. That is what happens, according to Jüngel, when theology says that Jesus is the Son of God. Moreover, theological metaphor not only brings a new horizon of meaning to reality but also brings reality to the possibility of its nonexistence, from which, alone, eschatologically new existence arises.[38] In that way, theology avoids speaking only in the present.

When the "first-order," metaphorical language of faith is reflected upon in the conceptual, "second-order," "dead metaphor" language which is often used in theology, even the latter language must be regarded as "live" metaphor, in order for it to tell the truth about God. None of that language, in other words, can bear divine reality within its literal or conventional meanings. At best, it can stimulate the imagination or serve as a vehicle through which divine reality can make itself known.

Jüngel is not unaware of the limitations of metaphor. He considers it an insufficient vehicle for attaining truth, because it can make the opposite of truth unfalsifiable and it can make appearances seem real. As with other forms of language, which are "dead" metaphors, it certainly has no intrinsic access to God. Indeed, he observes that the addressing feature of speech and metaphor can produce falsehood, too. All language, he notes, is ambivalent.

One way out of this problem is to deny the truth-value of metaphor and to hold to a system of words as designators of prescribed meanings. But another way out, Jüngel suggests, is to acknowledge a many-sided dialogue between Mythos and Logos, symbol and concept, address and

---

equated with a Hebrew vs. a Greek model, which amounts essentially to a dynamic model in which the components ultimately are out of one's control and may only be responded to (as in moments of insight), compared with a static model, in which one can and must manipulate the components and draw conclusions.

[37]MW, 110; ET, 58.
[38]PJ, 130. MW, 118; ET, 66-67.

statement, and to let a word have the most appropriate meaning it can have in a given context.[39]

Since Jüngel takes pains to explain how metaphor functions, why it must be the language of theology, and how language as word-event can be the vehicle or catalyst by which divine reality can reach people directly, it might be claimed that he is thereby engaging in a form of natural theology, wherein he makes preliminary preparation for the Word by studying and expounding on language. But he would argue that learning about language is not the foundation for understanding God. We do not necessarily learn anything at all about God when we learn how language can function. What we do learn is to understand and to appreciate what it is about language (namely, its metaphorical quality) that lets it play a significant role in divine-human encounter and why, therefore, at least some language about God can be meaningful even today.

Analogy

While Jüngel shares Barth's opposition to an understanding of the *analogia entis* (analogy of Being) that isolates (as by distilling out) God's Being from God's actions and that presumes to produce knowledge of God apart from revelation, he claims, nevertheless, that Barth misunderstands the *analogia entis*.[40] Jüngel has looked again at Roman Catholic arguments on behalf of the *analogia entis* and has concluded that that form of analogy should not be construed as dealing with a static residue of a God-similarity remaining in a fallen creation. Rather, the primary point that the *analogia entis* makes is that God is *not* at our disposal. It primarily shows dissimilarity between God and the world. In support of this contention, he quotes the Fourth Lateran Council (1215): "between creator and creature, no similarity can be expressed without including a greater dissimilarity."

But the doctrine that analogy always implies a greater dissimilarity leaves him unbearably uneasy, because it restricts human knowledge of God, thereby ensuring that God will remain unknown, and it does so within a context of presupposing that God is one without Whom nothing is. It is unbearable for God to be so necessary and also so unknowable.[41]

---

[39]MW, 98, 109-10; ET, 45-46, 57-58.
[40]GMW, 282n.2; GGW, 385n.2.
[41]GMW, 277-78; GGW, 378.

Moreover, if there is greater dissimilarity than similarity between God and the world, the result must be silence, for the greater dissimilarity keeps us from really knowing. Yet the Gospel pertains to a mystery that has been disclosed and is to be understood and declared.[42] And "there can be no responsible talk about God without analogy." Even Barth agreed with that statement.[43] So Jüngel chooses to follow Erich Przywara by arguing that God's great dissimilarity to us just makes us aware of the similarities that do, in fact, obtain between God and us.[44] Indeed, the Incarnation implies that the genuineness of the sacred can be measured by the extent of its penetration into the profane.[45]

Jüngel contends, therefore, based on Christian faith, that "the difference between God and man . . . is . . . the difference of a still greater similarity between God and man in the midst of a great dissimilarity," because God has identified with humanity in Jesus.[46] But analogy has the obligation to let itself be guided by the Gospel and by the history of Jesus Christ, so as to keep us from being deceived about the nature of God's similarity to us. Jüngel sheds further light on his notion by saying that a parable reflects a greater similarity than dissimilarity between God and human beings when, through it, the Kingdom of God makes itself less strange.[47] Here the similarity resides primarily in the Kingdom's being more familiar. The similarity also may involve the dynamic and open nature of both human and divine Being, which makes it possible for an event of the Kingdom's presence to occur.

Heidegger had said that analogy belongs to metaphysics, because where Being itself speaks, no analogy is needed. Jüngel disagrees. He is able to do so, because he proposes a unique way of understanding analogy. In his view, analogy does not seek to provide objective information

---

[42]Rom. 16:25-26; Eph. 6:19; Col. 1:26; 2:2; 4:3.

[43]GMW, 281-82; GGW, 384-85. Jüngel adds that Barth finally stopped being concerned about people trying to bridge the gap to God via the *analogia entis*.

[44]GMW, 284-85; GGW, 388-89.

[45]Bernhard Gerts, *Glaubenswelt als Analogie: Die theologische Analogie-Lehre Erich Przywaras und ihr Ort in der Auseinandersetzung um die analogia fidei* (Düsseldorf: Patmos-Verlag, 1969) 253.

[46]GMW, 288, 298; GGW, 393, 407.

[47]GMW, 285, 294-95; GGW, 389, 403.

about a highest existing Being or to demonstrate the similarity between two things based on the fact that they participate in one or more of the same qualities. Instead, Jüngel's concept of analogy lets Being itself speak. A traditional use of analogy, he points out, deals only with the things being related and not with the relations. Instead, "One must understand analogy as an event which [in the proportion x:a = b:c, for example] allows the One (x) *to come* to the Other (a)—with the help of the relationship of a further Other (b) to even one more Other (c)."[48]

This understanding of analogy, namely, as relation experienced as event, is the basis for what he calls his "hermeneutical thesis," namely, that within a great dissimilarity between God and humanity is an even greater similarity. It should be noted, however, that that similarity is not a static one but occurs as event, when God comes to us and thereby makes the similarity possible. The thesis reflects the gamble that divine reality can be conveyed by language that refers to human reality. The thesis also offers a formula, within the categories of linguistics, for expressing Barth's concept of subjective revelation. (Barth claimed that even though there was an "objective" revelation of God in Jesus Christ, people today will not understand that revelation unless God comes to them and reveals it to them personally [subjectively].)

Jüngel labels his view of analogy the "analogy of advent." He regards it as a conscious attempt to follow the revelatory movement of God in the Gospel. It bases the possibility of analogical talk of God on belief that God addresses us. Hence, he calls it language that is "appropriate to the gospel,"[49] since the Gospel is the good news of God coming to humanity.

The "analogy of advent" does not compare thing with thing. Rather, it compares relations with relations. But it goes one step further by treating relation as event (not unlike metaphor), thereby providing for the possibility of God "coming" to (or being perceived in) the relationship.

---

[48]GMW, 285; GGW, 389. As an example, in the parable of the treasure in the field (Matt. 13:44-46), the joyful experience of the unsurpassable worth of the Kingdom of God is related to the hearer of the parable just as the treasure that brings joy is related to the finder; viz., it comes to the hearer when he is drawn into the parable and has the unsurpassable value of God announced to him. PJ, 144.

[49]GMW, 261; GGW, 356.

Such a view of analogy can succeed because relations are "linguistic," that is, they are not frozen by predetermined definitions or structures but are open to new interpretations, as all Being is.
Jüngel applies the "analogy of advent" to God in the following way:

> When the analogy contains *God* as one of its members (x:a = b:c), then, on the basis of the relation of God (x) to the world (a), the relation within the world (b:c), which corresponds to that relation, appears in a completely *new*, eschatological light, which *makes* this relation within the world itself *new*. The relation within the world (b:c), which from within itself is simply incapable of giving any indication of God, begins then to speak for God . . . as . . . something even more obvious. . . . The God Who comes to the world (x→a) makes use of the obvious in this world in such a way that he proves himself to be . . . even more obvious. . . . But that can be experienced only . . . when b:c is *talked about* in such a way that it *corresponds* to the relation of God to the world (x→a), and God thereby ceases to be unknown (x). In the event of the analogy x→a = b:c, God stops being x.[50]

Jüngel applies his concept to the parable of the treasure in the field. Although the farmer (c) sells all that he has in order to buy the field containing the treasure (b) of even greater value that his plow blade has hit into, the lesson to be learned is not that people (a) should give up all they have in order to gain the greater treasure of the Kingdom of God (x). There is another relation in the parable: The treasure lets itself be found. When God comes to the analogy by providing the insight that the latter relationship holds the key to the relation of God to the world (namely, that the Kingdom lets itself be found [x→a]), then something new becomes known about God.[51]

---

[50]GMW, 285-86 (trans. modified); GGW, 389-90.

[51]The preceding quotation sparks another interpretation, which Jüngel may not accept fully. That interpretation runs as follows: We do not reason from the relations within a parable or an analogy to what God is or is like. Rather, those same parables (e.g., the parable of the prodigal son) that make us aware of God also cause us to see differently and more penetratingly the worldly relations that they employ, because *seeing them differently* (i.e., *as they should be*, as "something even more obvious") *and seeing God are the same thing.* God is said to have "come to the world" when the relationships within the world are *seen* as what they ideally *should* be (in a "*new*, eschatological light"). Such a view can change our behavior, thereby changing the relationships themselves.

We, however, are not in control of whatever creates the insight that enables us to see how b:c *"corresponds* to the relation of God to the world" and thereby makes God known. The ambience of language provides a hospitable context, but if it is to succeed in producing the desired but unpredictable result, God's revelation must occur. In analogy as in other areas, the ultimate hermeneutical path to knowledge of God, of Being, and of other beings does not reside in us and our constructions but rather in them and in their address to us.

Chapter 4

Interpreting the Bible

The Bible is the basic source of theology for Jüngel. His approach to interpreting it is consistent with his view of language. As an indication of that approach, this chapter considers his thoughts on hermeneutics, on the use of parables, on the historical-critical method, and on the problem of recovering the historical Jesus.

Jüngel's Hermeneutic

Jüngel's approach to biblical interpretation does not limit him to a single philosophy. He does not try to understand the Bible solely within the parameters and structure of any one philosophical system, as a natural theologian might do. He asks, with Barth,

> How can we bind ourselves to one philosophy as the only philosophy, and ascribe to it a universal necessity, without actually positing it as something absolute, as the necessary partner of the Word of God, and in that way imprisoning and falsifying the Word of God?[1]

Instead, Jüngel follows Fuchs in claiming that the function of a hermeneutical principle is not to explain the thing we want to understand, but to activate the *event* of understanding. Such a principle can sometimes be an artifice, established simply to set the event of understanding in motion, by getting the thing that we want to understand to appear as it really is. As an example, Fuchs suggests that a mouse can be said to be the hermeneutical principle for understanding a cat. Put a mouse in front of a cat, and the cat will behave in a way that exposes its true nature.[2]

---

[1]CD I/2, 733

[2]Fuchs, *Hermeneutik*, 109-10. The Bible could be viewed, therefore, as Christianity's principle artifice for activating our understanding of God.

Jüngel may be using his "hermeneutical thesis" as an artifice in this sense. By conceiving of analogy as relation experienced as event, and by believing that the anthropomorphic language in the New Testament can portray greater divine-human similarity than dissimilarity, he provides a device for provoking human thought in previously inactive areas, thereby also providing opportunity for God's own Self-disclosure in those areas. For when hermeneutics makes something intelligible, the thing becomes intelligible because *it* discloses itself and its relationship to us, not because it fits into a particular, overarching pattern of thought, as most conventional hermeneutical principles usually prescribe.

Stated simply, Jüngel's hermeneutic is to view biblical language metaphorically, looking for insights that result when he does so. Those insights expand his mental and spiritual horizon, and they may be signs of God's coming to him, bringing the truth or the more profound "dimension" to which the biblical language points.

This approach also can give a different "twist" to our conception of the Bible's role. The Bible's main purpose may not be to provide information about how we should think about God or how the early Church thought about God and Christ. Instead, it may be primarily about God's thoughts concerning us. Consequently, the Bible can become, when we read it, not an object for us to ask questions about but the Subject that questions us and our values and relationships.

When it does so, the Holy Spirit is likely to be at work. And the work of the Holy Spirit is a requisite part of Jüngel's hermeneutics, because the Spirit of Christ is the content of which the Bible is the form, and the two cannot be separated. The words of the Bible are the static deposit of the dynamic Spirit, and only the latter can unlock the significance of the former.[3] As the vehicle for God's own language, however, the Bible can "from time to time become God's Word,"[4] when God speaks through it. Apart from this happening even the Bible should not be called the "Word of God."

Jüngel's hermeneutic acknowledges that people come to the Bible with presuppositions; but it also provides for overcoming them. Jüngel

---

[3] In this connection, Fuchs comments that there is a "hermeneutical problem" simply because we cannot know truth at our own pleasure. *New Hermeneutic*, ed. Robinson and Cobb, 143.

[4] CD I/1, 131.

says that the truth of Scripture speaks when the literal text is juxtaposed to the present concrete situation, so that the latter can act as a catalyst in a metaphorical understanding of the text, thereby opening a new direction of thought and providing a vehicle for God to address us in the present. In such interpretation, the world of the reader and the world and God of the text merge in what Gadamer calls a "fusion of horizons." By pointing to the power of metaphor and of dynamic analogy to create new perceptions, Jüngel deals with the problem of our preconceptions limiting the ability of a text to say something new to us. At the same time, he acknowledges the force that our life's experiences exert on the hermeneutical process.

Although Jüngel considers hermeneutics to be the last avenue to certainty, he says that there is no single hermeneutical method in which theology can place complete faith. That claim certainly applies to interpreting the Word of God, for the event of the Word of God, he says, "is not a priori identical with any human linguistic context."[5]

Because the current situation into which the Bible is to be brought is always changing, and because sin is always corrupting subjective revelation, there is no eternally valid interpretation that can be given to the Bible, either. As Jüngel understands the matter, in biblical interpretation there is no final certainty.[6]

Parables of the Kingdom

God can provide certainty of a different type, however. This certainty can emerge when a person encounters parables.

A parable combines the intellectual experience of metaphor with the temporal involvement of narrative. Since Jesus often spoke in parables, Jüngel has given careful study to that linguistic form and has developed from it insights into Jesus' Being and significance.

Parable, like metaphor, is a nonconceptualizing language-event. Says Jüngel:

---

[5]Eberhard Jüngel, "God—as a Word of Our Language," trans. Robert T. Osborn, in *Theology of the Liberating Word*, ed. Frederick Herzog (Nashville: Abingdon, 1971) 41.
[6]PJ, 237.

If the parable were an equation, then it would be a thesis, and then its "content" would in fact be a theme which could be abstracted from the "form" of the parable. But a parable is not a thesis and has no theme at all. Rather, it is an event which then makes something else happen.[7]

What happens is that the audience gets a concrete understanding of what the parable is talking about. The parable "ignites" the point that it wants to make. Accordingly, he says, in Jesus' preaching the "Kingdom" was not conceptualized in a definition but let itself be grasped as Jesus talked about it.[8] The Kingdom is not like a woman (or any other noun) who did something but is like *when* something takes place.

Jüngel claims that, because of their analogical power, Jesus' parables express God's future in such a way that they themselves bring an eschatological "taste" of God's future.[9] Jesus' parables provide a "*sacramental* relation" of sign and thing signified, so that the sign becomes efficacious.[10] The parables can be divine events, because they are generated eschatologically by the Kingdom (reign) of God. Hence, "the new time of God's reign is already present in Jesus' parables."[11]

One needs a particular concept of time in order to understand how the Kingdom of God comes into language in Jesus' parables. Jüngel teaches that God's future, in Jesus' view, was a real happening in time and not an eschatological point at the end of time. Jesus accepted the Hebrew understanding of time. For the Hebrews, time was not a continuously running line, measurable in pieces, as in Western thought, but was or could be what was filled by God. Time was moments of significance:

---

[7]GMW, 293-94; GGW, 401. See also PJ, 107, 135, ##1-2.

[8]PJ, 87, 110.

[9]PJ, 134.

[10]GMW, 294; GGW, 402. In that Jesus (who, according to Jüngel, was determined fully by his faith in the Kingdom) was present, the Kingdom was present as he spoke of it. The specific formulation of his words did not evoke it any more fully. He could have given his disciples a direct answer instead of telling a story. The answer would have been the point of the parable. But the function of a parable, in Jüngel's view, is not to help people understand the Kingdom of God but to help them experience it in the present. Jesus' parables do not have a meaning, Jüngel adds. Their function is to help (*zuschanzen*) a person to the Kingdom.

[11]PJ, 101.

fullness of time, rather than duration of time. This understanding is evident when Jüngel says,

> The nearness of the Kingdom of God is so near that it requires the linguistic form of the parable, in order really to come to language in such a way that man is able to adjust himself to it. Then the parables of Jesus help us to understand the near future of the Kingdom of God . . . as a power that invades the present.[12]

As much as a parable can offer to the hearer the power of God or of the Kingdom of God—Jüngel equates the two[13]—the result is not that the Kingdom thereby becomes encapsulated on earth. Jüngel is careful to say that in place of the law and the prophets is not the Kingdom but is simply the preaching of it and the power of the Kingdom in that preaching. That care is evident in the statement that he considers to be the key to understanding the parables, namely, *"The Basileia comes to language IN parable AS parable. The parables of Jesus bring the Kingdom of God to language AS parable."*[14] Only a parable of the Kingdom can be put into words. The ineffable, itself, simply cannot be captured. As a result, what is present when the Kingdom comes into the world, namely, parable, preserves the distinction—the eschatological distance—between God and humanity. At the same time, even in parable the Kingdom can qualify humanity's present, since the parables offer a contrast between the divine and the mundane, and since the parables' words, themselves, can enable the hearer or reader to confront the reality of the Kingdom (that is, the reality of God), if the hearer "gets" the point of the parable. "In that way the creation appears in a new light, in the light of the dominion of God that ends the old."[15]

The Historical-Critical Method

In view of Jüngel's emphasis on the dynamic and nonobjectifying aspects of language, what role could there be for objective, critical study of the Bible?

---

[12]PJ, 168-69.
[13]GMW, 297, 353; GGW, 406, 484.
[14]PJ, 135, #3. See also 173, #1, 292.
[15]PJ, 138, #9.

Jüngel does find value in critical study of the Bible, and he endorses use of the scholarly tools. Indeed, he uses them with distinction, especially in his exegesis of the parables.[16] He comments that although we cannot come to Jesus Christ *by* (*aus*) our own reason and strength, we are expected to come to him *with* them.[17] Accordingly, he calls us to do exegesis in light of the present time and to avoid "text fetishism," because, he says, the *kerygma* is the Word of God only when it acknowledges historical restrictions and does not try to preserve itself from the changes of history.

The historical-critical method can prepare people to read the Bible intelligently. For example, use of critical tools shows that the Gospels are not histories. Those tools also help us to understand how the Gospels group their materials.

Jüngel holds that the literal words of the Bible provide the criteria for theology. Otherwise, theology would be based only on subjective interpretations of the world around us. To interpret those words appropriately, he engages in careful criticism of the Bible's own theology, of the theology that has developed during the Church's history, and of the theology stemming from his own German culture. By these means he also deals with the problem of presuppositions. Since he is not content with the sociological conditioning of knowledge, he calls for crossing cultural borders in the interest of apprehending more universal truth. The value of considering the world outside the Bible and the Church lies in the insights that such consideration can stimulate, with regard to the meaning of the Bible.

Jüngel teaches, therefore, that one cannot move directly from biblical text to sermon without critical evaluation of the text. But he also cautions against being satisfied with moving from the received text simply to a criticized text. Instead, the text must be related imaginatively to the present context, with the hope that input from the Holy Spirit will ensue.

---

[16]PJ, 83, 85, 142-45, 148-51, 169, 203, 236, 277.

[17]"Womit steht," 162. This comment sheds much light on Jüngel's relation to Heidegger. As a Christian, Jüngel is committed first to Jesus Christ. But he comes to that relationship with his reason and therefore is willing to consider Heidegger's ideas for whatever insights they might provide, as his faith seeks to develop understanding and to express it.

He endorses Bultmann's concern for demythologizing, as a historically necessary step in developing an existential, that is, experiential—not philosophically existentialist—interpretation of the New Testament. He disapproves of Bultmann's effort to separate biblical form from content, however. He holds them together by claiming that demythologizing means understanding the myth, and by saying that content is encountered along with form.

He warns that there is a danger that the form-critical method may tend to limit interpretation to sociological phenomena, but he suggests that critical study is needed for the same reason that one needs to understand conventional relationships before one can "get" a joke, or that one needs to know the meaning of philosophical concepts before they can be used properly in theology. Specifically, he says that "the historical-critical method practiced in *theology* has the task of delivering up the phenomena . . . unimpaired in their concretion."[18] For Jüngel, the historical-critical method is phenomenological examination of the text, so that the words of the text itself can create an entrance into us.

In summary, Jüngel finds the truth of God not in the objective facts or probabilities uncovered by the historical-critical method, but in the insights and in the changed relationships that can be generated (by God) by means of those facts. The scholarly tools are needed to uncover the facts, however, so they can perform their catalytic function. In that way they can become vehicles for God.

Finding the Historical Jesus[19]

When it comes to applying those tools to a search for the historical Jesus, Jüngel has a greater appreciation of the value of such an effort than either Bultmann or Barth had, although he, too, shares with them a recognition that the significance of Jesus for today does not lie primarily in historical data about him.[20]

---

[18]Jüngel, "Der Schritt zurück," 115-16n.4.

[19]Jüngel has not developed a complete Christology. This section, the one on "Parables of the Kingdom," and his identification of God with the crucified Jesus (referred to in the next chapter) provide the most significant clues to his thinking on that topic.

[20]As was mentioned in chap. 1, Bultmann's study of the Bible caused him

Jüngel is less sanguine than Fuchs concerning what can be known about the historical Jesus. He doubts that we can get back to the actual life of Jesus or to Jesus' understanding of himself. Instead, he suggests that Jesus' reported actions should be regarded, for the most part, only as theological commentary on his preaching.[21] "But," he adds, "if one asks why the historical Jesus had to become the preached Christ, then the historical Jesus as a historical phenomenon must also be discussed."[22] In approaching the "historical phenomenon," the historical-critical method is to be used, even though the true Jesus is different from the Jesus discovered by that method. Nevertheless, the method assists in evaluating the texts that reflect on Jesus' life, thereby providing clues for interpreting his death and other dogma about him. The content of his life is important, because the truth of the story of Jesus depends upon it, even if our methods do not yield a very firm grip on that content.[23] That is the reason Jüngel finds the parables valuable: They capture linguistically some of Jesus' own reality.

Jüngel believes that Jesus' own parables, as we now have them, are generally reliable reflections not only of Jesus' teaching but also of his life. He holds this view because, with Fuchs, he claims that Jesus' behavior commented on his parables in such a way that his disciples could not miss their point. Jesus' conduct made his message clear. He not only

---

to conclude that the truth about the historical Jesus is beyond our reach. In addition, the N.T. itself found the historical Jesus to be of interest only because of what was *believed* about his significance. Knowing that the *kerygma* refers back to the demands and works of Jesus still does not provide certainty about the historical Jesus.

Barth, too, argued against using historical studies as the basis for knowing Jesus Christ. But his argument did not rest on the limitations of the critical tools or on the conclusion that there was simply no objective, firsthand evidence but on the inability of sinners to recognize the newness that was and is in Jesus Christ. If we were present with Jesus, we would have either deserted him or crucified him; so how does the historical Jesus help us to understand Jesus better? No, Barth said, we can know Jesus Christ only by faith awakened by God.

[21]PJ, 200n.6.

[22]PJ, 79.

[23]Jüngel adds, however, that Jesus' life is not more important than that Jesus is risen (metaphorically speaking), because the Resurrection reveals God's identity with Jesus throughout his life.

spoke of love, for example, but he went to those who needed it. And both his preaching and his action reflected the eschatological determination of his existence: He was empowered to be motivated solely by faith in God. Indeed, it is because Jesus' behavior revealed the power of the reign of God that his preaching had authority.

Furthermore, the ability of parable to mediate the extraordinary while, at the same time, maintaining a distinction between the ordinary and the extraordinary provides Jüngel with a conceptual device for understanding Jesus Christ himself. Jüngel calls him the "parable of God."[24] He teaches, also, that the humanity of Jesus so fully reflected God's love, that believers considered it appropriate to claim that Jesus' life was an analogy of "God's *nature* as event of eternal love."[25] Jesus can be this analogy and parable because, since both his actions and the parables that he spoke brought the Kingdom of God to expression,[26] his relation to other people must have been determined by God.[27] But his relation to God "is not to be sought in a quality of Jesus' person but in the eschatological qualification of his conduct, that is, not in Jesus but in God."[28] Jüngel is willing to say, as Rudolf Otto did, that Jesus did not bring the Kingdom to prominence, but the Kingdom brought Jesus to prominence.[29] Thus, "the Kingdom of God authorizes Jesus' preaching and Jesus' conduct, while Jesus, trusting in the power of the Kingdom of God, engaged in [that

---

[24]GMW, 288, 358; GGW, 394, 491.

[25]"Möglichkeit," 540.

[26]These events provided the basis for the argument that such a person could have been resurrected. Jüngel points out that faith in Jesus' resurrection presupposed a history that did not begin with his death and resurrection (PJ, 278). This awareness reinforces Jüngel's interest in the historical Jesus and in what created faith in him. Jüngel also writes that "if Jesus was the absolutely 'free man,' then we must inquire about the origin of his freedom" ("God—as a Word of Our Language," 35).

[27]PJ, 173, #5, 174, #6, 181, 212. Jüngel adds that Jesus' personal identity was grounded not in himself but in God (218). See also "Das Sein Jesu Christi als Ereignis der Versöhnung Gottes mit einer gottlosen Welt: Die Hingabe des Gekreuzigten," *Evangelische Theologie* 38 (November/December 1978) 517, #12.5: "Jesus' life and death was an ex-isting out of the coming reign of God and an in-sisting on God's fatherly will."

[28]PJ, 262n.3.

[29]PJ, 281n.1.

preaching and action] in a unique way."[30] Hence, "Jesus was present in
the authority of God."[31] The parables reflect that activity of God in Jesus
and in Jesus' experience of God's power.[32] It would appear that Jesus'
preaching, therefore, was based on his new Being, as determined by his
experience of the Kingdom, and not just on his intellectual understanding
of the Kingdom. Actually, the two are indivisible, since Jüngel's is "a
Christology of the conformity of the Being of Jesus to the Being of God,
which arises from the eschatological conformity of the Being of Jesus to
the Being of God that makes its appearance in the preaching and in the
conduct of Jesus." (At least, this conformity is present in the eyes of believers.) By "conformity to the Being of God" Jüngel means simply that
Jesus represents God's will.[33] Such an understanding reflects Jüngel's dynamic ontology, according to which God's Being is God's will in action.

As with human knowledge of God, no way leads to knowledge of
Jesus that does not begin in Jesus himself. For Jüngel, this "beginning"
takes a twofold form. It refers to the necessity of there actually having
been a Jesus of Nazareth who walked the earth, and it refers to the present, "resurrected" reality of Jesus. Hence, Jüngel says it is important to
do historical work on Jesus with the objective of letting Jesus himself
come to expression, that is, of bringing to light the historic, theological
significance and power of Jesus.[34]

Following this approach, Jüngel finds that God became understandable in the history of Jesus, "within which the 'arrival of God' is identified with the 'eschatologically qualified present'."[35] Jesus' own present
was eschatologically qualified, and he qualifies the present of others in
the same way: His reference to the time of the Son of man is a reference
to the time of the future judgment, which Jesus binds to the present and
to himself in such a manner that the way in which people relate to Jesus

---

[30]PJ, 196, #3. See also 212.

[31]PJ, 197, #7.

[32]PJ, 87, 119n.7, 157. GMW, 354-60; GGW, 486-94.

[33]PJ, 212, 262.

[34]PJ, 82-83. Here Jüngel unites Bultmann's interest in objective study with
Heidegger's claim that the phenomenon must reveal itself and with Barth's
endorsement of that claim, at least with regard to divinity.

[35]PJ, 187.

determines the way the Son of man will relate to them.[36] With Jesus' words and deeds modifying the present time eschatologically and also the future judgment, it was not a big step for the Jesus of history to become the Christ of faith as time passed. The step meant that people believed that Jesus conformed to God and therefore identified God's will.

Preaching about Jesus today can act as a vehicle for the Holy Spirit's action, just as Jesus' own person and preaching (now reflected in the *kerygma*) did in his day. But identifying the future judgment as occurring with Jesus in history does not bring salvation history to an end, as often appears to be the case in Barth's view. On the contrary, Jüngel perceives Jesus the Christ as inaugurating a new, continuing history, "which is determined by the *nomos tou Christou* [law of Christ] as a history of love, freedom, and faith."[37]

In sum, what we learn from the clues that we can establish about the historical Jesus is not details of his life, but what his function was (namely, being a parable of God) and what (transforming) impact he had on those who believed in him and his way. His impact continues, as people who believe in the grace of his way seek to give contemporary meaning to "love, freedom, and faith."

---

[36]PJ, 256, 261, 280.
[37]PJ, 282n.3, 288.

Chapter 5

Jüngel's Views of God

Jüngel's conceptual tools and his theological background lead reasonably to his doctrine of God. But just as many of his writings offer gems of insight on the way to rather orthodox—albeit cleverly stated—conclusions, so this chapter begins with typically Jüngelian prolegomena, on its way to his conception of the Trinity.

Barriers to Intellectual Acceptance of God

A logical first step in talking about God is to demonstrate the error in the thinking of those who can no longer conceive of God. Jüngel takes that step in connection with three considerations that are discussed in this section. He argues against the notion that God is necessary, since that requirement leads to the conclusion that God is dead, when God's necessity is no longer demonstrable. He also opposes those who work with a Cartesian-based metaphysics and those who reject God as a result of asking inappropriate questions about God.

The Necessity of God

The modern person, as represented by Descartes, guarantees the certainty of existence only in the moment of thinking, Jüngel says. Transitoriness is overcome only by systematically doubting the certainty of everything, including God. Such doubting results in the one certainty, namely, that "I exist, because I think." But by basing my certainty on my act of thinking, I discover that I have destroyed the very intransitoriness that I sought, Jüngel suggests, because I become aware of the highly transitory nature of my acts of thinking.[1]

---

[1]GMW, 186; GGW, 251

In addition, Descartes realized that his own ideas might not corre-
spond to the truth of the world outside his thought. Moreover, he could
not be sure that he was the same person as the one whose existence was
guaranteed by his previous acts of doubting. He turned to his faith in
God to assure himself on these matters, because a good God would not
rule a universe in which there was not usually a continuous and correct
relationship between one's thoughts and one's external world. By
reasoning in that way, he provided a function for God. God was the
highest Being, Who compensated for what was lacking. More pointedly,
God was considered to be necessary, in order to maintain the certainty
and the continuity of the thinking individual.

For that function to be performed, God's essence and God's existence
were separated. As a result, God's unity was destroyed. To assure the
certainty of God's essence, that essence was detached from the transitory
world and regarded as being above and beyond it. God's existence, on
the other hand, was considered to be present in the world and in our
thought, assuring the validity of our innate ideas. (This separation is the
consequence of Descartes' position, Jüngel argues, even though Descartes, himself, did not intentionally violate the unity of essence and existence that Aristotelian metaphysics found in God. In keeping with that
philosophy, when traditional Christian theology distinguished between
God's essence and existence, it understood that it was making only a
logical distinction and not a real one, since God was the absolutely
Simple and therefore could not be subdivided. It also considered the truth
of human perception to be upheld by the divine intellect and to be dependent upon it. That relationship was changed, however, when Descartes
grounded human thought in the thinking individual, rather than in God.)

It was that separation, Jüngel suggests, that led to the eventual denial
of God's reality. The thinking human subject had been inserted between
God's essence and God's existence in such a way that the thinker became
the guarantor of God's existence, rather than vice versa. Just as Descartes' faith in God was based on his certainty of himself, so, in this
case, God is considered to exist only as long as God performs a function
that one acknowledges that one needs.[2] When the modern mind increasingly saw itself as the measure of all things, it concluded that persons

---

[2]GMW, 106-108, 123-26, 141, 152; GGW, 139-42, 163-67, 187, 202-203.

could be human and that the world could be comprehensible without God. God, therefore, no longer performed a necessary function. Since the modern acknowledgment of God depended on God's being necessary, when God was no longer seen to be necessary for the technical functioning of the world, there was no longer a basis for acknowledging God's reality. Jüngel comments: "Proof of the necessity of God is the midwife of modern atheism."[3]

Jüngel argues against regarding God as necessary by pointing out that necessity is a mode of being that always involves a relationship. From that observation he makes two points. First, something can be absolutely necessary for something else while still being contingent itself. Consequently, proving that God is necessary does not establish the Being of God with certainty.

Second, the necessary thing must function in a way that is determined by the thing for which it is necessary, which means that the necessary thing cannot be independent. Accordingly, Jüngel argues that God viewed as necessary would indeed be dead, because such a God would be determined by that for which God is necessary. Stated another way, because people are not complete, they need One more complete than they; but thereby they relativize God and make God dependent on their being dependent on God. If humanity is necessarily grounded in God, then God is too greatly reduced to the world and is held hostage by the world's needs, Jüngel concludes.[4]

Cartesian-Based Metaphysics

Jüngel also argues that God has become unthinkable for many people as a result of metaphysical thinking grounded in Descartes' *cogito*. With their deliberations resting on the certainty of their own thought, they had to draw the conclusion that God is unthinkable because God does not reside in the *cogito*. Limiting their "knowledge" of God to their own sub-

---

[3]GMW, 19; GGW, 23.
[4]GMW, 24-28, 122, 19-20; GGW, 30-35, 161, 23. He does not take up the topic of philosophical necessity, because God is encountered existentially and not in the philosophical arena, where the concept of "necessary principles" is employed. He would not deny, however, that God exists necessarily, i.e., that God's reality is not contingent upon something outside God.

jectivity, they developed a metaphysics that culminated logically in the death of God.

With reason grounded in certainty of the self, the self came to be treated as the infinite. Finite reason became the absolute point of view. And finite reason ruled that God cannot be known but can only be believed, because reason sees only what it projects. But if reason can think and project God, it also can think the negation of God. That it did, thereby eliminating God, since God had been grounded in the certainty of human thought in the first place.

Toward More Appropriate Questions

As a consequence of the Kantian argument against human ability to know the thing-in-itself and the further argument that leads to our thinking God out of existence, Jüngel points out that human reason itself has come to recognize it does not have the ability to know the nature of God. If it is to say anything at all about God, it must be more humble in its claims.

Providentially, perhaps, after the First World War interest shifted (in some quarters) away from questions concerning God's nature to a question that Jüngel finds appropriate for coming to grips with God's reality. The Existentialist experience of Nothingness, the events of the Holocaust, and the experience of economic and political powerlessness have driven people to ask not who or what God is but *where* God is, if at all. Jüngel agrees with raising the question about God in this way. He says that whether there is a God at all and what characteristics God might have are to be answered best by asking where God can be found and where people can be addressed by God. Such questions provide for the absence of God, a possibility that is excluded in principle when it is presumed that it is God's nature to be omnipresent and omnipotent.

Since "presence" and "absence" are merely human categories, however, Jüngel suggests that the question of where God is is not posed radically enough if it can be answered fully and literally in terms of presence and absence. A God Who is present in a worldly sense, that is, Who is palpably present in one location or situation and absent in another, Who is simply an exponential increase in mundane availability, is not God.[5] We shall see how Jüngel handles the question of where God is, as we

---

[5]GMW, 103, 54, 62; GGW, 135-36, 70-71, 81.

consider his approach to the question of whether or not God is conceivable.

Thinking and Speaking about God Today

Jüngel is concerned to show how we may speak and think about God today, while avoiding the destructive rocks of both theism and atheism. He includes within theism the practice of treating the word "God" as a sign that gives us a content-filled object that is amenable to human understanding.

Silence and the spoken word have been used over the centuries both to affirm and to deny God. Jüngel summarizes the four combinations. (1) It is possible to *affirm* God by being *silent*, because you consider God to be inconceivable and inexpressible. This has been the way of mysticism. (2) It is possible to be so untouched by claims of God as to ignore the matter completely, thereby *denying* God by being *silent*. (3) It is possible to *speak* about God as being inconceivable and inexpressible and therefore as being worthy only of *denial*, which is what atheism does. (4) And it is possible to *affirm* God by *speaking* about God, in the way that theism, Deism, and the metaphysical tradition in Christian theology have done. He then comments that "[t]he Christian faith, if it understands itself properly, can only protest against each of these possibilities as well as against any combination of them."[6] Jüngel's alternative to these approaches is considered in this section.

Conceiving of God

Thought via Address. The section of chapter 3 on "Thinking with Faith" considered one of Jüngel's approaches to conceiving of God. That view stated that we can think of God when God addresses us in an event. In such an occurrence, metaphysical thinking about God, which separates God's essence from God's existence, is overcome, because God is not fragmented but is fully present in the revelatory Word of address. In addition, by thinking after the "Object" of the event, correct theological thinking avoids the tyranny of the spirit of the times. Instead, since God is always coming (as will be discussed below), thought is led out of the

---

[6]GMW, 252-53; GGW, 344. It is not the case, e.g., that we know about some facets of God but that others are a mystery.

circle of itself and is drawn to imagine things differently from what they presently are. Accordingly, however, it should be noted that "God can be thought only as something constantly to be thought anew."[7]

In Jüngel's second approach, he discusses thinking about God based on the fact that God can be talked about. In that case thought follows language, instead of preceding it. But that language has a particular content; it is not just language-in-general. Here Jüngel has a material and not a temporal sequence in mind: It is only when *particular* things are said about God, and not simply the fact that people can use the word "God" in conversation, that our language can be said to precede our thoughts about God. Those particular things deal with God's historical revelation in Jesus Christ. But even that language requires God's presence in order to stimulate proper thinking about God, since God alone speaks adequately about God.[8] So even when the unthinkable becomes thought on the basis of our speaking about God in Christ, that thought is effective only in the context of a language-event through which God makes God's own reality known.

By now it should be evident that, for Jüngel, human language is the earthly locus of our ability to think about God (when the Word, as the heavenly source of that ability, is combined with it). That is his answer, also, to the question of where God is. He gives that answer because the word can bring people and God together, since it accords with both God, as the Speaking One, and with the linguistic nature of human beings. God and people come together linguistically not simply *because* language about God is used, and not *every time* that that language is used, but because God can and does use language, from time to time, as a means of making divine reality known. Jüngel claims that language can be where God is, also because words can unite the past (for example, God's past revelation), the present, and the future (for example, God's new address to us) with an immediacy that history, for example, cannot offer. The word is the instrumentality for capturing reality. At the same time, therefore, it is also the means both for distorting the fluidity of reality and, by implication, for pointing to the surplus that was not encapsulated. It functions much like God's own being in the world, therefore, a Being that

---

[7]GMW, 227; GGW, 309.

[8]One way of understanding the use of language under those circumstances is to regard it as speaking of God listeningly.

exists when it acts in revelation and, when acting, is both present to our ken and absent from our ken.[9] (We cannot comprehend the entirety of God, even when we encounter God's revelation.) Accordingly, because the word's function is similar to God's Being, in that the word, too, makes (a partial reality) present while also implying absence (of a more fluid and total reality), Jüngel finds the word to be the fitting earthly "location" of God.

God's Unity with the Transitory. The claim that God is in the Word of address to human beings, however, means that God also is in transitoriness, perishability, and change, a feature that is crucial both to Jüngel's understanding of God's reality and to his understanding of the possibility of human understanding of God. And since thought is transitory and occurs in a transitory setting, if God is in the transitory, too, then God can be thought. Jüngel notes that this claim about God stands in contrast to the Anselmian claim that God is "that than which nothing greater can be conceived," because such a God also is beyond being thought. Moreover, since faith, too, is in the flux of time, and since God and faith maintain (from a human perspective) a symbiotic relationship, yet another reason is provided for not excluding God from transitoriness.[10]

Jüngel tackles the question of God in the transitory by examining carefully the nature of transitoriness. He concludes that "[t]he being of what is perishable is . . . basically a *struggle . . . between possibility and nothingness.*"[11] He then notes that sometimes possibility can occur only after Nothingness has been experienced. He urges, in other words, that there can be value in obliteration or in the ability to cease. Negation can be evaluated positively, for example, in connection with the cessation of pain. Similarly, good can be derived from the fact that we can stop or radically change practices that we or others have initiated, if those practices begin to have unfavorable consequences. Nothingness, therefore, does not have to imply the absolute termination of all Being but can be viewed, instead, as the delimitation of reality. Thus, a function is provided that need not be assessed negatively. Indeed, there is great value in transitoriness, for not only does it encompass a ceasing to be, but it also includes a coming into being. Accordingly, the great value of

---

[9]See "The One Who Comes but Is Also Absent," below.
[10]GMW, 198, 202-203; GGW, 268-69, 274-76.
[11]GMW, 217; GGW, 294.

change, Jüngel suggests, is possibility. But possibility offers only limited hope, if God cannot be engaged directly in the transitory world.[12]

When he considers that matter specifically, Jüngel makes clear that his perspective is not grounded in abstract principles. On the contrary, he conceives God to be in the transitory world solely because Christians have experienced God in a particular history, namely, in Jesus Christ. Accordingly, God is to be thought of not in contrast to the changing world but in unity with it.

Jüngel presses his case by narrowing his focus to God's unity with the crucified man Jesus. This unity shows that a critique of theism, with its separation of an infinite God from finitude, is found in Christianity itself, where God is believed to be self-revealingly present in weakness on the Cross. Consequently, Jüngel opposes the concept of "God as only a highest, absolute, and independent essence." According to this concept, a God involved with the transitoriness of this world would be unthinkable. Instead, God is to be understood from the death of Jesus. And God's identification with the Crucified means that the Christian God must be understood as One Who dies. The death of God on the Cross does not mean merely that God is involved in the transitory, however. Even more significantly, it means that God is in the very midst of the struggle between possibility and Nothingness. But God does not merely contest against Nothingness. "In that God identified himself with the dead Jesus," Jüngel says, "he located nothingness *within* the divine life."[13] Hence, God

---

[12]GMW, 212-17, 225; GGW, 289-95, 306.

[13]GMW, 219; GGW, 297. See also GMW, 47-48, 74, 220, 362; GGW, 61-62, 98, 298-99, 496. Here Jüngel reinterprets the significance of Heidegger's claim that Nothingness is in beings (WM, Ger. 34-35, 40), by locating Nothingness also within the creative power of God, thereby overcoming the annihilating power of Nothingness.

By depicting God as involved in nonbeing, Jüngel evidences some similarity to Paul Tillich, who wrote of God's "participation in existential estrangement and its self-destructive consequences" (*Systematic Theology* [Chicago: University of Chicago Press, 1957] 2:174). But Tillich equated God with Being-itself, which eternally conquers nonbeing; whereas for Jüngel, both Being and nonbeing are in God. Barth comes closer to Jüngel, since the former conceives of God as bringing Nothing into "the service of being" (CD III/3, 348).

can be intimately involved in the transitory and yet not be overcome by it. Instead, God is present even in death.

God is not merely "the infinite power of being which resists the threat of nonbeing," however.[14] Since Nothingness is within God, God's power is in Nothingness, giving it the creative function of clearing the way for new possibilities of Being, as symbolized by resurrection. God relates lovingly and therefore givingly to Nothingness and brings something good out of it.[15] Thus is God the creator *ex nihilo*. Thus, too, do the Cross and Resurrection reveal God (as Self-giving love and as creative even within death) as encompassing death and giving it new meaning. In his own original phrasing, Jüngel conceives of God as the "unity of life and death for the sake of life."[16]

From this understanding of God's relationship with the world, he draws at least four conclusions. First, nothing—not even Nothingness—is outside God. Second, the eternal God is radically temporal. Third, God's essence must be thought of *as* God's existence in Jesus and as being present in Nothingness. Fourth, since God is in union with the transitory, there is a basis for claiming that God can be thought (as already noted).[17]

Speaking about God

It follows from Jüngel's approach to conceiving God that God can be spoken about meaningfully because God is thinkable, and God is thinkable because God is believable. One can believe in God because God came to the world in the history of Jesus. God thus was self-revealed and provided the basis for believing that events of God's Self-revelation continue to occur.

It will be noted that Jüngel does not try to prove that God identified with the dead Jesus. He is content to speak as a believer to believers (since the inception of faith is the work of God, anyway) and seeks "merely" to plumb the depths of Christian faith, identifying hitherto unrecognized implications.

[14]Paul Tillich, *Systematic Theology* (Chicago: University of Chicago Press, 1951) 1:64.

[15]GMW, 210, 218-21, 223, 339; GGW, 285, 296-300, 303, 464. That is why (to answer Heidegger's question) there is something and not nothing—namely, because God is Love.

[16]GMW, x, 299; GGW, xiii, 409.

[17]GMW, 222n.66, 189, 209, 223, 184; GGW, 301n.66, 256, 284, 303, 248.

The chief characteristic of effective talk of God is that it lets God come to expression. We already have considered Jüngel's view that the most appropriate language for letting that happen is metaphorical, analogical (in Jüngel's special sense), parabolic, and narrative.

Although appropriate language about God can take only those and similarly inadequate, nonobjective forms, the value of those forms is that they let *God* make the language adequate. The important point that Jüngel draws from his understanding of the relation between God and language is that God is not *brought* to language by human beings. We cannot construct statements that will coincide with the truth of God. Rather, God *comes* to language that deals with God, and God comes in freedom (that is, unpredictably). Jüngel suggests that the commandment against making a graven image means "you shall let God come to speech."[18]

He reinforces his position by arguing why the venerable apophatic tradition should not be followed and by identifying circumstances that provide the most appropriate context for meaningful talk about God. We deal with these topics next.

Imperatives and Restrictions. Jüngel wrestles with the classical, apophatic doctrine that "the divine is ineffable and incomprehensible" and finds it unsatisfactory because it does exactly what Cartesian metaphysics does: It separates God's essence from God's existence, and as long as it insists that God's essence is ineffable, it leaves the existence of God's *Dasein*—which it claims to be self-evident—in doubt. It asserts that God, as an entirely other, does indeed exist; but Jüngel asks, What justifies calling this unknown being "God"? He suggests that the doctrine is grounded, unbiblically, in Plato's statements about the impossibility of reducing "the beyond" to language, whereas God has seen fit to set limits to the divine mystery by means of events of revelation.[19]

Jüngel builds his positive argument on the biblical claim that although no one has seen God at any time, the Son has made God known. Accordingly, contemplating the Being of Jesus Christ makes talk about God necessary, in order to understand Jesus. "Whoever understands Jesus Christ experiences the one described by the word 'God' as the one of whom one is compelled to speak," Jüngel writes. For when we under-

---

[18]Jüngel, "God—as a Word of Our Language," 34. See also GMW, 289; GGW, 395.

[19]GMW, 232-37; GGW, 316-22.

stand Jesus, God makes a personal Self-disclosure wherein we are given the power of faith and we *must* speak of God. If, under such circumstances, we were not to talk about God, we would be equating God with idols, who are worthy only of being ignored. It is better, therefore, to talk about God, for even if we show thereby what we cannot say, we at least assert the reality of the divine mystery.[20]

Jüngel also offers another argument for the possibility of human talk about God. As love, God is engaged in Self-communication. If something is communicated, the recipient must have understood it in thought and language that is bound to the world. That means that the recipient can relay, in the same language, what has been understood. And that means that human beings *can* speak about God.[21] The language used to speak of God will not be able to capture the fullness of God, but it can communicate as well as people are able to communicate about God.

Jüngel is careful to place limits on the ability of human language to speak of God. He realizes that "human speech as such"—because it is merely human—"is not suited to speak about God."[22] Against Ebeling he argues, therefore, that human language and its syntax do not determine the function of the word "God," at least with regard to whether or not that word conveys the truth of God. Only God can do that. And God can do it because God is not limited to human linguistic capacity.

God is spoken about, however, only when a fundamental difference between God and the world is expressed. Indeed, one can talk about God precisely because God is not identical with Being and time. So, Jüngel writes, "to talk of God makes sense only when . . . the word 'God' . . . cannot be replaced by the function of another word."[23] Accordingly, God is not simply part, unity, ground, ideal, or consummation of the world.[24]

The Appropriate Context. A fundamental difference between God and the world became evident in the history of the God Who came to the world. It is that history which, according to Jüngel, brings the Being of God to human language. According to those who claim that human beings can say only what God is not (the *via negationis*), God certainly

---

[20]Jüngel, "God—as a Word of Our Language," 29-30, 33, 36, 45.
[21]GMW, 260-61; GGW, 355-56.
[22]T, 94.
[23]Jüngel, "God—as a Word of Our Language," 37.
[24]MW, 111; ET, 58.

does not come to language. Nor does God come when only superlatives—and certainly not deficiencies—can be attributed to God (the *via eminentiae*).

People can talk about God when they experience the humanity of God[25] in Jesus Christ, thereby understanding themselves out of the new relation between God and humanity that Jesus' life reflected. Appropriate talk of God comes, in other words, only where God is having an impact on humanity. That is why both Fuchs and Jüngel call love the situation in which people speak about the true God genuinely.

Love that bespeaks God and self-understanding that comprehends Jesus' relationship with God derive from faith in God. As with correct thinking and knowledge of God, so, too, correct speaking of God requires faith. Faith is needed for "God" to be an authentic word. A theological statement *becomes* true via faith, Jüngel says.

He also avers that only a person who believes in Christ crucified will be able to think of the appropriate metaphors to apply to God, because a person who believes has, in some way, been addressed by God's Word and "God's Word (that is, God's 'Yes') frees man for a word that corresponds to the Word of God."[26]

Characterizations of God

Based on his understanding of God's unity with the perishable, as revealed to faith in the Crucifixion and Resurrection and in God's Word of

---

[25]Jüngel uses this phrase from Barth in several ways. He states specifically that it means "the identification of God with the *one* man Jesus *for the sake of all men*" (GMW, 299; GGW, 409). See also GMW, 310; GGW, 423. He also says that "the word which corresponds to God [or expresses God] [is] the location of the humanity of God" (GMW, 300-301; GGW, 411). Here the word is both Jesus and language about him that serves as a vehicle for God's Self-expression. Again, God's humanity is a story (both of God's love for the world in Jesus and of God as love *in se*), the telling of which lets God be the subject of a continuing history, as that story from the first century is made contemporary in the human and divine interpretations rendered in its retelling (GMW, 304; GGW, 415). As discussed below, God is human, also, in participating in human love. The foregoing implies that the humanity of God is God's will for humanity: humanity as (at a given time) it should be.

[26]PJ, 271.

address, Jüngel delineates several features of God in a unique way. On the negative side, he opposes the concept of God as a being. On the positive side, one feature depicts God as "more than necessary," within the parameters that the world sets for necessity. Another cluster of characteristics identifies God as the One Who speaks and therefore as the Coming One, Who is present as absent.

Not a Being

Because of its heritage of anthropomorphic language about God, Christian theology seems trapped into speaking as though God were a being—traditionally, "the highest being." Even though Barth, for example, spoke of God as "the becoming" and explicitly repudiated the notion of God as a being,[27] it is difficult to read this theology without falling into the traditional assumption that he is talking about some sort of entity.

It is important, therefore, to recognize that Jüngel, too, opposes[28] the notion of God as a being, even though he refers to God as "He" and speaks of God as "the One Who comes." Then what is Jüngel talking about, when he talks about God? The question is inappropriate, if it assumes that it can have an objective answer. Jüngel's basic answer is that God provides the answer. The answer is not provided merely to idle curiosity, however. It is provided under circumstances when God is an event in a person's life, an event that leaves a person confident of having encountered or participated in ultimacy, an ultimacy that is presently or potentially good.

More than Necessary

As we have seen, in Jüngel's view belief in the necessity of God is at the root of contemporary denial of God's reality. Jüngel believes that contemporaries will understand his biblically based alternative to that belief if he proceeds by means of an argument based on the experience of Nothingness. He argues, therefore, that modern people and modern philosophy are aware of nonbeing and have experienced its possibility. A person experiences nonbeing in such a way that subsequent events are experienced in a new way. One savors life more fully when one is struck

---

[27]CD II/1, 231.
[28]Jüngel "Möglichkeit," 556. "Der Schritt zurück," 121n.4

by the possibility of vanishing. When faced with the possibility of nonbeing, one experiences something qualitatively new, which Jüngel calls "an experience with experience,"[29] because in it experience itself is felt in a new way. But this experience in the face of the possibility of Nothing is an ambiguous one. It could fill a person with anxiety. Alternatively, it could fill a person with thankfulness and be experienced as creation. There is nothing within the world's own structure, however, that requires a person to adopt that view. Since there is no reason why a person should choose to see (or should be able to see) the experience as an affirmation of Being, rather than as a cause for anxiety, Jüngel says that when that positive experience occurs, it can be understood only as the revelation of God. He adds that people begin to take the reality of God seriously, only when circumstances force them to confront the distinction between Being and nonbeing. Later he says that they can know God only when they know the void (*das Nichts*).[30]

In laying down the proposition that confrontation with nonbeing, the "experience with experience," is the place where talk about God becomes meaningful, is Jüngel doing something very similar to what Schleiermacher did when he located the point within human experience at which one could first begin to talk with certainty about God (namely, in Schleiermacher's case, in a person's "feeling of absolute dependence")?[31] In view of everything else that Jüngel says about God's free Word of address and about the historical and risen Christ as the basis for conceiving of God, it would be incorrect to assume that here he wants to establish a particular human capacity or to locate a universal human experience in which he can guarantee that God will be found. He does not claim that *all* "experience with experience" is experience with God. Encounter with Nothingness also can be resolved negatively in *Angst*. Rather, he is saying simply that, based on his interpretation of the Cross

---

[29]He derives the expression from Ebeling. GMW, 32n.49; GGW, 40n.49.

[30]GMW, 32-34, 189; GGW, 40-42, 255. Jüngel also has suggested, however, that most positive experiences can provide intimation of the *Nichts*, too, by implication from what they exclude.

[31]See Garrett Green, "The Mystery of Eberhard Jüngel: A Review of His Theological Program," *Religious Studies Review* 5 (January 1979): 35, 38-39.

and Resurrection, when an encounter with God occurs, it is *described* best as entailing distinctions of ultimate contrariety.[32] He does claim that, for faith, God can be found in conditions of extremity. But he does not base that claim on universal experience of Nothingness—which relates to the matter only ambiguously—but on his understanding that Nothingness is within the divine life. It is the Word of the Cross, namely, the message that nonbeing is within God's power, that makes possible the qualitatively new experience that *can* result from the "experience with experience."[33] It should be evident, therefore, that Jüngel does not turn to universal human experience as the basis for understanding the Cross and Christian theology, as Schleiermacher did. Just the opposite occurs. Jüngel suggests that understanding God via Cross and Resurrection (and hence understanding that God is the unity of death and life for the sake of life) explains why universal human experience can sometimes become qualitatively new in the face of nonbeing. Accordingly, he does not establish an anthropological point of contact with God any more than did the psalmist who cried to God "out of the depths" (Ps. 130:1).[34]

Continuing his analysis of confrontation with nonbeing, Jüngel contends that in the event in which a person affirms Being, God decides between Being and nonbeing; that is, the experience that affirms Being is

---

[32]In view of his emphasis on the thoroughly metaphorical nature of theological language, his reference to experiencing God in the distinction between Being and nonbeing is a purely formal way of speaking of a variety of other conditions of extremity in which God is present, e.g., life or death, "old" life or "new" life, dying and rising, freedom or slavery, justice or injustice, the choice between eating or heating. From that perspective, when the Prodigal Son, in conditions of degradation in the far country, "came to himself" (Luke 15:13-17), he was encountering God in the *Nichts*. In sum, Jüngel is saying that when the word "God" is related to lesser concerns, it is being used too casually.

[33]GMW, ix; GGW, xi. In the passage cited in this note, Jüngel implies that the Word of the Cross, itself, causes confrontation with nonbeing, pulling the rug out from under our self-contentment and self-certainty and providing the interruption through which truth is encountered. But he also says that the Word of the Cross makes possible a *favorable* or *positive* "experience of experience," because the possibility of nonbeing is conquered on the Cross.

[34]This paragraph and the preceding one were read by Jüngel and endorsed by him in a letter to me dated 27 May 1983.

provided by God, is a manifestation of God, or is interpreted as revealing what would properly be labeled "God." But for God to decide freely between Being and nonbeing means that God is not grounded in either of them and therefore is not grounded outside God's Self. It also means that God is not dependent upon anything that exists. But since God is not grounded in anything, God is not necessary for anything and therefore is not the necessary grounding of the world. God is not necessary, because, as Jüngel has already argued,[35] if God were necessary, God would be tied to the created order and to that extent would be grounded in it.

Instead, God is in a position to be a "plus" for the creation: God is more than necessary; that is, God's reality is neither created nor conditioned by the world's understanding of its own needs. God is above the order of necessity and contingency—although also in the midst of it, as the Crucifixion and Resurrection reveal. Hence, God is unrestricted, free, and self-determining.[36]

Jüngel also indicates from a biblical perspective what he means when he says that God is "more than necessary." When God is found in the *particular* historical reality of Jesus, God cannot be thought of as being *logically* necessary. God then is significant for God's own sake and not because God serves the function of meeting our individual needs. But if we think about God just to acknowledge God's reality, and especially if that thinking is based on a joy that God personally has called forth, then we show, by the very motivation of our thought, that God is "more than necessary," that is, God's status exceeds that of merely meeting a requirement.[37]

From another biblical perspective, God is more than necessary because God freely and unpredictably saves the world by "turning it around" and transforming it.

God may be more than necessary in the same way in which the owner of the vineyard in Jesus' parable (Matt. 20:1-15) may be said to be "more than fair." The owner does not simply act fairly, giving to

---

[35]See above, 79.

[36]GMW, 33-36, 59, 210, 217; GGW, 41-45, 78, 285, 295. Jüngel is able to employ a concept of Being-that-exceeds-necessity because of his understanding of the event-nature of Being and of the freedom of Being, both of which make it possible to understand both chance and revelation.

[37]GMW, 192-93; GGW, 260-61.

everyone his due. Instead, he gives to those who worked all day the wage that was agreed upon, and then he exceeds the conventional standards of fairness by giving the same amount to all of the workers. This Christian view of God as uncalculating love is reflected in Jüngel's characterization of God as being more than necessary.

Accordingly, God is more than necessary because God is love; and love shares freely, not out of necessity. Love cannot be demanded, no matter how much we need it or want it. We can neither force it to be present nor include it automatically in a calculation. In sum, it does not bear the characteristics of something that is necessary.

By engaging the contemporary, secular concern with nonbeing and with God's necessity, Jüngel takes up the concerns of his culture and then directs a Christian answer to them. But his Christian response does not conform to the answer provided by a philosophy that the culture endorses, even though he uses its categories.

The One Who Comes but Is Also Absent

Jüngel's dissimilarity to Schleiermacher is confirmed further in the former's view of God as One Who speaks. Here Jüngel speaks metaphorically, of course, with the purpose of making the point that that Ultimacy that bears the label "God" both can and does make its own reality known. As a variation on Barth's concept that God's Being is "in act," Jüngel writes that "God's Being is in coming."[38] God comes internally, in the dynamism of relations within the Trinity, and God comes externally to us in revelation and in God's Word that addresses us. In coming to us, God provides paths to God's self, paths that, following the logic of the void being in God, also include experiences of distance or alienation from God.

Faith enables a person to be open to God and to let God come, even when God is perceived as absent. (Without faith, God would not be missed.) Whenever a person speaks or acts from faith in the true God, God is "brought" onto the scene and thereby is confirmed as the Coming One. Jüngel suggests that such a concept of God's Being explodes the alternatives of transcendence and immanence.[39] As the One Who speaks, both directly and through others, God is neither continuously immanent

---

[38]GMW, 159; GGW, 213.
[39]GMW, 300; GGW, 410. "Womit steht," 173-74.

nor continuously transcendent. God is immanent in the faith that believes that God will speak again. But in that God is not speaking at a given moment, God is transcendent.

Even when God does "speak," however, God is not solely immanent. Jüngel writes that God's Word of address

> preserves . . . a relationship to which faith corresponds: a relationship in which God comes near to us without setting aside his apartness in this nearness. The presence and absence of God are no longer to be thought of as alternative in the word of God. Rather, God is *present as the one absent* in the word.[40]

God's presence as the Absent One can be explained also by means of an analogy to human beings. Jüngel points out that even human beings are both present and also removed or absent from themselves, in that they have potential that transcends themselves. So it is with God's relation to the world. God's presence is not simply sheer availability. God is always more than what the world experiences. Hence, we experience God's absence along with God's presence. And when God's "more" is experienced, it is experienced as revelation, since we have no control over its appearance. Revelation, therefore, is at the core of God's Being, a position that is congenial with the claim that God's Being is in coming.[41]

But even to employ the distinction between God's presence and absence is less than fully adequate, in light of God's reality as Jüngel understands it. Working with Dietrich Bonhoeffer's assertion that God is omnipresent only in that God comes to the world as One Who condones being forced out of the world, Jüngel notes that God in Christ was forced

---

[40]GMW, 165-66; GGW, 222. See also GMW, 182; GGW, 246.

One could say that God is present when we acquire a new vision of a better world. But since even that vision is incomplete and since that vision is not yet a material reality, God, Who will one day (so to speak) be All in all, is still absent.

Louis Dupré captures a version of Jüngel's concept when he writes that "silence itself would not have become manifest as silence if it had not negated itself and become *present* in speech. God is the silence present in the voice of speech, the silence 'naming itself in its exile from itself'." Review of *The Self-Embodiment of God,* by Thomas J. J. Altizer, in *Cross Currents* 27 (Winter 1977–1978): 468.

[41]GMW, 60-63, 104; GGW, 79-82, 137.

out of the world onto a cross. The event of being forced out is therefore to be viewed soteriologically. It demonstrates the ontological uniqueness of God's Being and destroys the alternative of God being either present or absent, since God, in being made absent, nevertheless was present to save—as the Cross came to indicate and as we have already seen in Jüngel's concept of Nothingness being in God. Hence, God can save us even when God appears to be absent.

The Triune God

Since, in faith, Christians can and do both think and talk about God, Jüngel eventually asks how we can best describe what we are talking about: What is the Being of the referent of the word "God"?

He begins his ontology of God with the biblical witness to Jesus Christ. This point of departure differs noticeably from that of other contemporary theologians who begin with Schleiermacher, Jung, Whitehead, Hegel, or Marx. He then thinks about the implications (1) of God's self-revelation as recorded in the Bible, (2) of the Crucifixion and Resurrection, and (3) of the biblical claim that God is love. These thoughts lead him to proposals for understanding God's very "Being." But he reminds us that the concept even of the "Being of God" is at best metaphorical or analogical. He insists that there is always a difference between God and Being.

His ontological formulations are, naturally, abstract. But he justifies them by treating them as aids to understanding the mystery of God, a mystery that is concrete in other forms, especially in faith, in the Bible, and in liturgy. Indeed, the goal of Jüngel's theological effort is, in his own words, "to increase concreteness through thoughtful abstraction."[42]

He offers two major ontological statements. Both are, not surprisingly, trinitarian. The first is indebted to Barth and is based on faith in divine revelation. The second is much more Jüngel's own creation, although in its focus on love, it cannot disavow an Augustinian heritage.

Before considering both formulations, it is important to take cognizance of what Jüngel considers to be the basis of the doctrine of the Trinity. He does not ground that doctrine in the immutability of God or in efforts to avoid tritheism, as theology has done in the past. Nor does

---

[42]GMW, 35 (my trans.); GGW, 44.

he claim that the Trinitarian dogma was a revelation. Rather, the dogma
formulates the Christian response to an event, namely, the death and
resurrection of Jesus, in which God is seen as abandoning the Son on the
Cross, thereby calling a monistic concept of the Being of God into question and requiring a Trinitarian formulation. The Cross, therefore, is
Jüngel's basis for the doctrine of the Trinity. As the event of salvation
(Heb. 9:14), however, it cannot be separated from the person of Jesus
Christ. And the person of Jesus Christ evokes faith. For that reason, he
finds the doctrine of the Trinity to be grounded not only in events of the
past but also in the recurring event in which Christians are impelled to
confess Jesus as God and God as Jesus.[43]

Revelation and the Trinity

Jüngel's first published work on the Trinity placed him in the middle
of a debate between students of Bultmann and Barth. The Bultmannians
sought to assure that God's Being be in history, by arguing that God is
a hermeneutical relation, the word applied and limited to interpreting the
event in which a person encounters God. The Barthians, while not
denying God's historicality, argued that God also is "in-and-for-Himself."
Jüngel claimed that Barth's doctrine of the Trinity had transcended those
alternatives, and he showed how.[44]

Jüngel claims that Barth teaches that God is in history, because God's
revelation occurs there; but God is not tied to history, so God is also "in-
and-for-Himself." Nevertheless,

---

[43]Eberhard Jüngel, "Das Verhältnis von 'ökonomischer' und 'immanenter'
Trinität: Erwägungen über eine biblische Begründung der Trinitätslehre—im
Anschluss an und in Auseinandersetzung mit Karl Rahners Lehre vom
dreifaltigen Gott als transzendentem Urgrund der Heilsgeschichte," *Zeitschrift für
Theologie und Kirche* 72 (1975): 365-57, 362, summarized in "The Relationship
between 'Economic' and 'Immanent' Trinity," *Theology Digest* 24 (Summer
1976): 180, 183; T, xiv; GMW, 351-52nn.21-22; GGW, 481n.21, 482n.22.
[44]Barth endorsed the formula that Jüngel worked out. Karl Barth, *How I
Changed My Mind*, with an intro. and epilogue by John D. Godsey (Edinburgh:
Saint Andrew Press, 1969) 82.

> we would have little grasp of the distinction between God and the world
> if we set God in and of himself over against the world. For then God's
> being would be thought of as another world,[45]

which Jüngel does not wish to claim. However, God does not "exist in
his own right" as unchanging subsistence or as an idea, because this view
would exclude the event in which God's Being is Being-for-us, as
confessed in the Judeo-Christian tradition. In fact, it is precisely in that
event that we know God at all, and it is precisely that character of God's
Being that we are most sure of. God's Being as Being-for-us, however,
demolishes the distinction between God *in se* and God in history.[46] The
reality of God *in se* is a reality that is only in history, for us.

Let us examine how Jüngel develops this conception of God, which
essentially obliterates the distinction between God and God's revelation.
He proceeds by elucidating Barth's doctrine of the Trinity, and he begins
where Barth begins, namely, with revelation. Barth understands revelation
to be not only God's presence but also the event of God's personal Self-
interpretation and "thus an event that does not let itself be distinguished
into form and content."[47] Because God's revelation is also God's Self-
interpretation, Barth draws inferences from God's revelation to God's
"inner" Being, by means of the analogy of relations. "In the light of what
[God] is in His works," Barth writes, "it is no longer an open question
what He is in Himself."[48] Accordingly, what we know of God from our
experience of revelation which leads us to speak of the economic Trinity
(God as triune in relations with us) is a true reflection (within the limits
of the capacity of language) of the relations within God the immanent
Trinity.

Barth also suggests that revelation is "not an other over against God"
but "a reiteration of God."[49] Jüngel picks up this "reiteration" theme,
saying that the fact that God can reiterate, does reiterate, and has reiter-

---

[45]Eberhard Jüngel, "The World as Possibility and Actuality: The Ontology
of the Doctrine of Justification," in *Theological Essays*, trans. and ed. J. B.
Webster (Edinburgh: T.&T. Clark, 1989) 112.

[46]T, 92-93.

[47]T, 16

[48]CD II/1, 260.

[49]CD I/1, 299.

ated "Himself" enables us to identify differentiation within God's Being.[50] With Barth, he presents a schema that provides not only for revelation and revealedness (that is, human experience of revelation), but also for a revealer (that is, God *in se*).[51] Then he bridges the ontological gap between God and humanity, by emphasizing the "for us" character of God's Being. He bridges the gap by treating God's Being as a series of events. Understood in that way, God's Being-for-us is not the continuingly favorable disposition of an entity (God) towards another entity (us) but is a specific instance thereof, involving simultaneously both God and one or more human beings (or, stated from an anthropocentric vantage point, involving human beings experiencing God-for-us, but where the human beings are not simply conjuring God up).

---

[50]T, 17.

[51]Jüngel feels that this understanding of the doctrine of the Trinity "protects the Christian doctrine of God from becoming mythological or slipping into metaphysics" (T, 21). When Barth and Jüngel inveigh against metaphysics, what they probably oppose is the use or development of a universal metaphysical system. Their own writings indicate that they do not oppose the development of models for understanding the God of the Bible, even though those models would appear to qualify as metaphysics (since they do not deal with the realm of nature and science)—unless even the models are to be viewed metaphorically. That Jüngel endorses the latter suggestion may be seen in his next comment in this note.

Barth says that God is who God is "not . . . only in His works. Yet in Himself He is not another than He is in His works" (CD II/1, 260). Jüngel comments that this statement means that God's Being is to be understood neither as static nor as dynamic and therefore not metaphysically ("Der Schritt zurück," 118). It is important to note that this comment applies also to Jüngel's own models of God, including his view that God's Being is in becoming. He rejects any model or statement that is understood as a metaphysical description of God. It would be better to think of those models on analogy to plaster of paris molds that have to be broken in order for the product to be seen as it truly is.

The problem that Jüngel's "reiteration" schema addresses is somewhat analogous to the one of trying to substantiate the assertion that in the act of speaking, the spoken word does not follow after a thought but occurs simultaneously with it. Although we hear only a voice, that does not mean that no thought is occurring. Application of Jüngel's formula would yield the statement that a silent manipulation of words (i.e., thinking) reiterates itself simultaneously in an audible manipulation of words (i.e., speaking).

Jüngel finds additional meaning in the event of God as revelation. He points out that God is for us in history, but not as a deposit. God is in history as the continually recurring event of revelation. One can note, therein, "the distinctions between revealer, becoming revealed and being revealed which constitutes this event." From those distinctions Jüngel concludes that God's Being "is a being structured as a relationship," with each distinction constituting a mode of being. And "the differentiation between these three modes of being is to be understood from the relationships which hold them together."[52] The divine "Persons" distinguish themselves in that they relate reciprocally to one another; and they are united as one in the process of relating to one another. God's Being, in itself, therefore, clearly is pure event, the event of "living" relationships.

And since live relationships are not static, it can be said, figuratively, that God's Being is in motion. Motion within God first becomes conceived appropriately, of course, as the result of revelation, which implies a movement from God to humanity. Barth speaks of that movement as "The Way of the Son of God into the Far Country," which is the result of God's "primal decision" to make that move, in God's eternal and gracious election of humanity. Jüngel points out that this theology depicts God's Being as being "*in motion* [and therefore also in becoming] from eternity. God's being is moved being: 'Being in the act of his revelation'."[53]

God's revelation was most clear in Jesus Christ, "God's existence as man," which was "at the same time God's surrender of himself to the opposition to God which characterizes human existence. The consequence of this self-surrender of God is God's *suffering* . . . even to *death* on the Cross." Such suffering is a possibility of God's Being, because what is possible for God is determined by Jesus Christ and not by any concept of God that is independent of him. We suspect that God's Being is in becoming, therefore, because in Jesus it was "swallowed up in perishing." Yet in God's own freedom, the message of the Resurrection, according to Jüngel, is that "the perishing was swallowed up in the becoming."[54] Perishing is what God freely chooses to be—and to overcome.

---

[52]T, 25. See also 27.
[53]T, 1-3.
[54]T, 83-85, 102n.155, 107.

When Jüngel speaks of God's "being-for-himself" or of God's essence, he does so simply to make two points: first, that God is to be distinguished from the mundane created order, and second, that revelation is the revealing of something other than the world as we normally experience it. In speaking of God's essence, he is not claiming that there is a divine substance.

He speaks of the immanent Trinity in three compatible ways: in terms of decision and correspondence, self-affirmation, and relations. When presenting the first way, he notes that the distinction that Barth sees within God is cast in terms of God's eternal decision of election. This is God's Being in act, affecting God eternally by differentiating modes of God's Being, in that God determines Godself, in the Son, to be the electing One. In acceding to the Father's will, the Son participates in the decision of election. Jüngel's word for this agreement is "correspondence." He applies it (in terms of the second way) to God's Self-affirmation, which "constitutes the historicality of God's being," in which Father, Son, and Holy Spirit say "Yes" to one another. Both Barth and Jüngel understand this affirmation to occur not only because there is an affirmer and an affirmed but because there is mutual affirmation, and Jüngel speaks of it as God's Being corresponding to itself as Father, Son, and Holy Spirit. The affirmation is mutual, because (in the terms of the third way) each mode of God's Being becomes what it is in relation to the other modes. That is another reason that God's Being is essentially relational.[55]

Since relationship is always becoming, God's Being is always becoming—within itself. But "the becoming in which God's being is, can . . . signify neither an increase nor a decrease of God's being." Rather, "becoming" simply "indicates the manner in which God's being exists." It does not mean that God becomes someone else or that God becomes

---

[55]T, 35, 68-73, 96, 107, 63, 102. Robert Jenson captures this relationship when he writes, "God is not first the Father, who then begets the Son—begetting the Son *is* the Father. And so for each of the modes of being. Each of them is . . . being for the others, with nothing held back." *God after God: The God of the Past and the God of the Future, Seen in the Work of Karl Barth* (New York: Bobbs-Merrill, 1969) 111. And since relationships exist concretely, God's Being is *concrete* in its internal relationships.

different from what God had been previously.[56] The notion of mutual affirmation within the Trinity also is intended to make that point. God's becoming also is not to be thought of as being determined or even guided by God's relation to the world. Jüngel endorses Barth when the latter says that "God's being is being which knows, wills and decides *of itself,* and is moved by itself. Inasmuch as God's being consists in God's act, it reveals itself as being which is *self*-moved."[57] Jüngel adds, "God is fully subsumed in his relation and attitude to himself as Father, Son and Holy Spirit." Hence, we have to distinguish between the event in which God interprets Godself (in revelation in history) and "the event in which God himself assigns to himself his being as Father, as Son and as Spirit." That assigning is the becoming and the Being that is uniquely God's: It is the form of God's own self-relatedness and of God's own becoming. If we do not acknowledge God's own particular type of "becoming," we may make the mistake of thinking that God "becomes" as the result of a relationship to someone or something other than God.[58]

---

[56]T, 32, 63, vii, 106n.159.

[57]CD II/1, 260, 268; emphasis added.

[58]T, 64, 39, 100-101. At this point Jüngel voices opposition to Schubert Ogden, who distinguishes between God's existence and God's essence and wants to make abstract statements about God's essence, based on the "concrete actualizations" of revelation. Ogden quotes Charles Hartshorne to the effect that "philosophy seeks that general principle or essence of the divine being of which such concrete actions of God are mere contingent illustrations." Jüngel argues that God's Being is only concrete (or only in the concrete act) and therefore is not subject to abstraction from the becoming that is peculiar to that Being. God's own mode of becoming is not such that it provides contingent illustrations of a more permanent divine essence. (One might say that God's Being is like a song, which exists only while it is being sung. Any abstraction does not begin to capture the reality of the song.) Accordingly, he opposes applying to the Being of God Heidegger's distinctions between *existentiell* and *existential* and between ontic and ontological, which Ogden uses. This way of arguing illuminates Jüngel's view of objective revelation (e.g., Jesus Christ and his suffering), his own language to the contrary notwithstanding. He regards objective revelation not as something given at face value, from which we can draw appropriate conclusions, but as a catalyst through which God can reiterate God's Being to us individually.

Jüngel's argument also sheds light on his understanding of the relation between God and Nothingness. When he says that Nothingness is in God, he

Just the reverse is true. We derive the fullness of *our* being from God, but "God's relation to us is . . . correspondence to God's self-relatedness: *analogia relationis.*"[59]

The revelation that we experience as grace and as relationship with God is but a repetition or a parallel, following the analogy of relation, of God's own Self-affirmation. Says Jüngel: "The grace of God's being-for-us must be able to be a 'copy' (*Abbild*) of the freedom of God's being-for-himself, so that this freedom as the 'original' (*Urbild*) of that grace becomes visible in that grace."[60]

Revelation tells us that God's becoming-type Being is not only within God. Because of God's primal decision, both Barth and Jüngel say that God always has been turned towards humanity. Accordingly, Barth says that God "does not will to be *himself* in any other way than he is in this *relationship*" of being for humanity.[61] It is not surprising, therefore, for Jüngel to teach that God's Being has time (and therefore space, as in "a space of time") for human history.[62]

Just how is God's Being related to human history? Jüngel's innovative answer centers around "double relational being." He summarizes the problem and his solution as follows:

> The fact that God *becomes manifest* means that God's being is relational being. But . . . if God's being is to be comprehended as *in relation to something* . . . and yet to remain protected from being dependent on every *other thing* . . . without on the other hand the relation becom-

---

means, in part, that concrete reality—which is the only kind that there is—at its *best*, in a given time and place and under particular circumstances, does not exclude suffering and Nothingness. When he says that God is in Nothingness, he means that something good *can* come from Nothingness, but it does not have to. When it does, we experience or God reveals God's Being as the unity of life and death for the benefit of life, and that formula serves as a vehicle for expressing the truth that is true on that occasion, in the act or the coming of God.

[59]T, 104.

[60]With that pattern in mind, he adds that God "is, *in another way, the same* for us as he is for himself." T, 93-94.

[61]CD II/1, 274.

[62]T, 98n.147. God's Being has time at all, because in God's Self-affirmation God continuously makes space for time, which is reflected in God's being in motion, in relationship, and in becoming.

ing the *accidens* of a substance existing in and for itself, then one will have to understand God's being essentially as *double* relational being. This means that God can enter into relationship (*ad extra*) with another being (and just in this relationship his being can exist ontically *without* thereby being ontologically dependent on this other being), because God's being (*ad intra*) is a being *related to itself*. The doctrine of the Trinity . . . attempts to think out the self-relatedness of the being of God . . . appropriately when it understands God's self-relatedness in his modes of being . . . as the *power* of God's being *to become* the God of another.[63]

Since God is *essentially* relational (via the relationships within the immanent Trinity), God clearly has the capacity also to relate to the world. Therefore, when God relates to the world in revelation, God is paralleling God's own Self-relatedness. So God's Being is internal event of relations and, simultaneously, external event of revelation and love, in which the internal event is repeated in an earthly setting. With this double relational Being, God can be simultaneously in intimate relation with the world and distinct from that relationship, "in-and-for-Himself."[64]

The significance of Jüngel's formulation is that it depicts a God Who is not at our disposal, in that God is not a static reality, about Whom we can learn facts, which then serve as indisputable foundations for the practical implications that we choose to derive from them. By depicting a self-consistently changing God, Jüngel encourages us to be open—in a

---

[63]T, 99.

[64]One way of understanding God as 'ontologically unified internal and external relationship that is always becoming' is to conceive of God as, minimally, the unity of ideal and actual, which changes with every situation. So conceived, changing relations within the immanent Trinity would mean reconstructing the ideal for each new situation as situations change. The form of divine "becoming" that is external to the immanent Trinity would be that of people experiencing and even implementing the ideal concretely in the world, in small ways from time to time, as they are inspired by (related to) God. To claim, however, as process theology does, that the changing situation within the world causes God to change is to work unnecessarily with what might be called a "visual" model that assumes that God continuously *was* a certain way and now must be modified (as the lines in a picture might be modified), rather than with a "musical" or "oral" model, according to which God as a different ideal for each situation would be simply the appropriate (not previously played) "note" or "word" for that situation.

way that belief in a static God does not require—to the "new slant" or
to the necessary theological modification that the next revelation of God's
present Self will demand. Indeed, the very occurrence of such openness
would be a sign of God's present relationship with us. At the same time,
Jüngel's formulation does not permit the content of divine reality to come
under human control.

Love and the Trinity

Jüngel's second major treatment of the doctrine of the Trinity occurs
in *God as the Mystery of the World*, his attempt to justify God-talk in a
skeptical world. His first method is hermeneutical; his second is phenomenological and ontological.

His efforts to interpret the Gospels lead him to an understanding of
language that makes it possible to comprehend how, through an analogy
of relation, God can come to us as we talk about God and thereby can be
more similar to us than dissimilar, as was discussed in chapter 3. When
he asks what it is about God's Being that would account for that greater
similarity, his interests become ontological. He finds that what hermeneutics reveals concerning our ability to talk about God can be expressed
ontologically as love.[65]

Jüngel can appear to derive his ontology of God from his hermeneutic,[66] simply because their foundation is the same. He would not want his
readers to lose sight of that foundation, however, which is the Word of
God that reveals the love of God in the life, crucifixion, and resurrection
of Jesus. That is the basis for his claim that God is love.

It is also the basis for his second development of the doctrine of the
Trinity, for he teaches that God as love can be conceptualized only as
Trinity. A Trinitarian conception of God is necessary to explain how God
can *be* love and not only have it for others. God can be love because
love exists (as Holy Spirit) *within* God or "between God and God," that

---

[65]In Jüngel's own words, "the basic hermeneutical structure of evangelical
talk about God, namely, analogy as the still greater similarity within such a great
dissimilarity between God and man, is the linguistic-logical expression for the
being of God, which being realizes itself *in the midst of a still very great self-
relatedness as always still greater selflessness* and, in that way, is *love*." GMW,
298 (translation modified); GGW, 408.

[66]Recall esp. his "hermeneutical thesis."

is, between Father and Son. Moreover, God's acts of revelation—the basis of Jüngel's first work on the Trinity—established God as love, in that they show that God willingly enters into relations with human beings.

Jüngel claims that there is no ontological difference between God and love. He is even willing to say "love equals God," provided that God is permitted to define what love is.[67]

Love bridges the gap between God and humanity, since love is found in both. Human love derives from the God Who already *is* love and therefore can set love in motion by having love for others. As the One that makes love possible, God is present in a hidden way in every event of true love, including human love. Accordingly, Jüngel claims that everyone is ontologically united with God, when love occurs. In that way, too, God is more similar to us than dissimilar.[68]

Because love applies both to God and to human beings, Jüngel believes that a phenomenological analysis of human love can yield insights into the Being of God, especially as that Being is conceived in the doctrine of the Trinity. That analysis can make the traditional doctrine more comprehensible, although Jüngel is quick to deny that a correct understanding of the Being of God can simply be deduced logically from the nature of love, because such a deduction would imply that God's reality does not exceed the human understanding and experience of love. The remainder of this section presents Jüngel's analysis of human love, accompanied usually by its application to the doctrine of the Trinity.[69]

Self-Related Selflessness. Jüngel begins by noting that love is not selfless without being self-related. It is directed toward a particular beloved and wants to *have* the beloved. In that way, a lover is self-related and selfish. Indeed, without self-relatedness love would be only an abstraction. Accordingly, Jüngel opposes making *eros* and *agape* alternatives. He argues that selfishness and selflessness are combined when I, as a lover, do not want to have myself without having my

---

[67]GMW, 314-17; GGW, 430-34.

[68]GMW, 326-27; GGW, 447-48. "Gelegentliche Thesen zum Problem der natürlichen Theologie," *Evangelische Theologie* 37 (September/October 1977): 488.

[69]The headings in this section follow those that were added by the editor, when a version of this material appeared in *Dialog* 21 (Summer 1982): 220-23.

beloved and when only by having the other do I have myself in the way that I want myself (which is in a new way, that is, with my beloved). Wanting myself in a new way, I am willing to being myself again, as it were, this time with my beloved, whom Jüngel is willing to call the "lust-object." The lust aspect of love draws me outside myself, so that I must meet myself again. But when I become myself again, I do so this time with the other, so that I then understand myself *with* the other and therefore in a new way. (It makes a difference, Jüngel notes, whether I understand myself without another or with another.) When I am in love, then, I always want to be outside myself and with another.[70]

This understanding of love has clear implications for comprehending both the relations in the Trinity and God's love of people. God's reality as concrete love is affirmed, for example, by understanding God's triune Being as both self-related and selfless. Those relations are discussed below, at subsequent stages of Jüngel's analysis.

Reciprocal Surrender. Love is reciprocal giving or surrender, in which each party also receives: each party becomes the beloved. "In love there is no having which does not arise out of surrender," Jüngel says.[71] Love changes the structure of having; in love, I can have only as I give. In order to have my beloved, I must surrender myself to my beloved, that is, I must stop having myself. Moreover, in the giving of love, I am more interested in being possessed than in possessing.

Since love requires at least two for reciprocity, God shows that God is love itself by sending "His Son," thereby defining God as at least two persons. Differentiation within God is also shown when the alive God identifies with the dead Jesus by empowering his resurrection.[72]

---

[70]GMW, 317-20; GGW, 434-37.

[71]GMW, 320; GGW, 437.

[72]GMW, 327, 363-64; GGW, 448, 498. By distinguishing between Father and Son within God on the basis of the crucifixion of Jesus and the resurrection of that same Jesus by God, Jüngel claims that God is in relations, that God identified with Jesus' Godforsakenness, that God experienced death (whereas we do not experience our own death), and that God recovers from death (GMW, 363; GGW, 497). Thus, without resorting to Whiteheadian philosophy but by drawing out the implications of Christian faith in the Cross of Jesus Christ, he destroys the classical axioms of God's absoluteness, inability to suffer, and immutability (GMW, 373; GGW, 511).

This separation of Father and Son shows that God has someone to love, that God loves, and (since both Father and Son are God) that God is (the event of) love (between Father and Son). God's self-love is manifest in the distinction of lover, beloved, and the event of love. The Third Person of the Trinity is the *event* of love. As event, the Spirit is the Being of love, because that Being consists in the *relation* of lover and beloved, and the Holy Spirit *is* that relation.[73] And since that relation is one of total harmony, the "differentiation between God and God" within God "can never be understood as contradiction in God."[74]

Indeed, it is the harmony of the distinctions within God that characterize God's absolute freedom most adequately. God is free not simply because God is not dependent on the world but because God is internally free: God "has His own act together." Indeed, it is precisely because God is fully Self-governing that God can enter into a real relationship with the world without Self-compromise. This is the point that Jüngel wants to make when he says that the doctrine of the Trinity proclaims that God lives "of Himself in Himself," that God comes "from God to God as God," that the wherefrom and the whereto of God's coming is God's own Self, and that God "cannot be relativized by any other 'god'."[75]

Love Includes Self-Estrangement. Because love entails surrender to an other and therefore self-estrangement, it includes the dialectic of being and not-being. Jüngel says, "The loving . . . I is . . . related to the beloved Thou, and thus to his own nonbeing: without Thee I am nothing."[76] Not only does a lover reach out to someone else, but in needing the beloved, the lover is made aware of personal inadequacy or nonbeing. Thus does love conceal the dimension of death and Nothingness within

---

[73]Says Jüngel: "The Holy Spirit is . . . the relationship between the relationships of the Father and the Son, that is, the relationship of the relationships and thus an eternally new relationship of God to God. This *eternally new* relationship of God to God is called, christologically, resurrection from the dead and is ontologically the being of love itself." (GMW, 374; GGW, 513).

[74]GMW, 346; GGW, 474.

[75]Jüngel, "'Economic' and 'Immanent'," 179, Ger. 353. GMW, 36, 346; GGW, 46, 474. The event of God occurs in various contexts, yet the context does not contribute the divinity to the divine presence in those contexts.

[76]GMW, 323; GGW, 442.

itself. In love, power completes itself in weakness and is united with it. It is the same unity of life and death that Jüngel discovered first in the Crucifixion and Resurrection. A love relationship is strong, however, precisely because it contains within it a death that has been conquered, namely, the death of personal inadequacy, the death accompanying the risk of reaching out from oneself and being rejected, and the death of not loving. Indeed, Jüngel goes so far as to say that a paraphrase for the nature of love is "the unity of death and life for the sake of life."

Just as human love involves both confrontation with one's own nonbeing and extension beyond oneself to an other, so does God's love. God confronts and conquers nonbeing in the continuing relation of Father and Son in the immanent Trinity. God also moves out into the Void. Just as love unites life and death, with life going beyond itself (into death) in the event of love, so in God's mode of being God "is already beyond Himself: He already transcends Himself."[77] God's internal self-relatedness, which is what divine love *is*, occurs as God's radical relatedness to something absolutely other than God (which is what divine love *does*), namely (according to the New Testament), radical relatedness to human nature and to the world. This relationship causes Jüngel to emphasize the point that the difference between God and the world is grounded within God's own Being and not in the world's inability to overcome that difference.[78]

The way in which God overcomes God's own nonbeing (in the man Jesus in the economic Trinity) is, by the Resurrection, to pull the death of Jesus into God's eternal life. God thereby shows that God is for us as love, in that God conquers Nothingness for others (namely, for Jesus and us) and so lets us participate in the divine life.

New Being. Thus, love promises a new Being. It fulfills that promise, too, because "in the event of loving surrender, a radical self-distancing takes place *in favor of* a new nearness to oneself—a nearness, to be sure, in which the beloved Thou is closer to me than I am to myself," since I am engaged in self-surrender, lost in the beloved without whom I do not want to exist. I thereby *get* an unexpected new self, from my beloved. In

---

[77]T, 302.

[78]GMW, 380; GGW, 521. Jüngel sees this difference and its grounding as a positive relationship, in that it means that the world is not left to its own resources.

that way, I exist *ex nihilo*: "the loving I is given an existence which does not derive from it." Stated alternatively, "I am united with myself in a new way." I am gathered with my beloved into a new and more complete person, so that I can say that I was not whole formerly. From that perspective, Jüngel argues that there is no self-identity apart from someone else who can "bring me out," by getting me to forget myself and by giving me more to identify with. In love, therefore, there is a free creation of Being, at the risk of loss of Being.[79]

Within the triune Being of God, the designation "God the Father" means that God loves so fully within Himself that He gets possession of His Being, because "God the Son" is the beloved of the Father and always relates himself to *his* beloved (namely, the Father), thereby giving his Being to the full possession of the Father, who also does the same thing for the Son.[80] God's self-possession, Jüngel says, comprises God's selflessness, because the self-possession is based on a relationship of overflowing love between Father and Son.[81]

Drawing Others into the Relationship. Because an ideal love relationship is strong, the people in it, whose Being has been expanded and reinforced by each other, both want to and can reach out from themselves to encounter the world and to draw it into their relationship.

So it is, analogously, with God. God's Being *is* relation, and that characterization does not apply only to the immanent Trinity. Because on the Cross God expresses God's inner Self as love, and since revelation is God's Self-interpretation, it follows that God's innermost Being is a turning outward. God does not exist without relating to others. Stated more strongly, God does not want to love Godself without loving people. So God as Spirit "overflows" Godself and pulls people into the love of the Father and the Son. The Holy Spirit is the gift "in which . . . God relates himself to mankind in such a way that humanity is drawn effectively into the event of divine love." God's Being, in other words, is attractive. Just as the Father and Son are united ("by" the Holy Spirit) in love and realize themselves as lovingly receiving and experiencing each other, in just that way the Holy Spirit brings about loving human

---

[79]GMW, 321-24; GGW, 440-44.
[80]GMW, 371; GGW, 509.
[81]Jüngel, "'Economic' and 'Immanent'," 182.

acceptance of the Self-bestowing God, linking people into the loving relationship between Father and Son.[82]

Since God will not be without humanity, Jüngel says that God comes to Godself when God comes to humanity, that is, God carries out God's own will. Within a great self-relatedness is an even greater selflessness through which God freely overflows God's Being. God relates to Godself when God is selfless, because it is God's eternal will, reflected in God's election of humanity through the Son, to be *pro nobis*. In being selfless, the Son is being "obedient" to the Father (that is, the Son reciprocates the Father's selfless love) and thereby relates to Him (thereby maintaining God's self-relatedness). This inner-Trinitarian pattern is repeated when God becomes human. Since the Son represents humanity, God's Being exists in the act of loving people, both internally (in the Father's love of the Son) and in the act of coming to the world. Indeed, God's aseity *is* God's free decision to love. Because the triune God is, in the Son, eternally turned toward humanity, Jüngel can say that "in no case may God be thought of as *de facto* 'in Himself'."[83] However God may have to be treated theoretically, and in whatever way God may be depicted to preserve God's absolute freedom, Jüngel considers it godless to believe that God's essential reality is separate from humanity. The Trinity as he understands it is continuously turned toward and overflowing for people.[84]

A distinction is made between the economic and immanent Trinities because of the distinction between human experience of God and human theorizing about God. When those distinctions are viewed "from above"

---

[82]GMW, 220-21, 329, 364, 327-28, 375; GGW, 299, 451, 500, 449-50, 513-14.

[83]GMW, 384 (my trans.); GGW, 527.

[84]GMW, 37-38, 339, 369, 372; GGW, 47, 465, 506, 510. This is how Jüngel provides for God to be affected by humanity, namely, by being concerned for humanity thoroughly (or 'from the beginning of eternity'). Jüngel avoids applying a rigorous phenomenology of love directly to the human-divine relationship, because doing so would reduce God to human categories. Hence, although God loves us, God is not—unlike the case of love between two human beings—conformed to us (as God's beloved) or transformed by us. Jüngel applies his phenomenology of love primarily to intra-Trinitarian relationships and then says that God loves us only in an analogous way, thereby freeing God and God's love of us from any necessity of conforming point by point to our perception of love.

(that is, as though from God's point of view), the doctrine of the economic Trinity captures God's selflessness, while the doctrine of the immanent Trinity expresses God's self-relatedness or self-possession. When viewed "from below" (that is, from a human perspective), the economic Trinity pertains to the history of God's dealings with humanity, while the immanent Trinity pertains to the internal dynamics of God's Being. Jüngel's primary conclusion, however, is that the two are really the same. Just as the God Who is Love is both self-related and selfless, so God's internal dynamics do not function apart from God's coming to humanity. Jüngel considers the immanent Trinity to be a summarizing conceptualization of God's history with humanity, as reflected in the doctrine of the economic Trinity. He thereby reverses the traditional approach to these Trinitarian distinctions, by placing primary emphasis on God's history with humanity. In contrast to the Eastern Orthodox and other traditional approaches, his doctrine of the Trinity is a doctrine "from below." With Barth, he believes that what we see in God's work as the economic Trinity is true in God's essence. The unity of the immanent and the economic Trinity lies, according to Jüngel, in the fact that God's Being is in proceeding. God proceeds *from* God, so that not only is God unoriginated, but the Father's communication of Himself in the Logos is identical with the divine hypostasis of the Father. God proceeds *to* God, in the Father always having an eternal Son, and also in the Son delivering himself up to death, where God nevertheless is. And God proceeds *as* God and therefore, in the Holy Spirit, as overflowing love to what is distinct from God. Jüngel generally endorses Karl Rahner's claim that the immanent Trinity is identical with the economic Trinity, but he urges that they be distinguished in reason, so that they do not get reduced to a tautology, thereby denying God's freedom to be different from our preceptions of the economic Trinity.[85]

Love as Continuing Occurrence. Love's strength depends upon its not standing still but continuing to occur. "Love is the *living* unity of life and death," Jüngel says.[86]

---

[85]GMW, 346-47, 369-71, 381, 383; GGW, 475, 507-508, 522, 524. T, 45. "'Economic' and 'Immanent'," 183-84, Ger. 361-64.

[86]Jüngel, "Das Sein Jesu Christi," 511, #1.3.1.

A God Who is love, therefore, must be a continuing occurrence; and
so Jüngel finds God to be. God *is* in God's history, when history is
understood not as a record of the past but as continuing occurrence. And
God's history is a history of loving another, both within the Trinity and
outside it. Consequently, God is neither Self-contained, nor Self-centered,
nor satisfied with the earthly status quo.

Ludwig Feuerbach claimed that people identify love with God because love is the pinnacle of human self-realization. But such a god,
Jüngel argues, would mean that the possibilities of human being are ex-
hausted, because such a god, as (human) pinnacle, would have no more
potential—not even for self-surrender to another, which means that such
a god would be the end of love, for a love without potentialities is not
love.[87]

It is God's freedom as love that overcomes impossibility and makes
the possible possible. And a God Who creates and implements potential
is a God Whom Jüngel understands as event. More forcefully, he says
that we are not speaking of God if we are not speaking of event. He even
speaks of the Kingdom of God as "the Being of *God* as the event of
love."[88]

In Trinitarian terms, the Holy Spirit constitutes the divine Being as
event. And since, as the Being of God, the Holy Spirit is the ever new
event of love between Father and Son, God's Being must itself be future
and always in coming. "God the Spirit" means that while God is God's
origin, God is not already at God's goal, although God's goal reflects
God's origin. In the movement (which the Spirit is) from origin to goal,
God's Being is in coming and is God's own future.[89]

---

[87]GMW, 339; GGW, 464. Jüngel acknowledges that his claim on behalf of
love rests on faith. One has to *believe* that love is victorious and never ceases.
And one of his understandings of God is precisely that of the Spirit that arouses
faith in love.

His argument against God as merely the designation for the highest form of
human self-realization holds, abstractly, only when that pinnacle or goal is left
unspecified and is regarded as being static. When love, specifically, is named as
the pinnacle, however, the argument would appear to fail because of the very
quality of love that Jüngel attributes to it, namely, its inexhaustibility.

[88]PJ, 163.

[89]GMW, 374-75, 387-88; GGW, 513-14, 531-32. God's future has the con-

Indeed, Jüngel defines eternity as God's coming to God, which is what God's Being is. God comes to God eternally. In God's coming to Godself, which is God's self-affirmation, "God *makes space* within Himself for *time*."[90] This is one of the ways in which Jüngel subordinates time to God, while, at the same time, removing God's future from temporal causality.

Concurrently, since God comes "from God to God as God," that means that nothing is the source of God, especially not Being or Nothing (*das Nichts*). Thus, the concept of Being is subordinated to the concept of God. Both Being and Nothing are the consequence of God's coming to God. (God's coming provides or creates a Nothing—"makes space"— for God to fill.) In addition to the biblical basis for this movement, one can notice here the Heideggerian concept of Being as consisting in and resulting from action. God's Being consists in action; the world's Being results from that action. Jüngel writes that "in the statement 'God is,' the predicate is to be understood from the subject. That means that only to the extent that God comes from God does being result."[91] Being and Nothing are therefore primordially *within* God's self-relationship. But since, reflecting the Heideggerian view, it is the activity provided by Being and Nothing that creates time, time, too, is subordinate to God. At another level, Being and time are in God because neither of them is beyond the possibility of being affected by the extraordinary.

Jüngel sees the subordination of Being and time to God symbolized in the death of Jesus Christ, when that death is viewed as the death of the Son of God by whom our temporal Being was made.

The figurative use of philosophy, doctrine, and Scripture appears at another place in Jüngel's writing pertaining to Being and time. There, doctrine and Scripture are coupled with faith in such a way as to cause the reader to realize that Jüngel is not interested in developing a correct philosophy of the structure of the universe, or in describing the mecha-

---

tours of Jesus Christ, in whom God reached God's goal. The work of the Holy Spirit and the love of God for humanity mean that God does not want to reach God's goal without us: God wants to pull us into God's goal, just as Jesus was (GMW, 389; GGW, 533). God comes to people (as the Son came to Jesus) as their eschatological goal (GMW, 383; GGW, 525).

[90]T, 96.
[91]GMW, 381 (trans. modified); GGW, 522.

nism by which the divine and the human interact, or even in making incontestable statements about God. Rather, he is interested in uncovering the multifaceted significance that attaches to belief that God is love. When Being and time end or (as in eschatological experience) seem to end, he says, the Christian, who by faith sees himself and the world located and functioning within limits set by God, "knows" that it is God Who brings them to an end and Who therefore is present at their end. Unity is thus achieved by ending the distinction between them (since they both end in God) and (what is the same thing) by transforming human existence, which is limited by them, into unlimited fellowship with God.[92]

Essence and Existence United. Finally, love, as the essence of something, cannot be distinguished from its existence. The core and quality of love is to be found only where love is taking place.

Jüngel is willing to speak figuratively of God's "Being," when that Being, as love, is described by the doctrine of the Trinity, because that doctrine solves the problem of the separation of God's essence from existence, by holding that God's existence is God's essence, in that God's essence is constituted by relations (between Father and Son as Holy Spirit) and those relations are divine existence.

God as Mystery of the World

That Jüngel's models of the Trinity are to be understood only metaphorically is implied by his very clear statement that the Being of God is a complete mystery and is not a mystery simply because of the limits of human knowledge. The New Testament reveals God *as* a mystery, which, unlike a riddle, cannot be "solved," but which remains a mystery even when it is apprehended.[93] The mystery can be communicated linguistically (when it communicates itself), Jüngel allows, but otherwise it is inaccessible.

God is the mystery of the *world* because God empowered Jesus to be who he was, and Jesus was in the world. Because Jesus belonged to God and to the world, Jüngel concludes that the world belongs to God

---

[92]GMW, 380, 384-85, 394-95; GGW, 521, 527-28, 542.

[93]Jüngel apparently has not come across that view of riddle that regards it as a maintainer of tension as contexts and horizons change and therefore as only momentarily solvable.

(because it belonged to the Being of Jesus) and therefore does not possess itself. It nevertheless does not cease to exist. It must be the case that the world cannot fully provide for itself, neither understanding nor taking appropriate charge of all that can be known about it, because otherwise Jesus could not have brought anything new to it, which he did. The fact that the world can exist while nevertheless not possessing itself points to a mystery that is best designated "God."[94]

The world can exist without possessing itself,[95] because God comes to the world as love and as Holy Spirit, interrupting it and thereby strengthening it by bringing life out of death in unexpected ways. God is the mystery of the world *when* God comes to it. Hence, God is the world's mystery when love is awakened and when the Holy Spirit draws people to God. For that reason, Jüngel says that one must speak of God's Being as history and of this history as the mystery of the world.[96]

It is the mystery of the world because God is love. This assertion is significant because it means that God is in relationship with us, enabling us to see the world and its internal relationships as being ultimately in relationship with more-than-itself (God). Whenever that event occurs, we see the world with new eyes and experience it differently. Through an experience of God, we understand the world no longer from itself but in its true nature as standing before God's lordship. Just as light is the end of darkness, so God is the end of the world understood from itself, when God comes to it.[97]

Finally, God is truly a mystery because, even though we ask about God because God has already addressed us, God's response to our questions only causes us to raise more questions, as we are lead ever more

---

[94]GMW, 379; GGW, 519.

[95]Jüngel says that the world possesses itself only deficiently, because it has itself in such a way that no one or nothing else can belong to it or come to it. (By mentioning belonging, he provides for the possibility that God is part of the world even though the world does not recognize it. In that case, God's coming and the world's recognizing are two sides of the same coin.)

[96]GMW, 390; GGW, 534.

[97]GMW, 379; GGW, 519. "Gott—um seiner selbst willen interessant." "Säkularisierung—Theologische Anmerkungen zum Begriff einer weltlichen Welt," in *Christliche Freiheit im Dienst am Menschen*, ed. Karl Herbert (Frankfort-on-Main: Verlag Otto Lembeck, 1972), 163-65.

deeply into what turns out to be the unfathomable mystery of God's reality.

Chapter 6

Summary and Evaluation

Working with the Bible, with Barth's doctrine of revelation and of God, and with Heidegger's concept of Being, his use of phenomenology, and his understanding of primordial language, Jüngel has developed a homogenous theology that culminates in a Trinitarian doctrine of God. According to this doctrine, which is based on faith in the salvific value of the Crucifixion and Resurrection, internally and externally active divine love overcomes literal and figurative Nothingness.

This listing of Jüngel's sources, along with only a partial summary of his doctrine of God—and no mention of his Christology—makes the point that Jüngel's writings do not have a single focus. Correspondingly, that observation applies to the present work, as well. Most of the time, Jüngel writes to generate insights on a variety of basic theological topics. In so doing, he makes use—quite often—of revelatory metaphors, vehicles by which God can come to provide the precise truth to what he has to say. That device would seem to be the central feature of his theology.

This final chapter follows the sequence of the preceding ones in a general way, but it does not engage in a detailed critique of each subsection of each chapter. Rather, it seeks to shed additional light on Jüngel's thinking by means of comments that cut across the restrictions established by the chapters and that juxtapose categories from different chapters. It also makes note of methodological features that are missing, to a large extent, from Jüngel's work.

Much of Jüngel's writing is very nuanced and intricate in its development. Unfortunately, it also can be obtuse, as when he lets it appear as though he is talking about something objective, even though he knows that he is talking about a dynamic symbol. At other times, his writing is quite global in its approach, employing sweeping generalizations that are treated as fact, with no evident effort to substantiate them. His high esteem of metaphor and his objections to an "objective world" apparently let him feel justified in interrupting a logical sequence of thought with a bold assertion or a verse of Scripture, with either item being used to reach a conclusion not drawn in any other way. His rearranging and creatively juxtaposing concepts, verses, and metaphors do nothing less, however, than what any other approach to theology can do, namely, to serve as a vehicle through which Ultimacy can make Itself known. At least, that is one possible assessment.

But an evaluation of Jüngel's work does not hang on matters of exposition. His supporters and detractors will probably divide primarily over his view of natural theology and his concomitant emphasis on revelation, especially as that emphasis pertains to the role of language and to his concept of God. Given the breadth of his theological interest and competence, however, there are many other topics that bear scrutiny, as well. These topics include the method and scope of his theology, the role that history, context, human action, and the Bible play in it, his epistemology, his use of phenomenology, and hermeneutical considerations.

Jüngel's Theology and Its Source

Jüngel views his theological endeavors as consistent biblical exegesis, for the guidance of the Church. He regards much of his own theological language and the language of the Bible as figurative. Consequently, he sees his work as providing opportunity for divine illumination through "language-events." The orientation of his theology is existential, in that its objective is a transforming personal encounter with God, for the purpose of engaging one's environment in accordance with God's will. Jüngel's way of reasoning about God also calls for entering into philosophical dialogue and for applying the strictures of phenomenology to its subject matter.

Method and Scope

Jüngel is concerned, as are many theologians today, about the right method of thinking about God. Starting off in the wrong direction, in this regard, cannot fail to yield less than the most fruitful results, largely because of the blinders that methodological decisions affix. As Wittgenstein has suggested, theology is at least "grammar," and that understanding (that is, theology as the rules for determining the sense in which the word "God" is to be understood) is evident in Jüngel's approaches to the doctrine of the Trinity, in which he distills principles for thinking about God's Being, based on God's Self-revelation as love.

Jüngel's central theological "rule" appears sound. This rule states that thought must follow the nature of what is being thought about and must assume the right relationship to it. With regard to God, this rule means that people must be receptive to unexpected inputs and not impose pre-conditions on God's power. The rule also recognizes the necessity of interpretation, and it recognizes the historical Christian interpretation of God's mighty acts. Consequently, it calls for Christian theology to take its cues, both for stimulus and for interpretation, from the biblical revelation of God's will, especially in its most human form in the life and teachings of Jesus Christ. Finally, the rule recognizes the metaphorical nature of all language about God and acknowledges, therefore, that such language can serve only as a medium for a more immediate awareness of God's truth, which God alone can bring.

Following Jüngel's theological methods, one's theological skills may be applies in three ways. Primarily, one develops theological insights by being alert to metaphorical applications of the literal wording of the Bible, within the context of a present-day situation. In that way, one's imagination is both ignited and controlled.

When dealing with matters outside the Bible, there are two approaches. Often, one can come to understand a topic by applying Christian symbols or stories to it. Alternatively, one may muse upon a topic until one gets an insight into the human condition (alone in its secular form or as it is related to a more ultimate context). Then one should check the validity of that insight by trying to apply it to traditional Christian symbols and stories. If it is compatible with them, one has added another level of meaning to the Christian theological repertoire. If incompatible, one's insight may be distorted or, at minimum, one has identified an area of tension between one's own thoughts and traditional Christian understandings.

This approach makes it clear that theology is never completed, because the language and images of the Bible keep acquiring new meaning as the cultural and historical context in which they are read and preached changes and as theology enters into dialogue with its present context. That is partly why there is danger in constructing a theological system: It freezes one's thinking about God into a particular time and place. The other danger is that it ignores elements of revelation that do not fit into the system, thereby creating the danger of our distorting God's own address to us.

At a time when renewed interest is being shown in religious pluralism, does Jüngel not run a similar risk by limiting his theology to the norms of Christian theology? This question raises the ultimate one of what one is willing to risk putting one's trust in. At this point in time, Jüngel is willing to risk trusting that Jesus Christ is the full and final revelation of God, that is, that all significant knowledge and experience of the Ultimate can be related to him. This is not to say, however, that other religions cannot serve as catalysts—just as other extrabiblical phenomena have—to illuminate the fullness of the Christian revelation, and Jüngel's methodology does not exclude, in principle, the possibility of learning from them. If, on the other hand, one were to place one's ultimate trust solely in human reason and experience, and if those capacities, when directed toward other religions, could yield, with objective certainty, fundamental truths other than those acknowledged by Christian faith, then Jüngel's trust would be misplaced. But all experience requires interpretation—and commitment to the interpretation—in order to have meaning. If certainty can be attained, therefore, only through personal commitment, then the more basic risk is one that no religion can avoid. It lies in the locus of commitment and not, first of all, in restricted theological norms.

Jüngel's advance over Barth lies precisely in his efforts to cope with the intellectual restrictions that a faith-commitment can bring. He is willing not merely to interact with the world outside the Bible but to learn from it—not to learn about God directly from the world, but to acquire new angles of vision, which permit God's action in the Bible to be seen and understood more fully.

Even such dialogue should not be expected to establish the universal validity of Christianity's claims, however. To attempt to relate all truth to the Christian God would be to put God on the same plane as the created order and probably to misunderstand the extraordinary nature of God. The likelihood that at least some Christian claims will always have to continue to appear arbitrary is predicated on two of those claims, namely, the fallen condition of human nature and the necessity of God's Self-revelation.

Role of History

Included in theological method is the issue of the significance of history. Historical consciousness is not missing from Jüngel's theology, but it is not given the attention that some other theologies devote to it. Jüngel's work with metaphor certainly reflects his awareness of the historical nature of existence, since one must have historical experience that causes one to be aware of how words are commonly used, in order for the uncommon use of words in metaphor to be effective. Similarly, he acknowledges that reason is essentially historical.

Salvation, on the other hand, occurs, he would argue, in eschatological encounters (primarily in word-events) and therefore is technically neither inside nor outside history but on the horizon of history. God is never fully present in history. That is why even Jesus' life was only a parable of God's presence. Nevertheless, the impact of those encounters and of that life is felt in history: They change our behavior; we are able to love more fully, as a result of them.

Although faith experiences God in the context of previous experiences, the content or object of faith can be extrapolated neither from those experiences nor from the historical experience of the world *in toto* or in part (without the guidance of the Holy Spirit, in which case one would not be learning only from history). God's Being is historical only at the moment of revelation. God is not found in the mundanely given, because God is not a God Who *is* but rather one Who *comes* (as in a language-event). Hence, theology should not be carried out as a study of history. Such an approach only confirms what reason already knows. Besides, since history is usually written by the victors, the reality known by recorded history hardly can escape being distorted.

History understood as a record of and as the dynamics of past events constitutes what we have learned from the past and therefore what we have to build the future on. Its significance for faith is seen only by faith, however. As far as its use for theology is concerned, history is not self-explanatory, contra Pannenberg, nor will it ever be. But like language, history can be a catalyst by which God can stimulate us to envision reality in a yet more perfect way and to take the necessary next steps toward the realization of that vision. Jüngel pays little attention to this value in history.

History understood as current activity in the world is what Jüngel's God is all about, for it is there that God encounters people, through the Word, and empowers them to be doing God's will actively in the world. Jüngel is concerned with sparking that encounter linguistically. Once the Holy Spirit is at work within a person, that person does not have to be reminded to do deeds of love. That is one reason why Jüngel does not emphasize human action in history.

Role of Context

History is a part of the context that affects the scope of one's thinking. Also included in one's context are cultural and national environment, economic status, race, sex, and position within conflicts for power. Jüngel acknowledges social reality as part of what determines our consciousness. He also agrees that theological theory has political consequences and that it must question economic presuppositions.[1] His major works do not address these matters specifically, however. Nor is he preoccupied by the contextual nature of theology, as liberation and feminist theologies, for example, are.

The way in which he moves to overcome the problem of context in theology is to formulate metaphors and images that are sufficiently abstract to have broad application—even in contexts that are not his own. Thus, "Nothingness" can mean being laid off by one's employer. The "death" where God is at work can be a cold room in the house of a well-to-do family. God can be present anywhere as the basis for hope, even though otherwise absent. As in the case of all good general theory, his method of dealing with abstractions and the conclusions that he draws from them do appear to be applicable to a wide range of concrete situations.

He also recognizes the importance of context in meaningful talk about God. Particular contexts provide a purpose or point to God's presence, and in a changed context that point may be missing, thereby making references to God pointless (in the new context) and language about God meaningless. In such a situation, there is nothing that we or our language can do to speak truly of God. (Some forms of liberation

---

[1]T, Ger. 129-31. "Redlich," 476. Eberhard Jüngel, *Christ, Justice and Peace: Toward a Theology of the State*, trans. D. Bruce Hamill and Alan J. Torrance (Edinburgh: T.&T. Clark, 1992) 71-72, 77.

theology, with their claim that God is present only among the oppressed, appreciate this insight in a way that Jüngel, himself, does not.)

One context that Jüngel does embrace is the Christian one. He accepts the scandal that Jesus was God's unique revelation. Another context that he accepts is the Church, even though his ecclesiology is somewhat underdeveloped. Theology is to be done within and for the Church, because its role of guiding our thinking about God can be fulfilled only after God's own initiative has created faith. This role does not prohibit theology from performing a faith-producing catalytic function for curious nonbelievers, but it does mean that theology does not have the task of demonstrating God's reality. Jüngel acknowledges that God can speak from outside the Church, too, and he is always seeking to broaden his context and his understanding of the Ultimate. But he has yet to be convinced that the standards of the world (for example, economic analysis) should become theology's standards. Even within the Church, however, there are many contexts, especially economic, ethnic, and racial ones, that could enrich his theological perspective, if he were to immerse himself in them more fully, as he has in experiences of Nothingness and love. Theologians who do not seek such enrichment are unlikely to be able to comprehend the fullness of the Gospel.

Role of Human Action

History and context provide the foundation for human action, and considerable attention is being paid, nowadays, to the impact on a theologian's conceptual formulations of his or her active engagement with the world. Nevertheless, Jüngel objects to morally oriented activist[2] theolo-

---

[2]Jüngel is not against action per se. He believes in working for a more humane world, in taking action against unjust political systems, and in helping people to develop their potentiality. He does not believe in separating the spoken word from action, however. People's words are their acts and vice versa. Accordingly, he includes action within "linguistic existence." He writes, "Responsibility for the world takes place in linguistic existence, as man speaks, . . . thinks, . . . acts." *Unterwegs zur Sache: Theologische Bemerkungen*, Beiträge zur evangelischen Theologie 61 (Munich: Chr. Kaiser Verlag, 1972) 299. "Toward the Heart," 230. *Death*, 132, 134. "Grenzen des Menschseins," in *Probleme biblischer Theologie*, ed. Hans Walter Wolff (Munich: Chr. Kaiser Verlag, 1971) 204, #13.2.

gies that tend or appear (1) to be determined by action to the exclusion
of thought and argumentation, (2) to equate God's work with human endeavor, and (3) to confuse salvation with well-being. Such theologies do
not let God come directly, he complains. Yet only God's coming brings
salvation. Moreover, along with Ricoeur, he contends that more biblical
texts are to be regarded as metaphorical and poetical than as political.[3]

It is at this point that Jüngel relates human behavior to theology,
however, because he realizes that we can speak and write truly of God
only when we do God's will in faith, only when we love, and only when
we understand ourselves, as Jesus did, in the freedom of surrender to
God. He realizes (with Irenaeus), in other words, that good theology
stems from a right relationship to the God of Whom it presumes to speak
and, accordingly, from appropriate behavior.[4]

Indeed, his "hermeneutical thesis" implies just such behavior. That
thesis states that there is greater similarity than dissimilarity between God
and humanity when God comes to humanity. Such coming can have an
impact that can be seen: It affects our being and therefore should be
expected to be reflected in our doing. (In fact, the similarity *is*, I take it,
the quality of our being and action. It is, to borrow from Orthodox
theology, a moment of divinization.)

It seems inconsistent, therefore, for him to state quite so flatly that
"God does not come through our acts"[5]—unless he means merely that
God is not equivalent to our acts. For while "Word of God" becomes
meaningless if it is domesticated into purely mundane human experience,
that experience can be preparatory to the coming of The Extraordinary
(although not guaranteeing it), and it can provide the same catalytic vehicle for God's coming as language can. Indeed, if God has come through

---

[3]Paul Ricoeur, "Naming God," trans. David Pellauer, *Union Seminary Quarterly Review* 34 (Summer 1979): 227.

[4]If thought at its most profound really does follow Being, the depth of the
human predicament becomes clear: To the extent that Being is in a state of sin,
our thinking cannot escape that condition. At the same time, the significance of
a change in Being due to God's transforming action also becomes evident. The
possibility of such a change, within the presupposition that thought follows
Being, explains Jüngel's claim that close harmony with God is an essential com-
ponent in excellence of thinking about God.

[5]Jüngel, "Womit steht," 172.

the actions of Jesus of Nazareth, and if God comes to us again (and again) as the Holy Spirit (John 14:16-18) Who affects our actions, and if we meet Christ in our neighbor, it would not seem unreasonable to expect God also to come to us in, with, under, and through some of our acts.

The probable reason why Jüngel does not pay much attention to human action is his devotion to the doctrine of justification by grace. He understands that doctrine in the traditional Lutheran way, in accordance with which there is nothing that people can do to earn salvation. In the process of closing any loopholes in that claim, he finds that the doctrine provides for making a distinction between a person and her or his work. Our work produces things that we have. But God loves us and accepts us not for what we do but for who we are, in the light of Christ's perfect sacrifice on the Cross for all humanity. In other words, our value derives solely from God's regard for us as human beings. Hence, being is greater than having or doing. Jüngel underscores this conclusion by suggesting that human worth is reflected supremely in the unproductive "senior citizen."[6] Having thus secured the ultimate worth of even the destitute and the jobless in the unmerited love of God, Jüngel may fear that any emphasis on human action would undercut his argument and provide the basis for others to make assertions of personal righteousness based on works.

Yet the doctrine of justification by grace through faith has to do with more than just the circumstances under which salvation is attained or the status of human beings in the "eyes" of God. Luther's expectation was that the preaching of that doctrine, that is, the preaching of God's loving acceptance of us for the sake of Christ, would evoke a free and faith-

---

[6]Eberhard Jüngel, "Der alte Mensch—als Kriterium der Lebensqualität: Bemerkungen zur Menschenwürde der leistungsunfähigen Person," in *Der Wirklichkeitsanspruch von Theologie und Religion: Die sozialethische Herausforderung*, ed. Dieter Henke, Günther Kehrer, and Gunda Schneider-Flume (Tübingen: J. C. B. Mohr [Paul Siebeck], 1976) 129-32. See also idem., "Wertlose Wahrheit: Christlich Wahrheitserfahrung im Streit gegen die 'Tyrannei der Werte'," in *Die Tyrannei der Werte*, ed. S. Schelz (Hamburg: Lutherisches Verlagshaus, 1979) 45-75; idem., "Der menschliche Mensch: Die Bedeutung der reformatorischen Unterscheidung der Person von ihren Werken für das Selbstverständnis des neuzeitlichen Menschen," *Zeichen der Zeit* 39 (1985): 35-43.

filled response that would reflect God's love and issue in good works. Good deeds would be a sign that God had acted and that salvation had occurred. Moreover, Jüngel's anthropology is highly Barthian, which means, minimally, that Jüngel considers Jesus Christ to be the standard of what it means to be fully human. And a central feature of Jesus' life was his capacity to love. To be fully human, therefore, would be to be, by the power of the Holy Spirit, equally as loving as Jesus was. In either case, whether by responding with loving action to God's love for us, or by seeking to express our full humanity by following the high standards of Christ's love, Jüngel's theology provides all of the rationale needed for reaching out to others, either in helpful action or, as a minimum, in interest and concern. His theology also provides the basis for watching intently for where God is currently at work in the world, reflected in and encountering people through human action, and for how love and God's will can best be implemented in the world. To the extent that Jüngel is not attentive to these matters, he would seem to be underrating his own best insights into how to achieve excellence in theology.

Role of the Bible

Despite the importance of the preceding three sections, as long as Christian theology can be defended as a distinct endeavor, it will be proper for Jüngel's theology to be rooted in the Bible. Light from other sources is permitted to assist in illuminating the Bible's meaning for today, but the Bible remains the sole human criterion for judging claims to sacredness and ultimacy. All such claims must be compatible with the Bible, but even the Bible is the final arbiter only when illumined by the Holy Spirit.

Jüngel's use of the Bible focuses almost exclusively on the New Testament. As a result, he deprives himself of some channels for understanding God better. Moreover, he does not draw the life and teachings of Jesus adequately into his theology. He may be correct in thinking that we cannot know much about the historical Jesus. But even if the biblical accounts are mostly theological commentary, he does not pay attention to most of them. In limiting his interest primarily to the parables and the Crucifixion, he ignores or does not fully exploit the following features of Jesus' life:

• the freedom of thought and action that his faith in God gave him,

- his openness to people on the fringes of society and his astonishing acceptance of outcasts, tax collectors, Samaritans, and women,
- his ability to build community by giving people a sense of worth,
- forms of his love, such as his ethics and healings, and
- his willingness to oppose hypocrisy and to die for his beliefs.

These features, in addition to the ones that Jüngel does deal with, would seem to be important components of the foundation for all other claims of Christian theology. Without most of them, no one would have found any particular significance in Jesus' crucifixion, let alone come up with "resurrection by God" as an interpretation of the "appearances" perceived by Peter and others (1 Cor. 15:5); yet these categories are at the heart of Jüngel's theology. Even in view of the historical problems of the New Testament, Jüngel's Christology would have a more firm footing if it were related more directly to the features perceived in Jesus that caused him to be found to be so extraordinary. As a result, the contours of divine presence on earth might become more clear, as would the relevance of Jesus for today. While I do not object to the implications that Jüngel finds in the Cross and Resurrection, it would seem that if they cannot be found also in Jesus' life and teachings, they are subject to being dismissed as pure speculation. Jüngel's own theological method paves the way for him to develop his Christology further, because he does not limit himself to the conceptual molds of the past but provides for God always to reveal the Bible's fuller meaning from the perspective of contemporary experiences.

Jüngel's Epistemology and Hermeneutic

With these considerations of the biblical roots of Jüngel's theology, the methods that he employs, his non-Hegelian view of history, and the role he assigns to faith and action, we have already touched on aspects of Jüngel's hermeneutic and of his views of how knowledge of God can be obtained. We now turn more intensively to the latter topics, including an assessment of his use of phenomenology, his view of language, and his application of those conceptual instruments to natural theology.

Knowledge of God

Jüngel's assumptions concerning our knowledge of God may be reviewed quickly. He assumes a Western model of ultimacy, that is, he assumes that God takes the initiative and acts in the world. As a corollary, he assumes that human experience is occasionally affected by God's action or presence.

For human knowledge of God to occur, the Ultimate must encounter us again and again in acts of Self-revelation. This encounter not only makes a cognitive difference but also molds our being, changing behavior and generating a new interpretation of the world through a new perspective and new behavior. Nevertheless, faith is still needed in order to acknowledge God's presence in the encounter. Finally, therefore, knowledge of God is verified in the depths of our being, by faith. Otherwise, it cannot be verified.

Those who would hope for a more objective knowledge of God will find Jüngel weakest in his dependence on personal experience. But the logic of his epistemological claim seems strong. If we are dealing with what is indeed ultimate, our subject matter is outside our control. It is its own criterion of the truth about Itself, and if we are to know It, It must make Itself known. Jüngel avoids solipsism by providing for testing our interpretation of our experience of God by comparing it with biblical data and with other Christian experience, and to that extent we are not bereft of quasi-objective guideposts. Basically, however, since God is the final criterion, from a human point of view that means that whether or not we have encountered God will depend, subjectively, on the strength of our conviction that we have done so.

Hermeneutical Considerations

Jüngel's understanding of Being and of language have anti-Cartesian implications, which point to our inability to make definitive statements about an objective world, an objective metaphysics, and the objective truth of Christian doctrine. These implications get lost in some of his "dogmatic pronouncements" about God, but it is likely that, when pressed, he would agree that "objective theological knowledge" means "our community *believes* that that's the way it is."

For those who want to ensure that they are doing Christian theology, the value of his emphasis on "thinking after" is that it maintains the Christian criterion of truth about God, namely, God's "objective" revelation in Jesus as recorded in the Bible and God's present self-attestation in our subjective experience of revelation.

Jüngel is wise not to limit himself to a particular philosophical system. He also is wise to make judicious use of existentialism and phenomenology. Although he engages Idealism heavily, however, there is a noticeable absence of any confrontation with its historical alternative, Marxism. There are, of course, plenty of people currently bringing Marxist analysis into theology. But a follower of him who "went to those who needed love" cannot forever ignore that philosophical system most self-consciously devoted to people in concrete need.

Certainly an argument can be made for the theological use of some of the tools of Marxist analysis. It might run as follows: "Grace of God," "God's love," "Spirit of God," "power of God," and "Kingdom of God" are not discrete aspects of God but are symbolic expressions of divine reality in its totality. Rahner has made a strong argument for overturning a prominent medieval Catholic view of grace as a created supernatural substance, distinct from God, and replacing it with the view that grace is simply another word for God: grace and God are the same thing. To say that God acts graciously is not to characterize one mode of the behavior of an entity labeled "God." Rather, it is to claim that God is the quality, power, or event of grace. The newer view agrees with the position taken by Luther, Calvin, and other Protestant theologians. Following their lines of reasoning, "the will of God" could be yet another expression for the totality of God.[7] If that be the case, then understanding God's will would mean understanding God and not just understanding the ethical interests of God. God would not be distinct from God's will, in the strong sense that God's will would be the totality of God and not merely an aspect of God. The traditional argument for the simplicity of God would endorse this position. Similarly, God is not distinct from divine love, or from the Holy Spirit, or even from the reign of God (as Jüngel himself argues). It follows that reasoning about God should include trying to determine God's will, since determining God's will would be a valid route to understanding the totality of God. But God's will is done in terms of this world and its various structures (economic, political, social, cultural, religious, etc.). And surely the God Who knows the number of hairs on

---

[7]This possibility provides a hitherto unconsidered view of God's Being that would justify much of the work of liberation theology. With regard to Rahner and Luther, see Karl Rahner, *Nature and Grace*, trans. Dinah Wharton (London: Sheed and Ward, 1963) 20-21, 24; idem., *The Trinity*, trans. Joseph Donceel (New York: Herder and Herder, 1970) 101; and Ewald M. Plass, ed., *What Luther Says* (Saint Louis: Concordia Publishing House, 1959) 611.

the head of each individual must be conceived not as having simply a will-in-general but as having a will for each specific situation. Indeed, following the proposal to equate God with God's will, God would *be* the best that could occur in every specific situation. Understanding the will of the God Who (in traditional terms) relates concretely to the concrete world, therefore, would seem to require employment of the social sciences—not as standards, but as analytical tools—as much as it requires employment of philosophy, in order to comprehend the components of God's will being done. Such an effort to understand God would also justify theology's venturing into the hazards of identifying the characteristics of God's presence on the current scene, just as theology has identified God's presence at the scene of the Crucifixion.

Phenomenology

Among the hermeneutical strategies employed by Jüngel, the principles of phenomenology are present. Jüngel agrees with Heidegger[8] that theology is a phenomenological study, and he identifies the focus of that study as the central phenomena of Christianity, namely, Jesus Christ and the basic writings about him. That study leads Jüngel to contend for a similarity between divine and human love, thereby providing justification for a phenomenology of human love as a basis for gaining insight into the Being of God.

At a time like the present, when the Bible's metaphors do not always work, he does well to consider phenomena outside the Bible that nevertheless are related to the Bible. In making that move, he enters the realm of natural theology, of course. He can justify doing so on the basis of faith seeking to explicate what it already knows.[9] If it be asked how a

---

[8]As a means of ensuring that the truths of Barth's theology will not be dismissed out of hand, Jüngel does well to borrow from the pagans in order to make a Christian point. In other words, he uses Heideggerian concepts when he thinks they will help "modern man" understand the Gospel, since he believes, as Barth does, that God is able to work through any conceptual system, but he does not commit the totality of his theology to Heidegger's philosophical framework.

[9]Contrary to the opinion of Walter Kasper ("Abschied vom Gott der Philosophen," *Evangelische Kommentare* 10 [October 1977]: 622-23), he does not use his phenomenological reasoning for purposes of verification, as though he were in control of the subject matter, but merely as an aid to understanding.

phenomenological study can tell us about God if God's Being is in coming and therefore not present in the phenomena, the answer is that God can come to illumine our understanding of those phenomena, especially those that have been associated with God in the past.

But Jüngel does run the risk of turning the object of study into an independent source of new truth about God. His study of love succeeded in avoiding this problem, however. Postulating the divine in human love did not result in self-awareness becoming a type of direct awareness of God. The intent behind his use of phenomenology can make all the difference. He takes fewer risks if he uses phenomenology for biblical illumination than if he uses it for theological discovery or demonstration, because the latter two instances presuppose a much lesser dependence upon God's own Self-revelation than does the former.

Accordingly, he does not examine religious experience to develop an understanding of why certain religious symbols "work," because the ultimate answer to that question lies in God and because answers of a preparatory or anticipatory nature encourage the belief that human wisdom can provide adequate explanations of divine revelation. He does not seek a phenomenology of faith eidetically reduced and organized, because the eidetic elements do not automatically lead to their Essence. As Gordon Kaufman has said, theology cannot be based on the "essence" found in a phenomenological analysis of the religious experience common to all people, because in order to understand and talk about any experience—even before submitting it to analysis—it must be brought into the language of the experiencer's culture and therefore will be shaped by that language and will not be presented in pure form.[10] Since the divine element in human religious experience (experience that contains a mixture of God and sin) is not much more available to us than the

---

[10]Gordon D. Kaufman, *An Essay on Theological Method*, American Academy of Religion Studies in Religion 11 (Missoula MT: Scholars Press, 1975) 4-6, 17. But, against Kaufman, Jüngel does not believe that theology is reduced to studying cultural apprehensions of God. Nor does theology have the task of imagining God *de novo*, totally apart from God's own reality, which reveals itself.

Studies of mystical experience do not produce new raw data about God, either. They tell us merely what the human experience called "union with God" feels like (e.g., existential joy, or a feeling of oneness with the creation and with more than the creation).

historical Jesus, whom Christians believe to have manifested God in pure—albeit culturally conditioned—form, there would still seem to be merit in arguing for concentrating attention on the purer source, as being more likely to lead both to God and to the conditions that would not only call for but manifest God's presence. This orientation makes sense especially for those who believe that the constellation of forces that evoked the title "Son of God" for Jesus also applies to God's presence today.

Jüngel prescinds completely from the even broader interest of much North American theology in the phenomenological study of ordinary human experience in general, an interest devoted to proving that "God" is still a meaningful word by showing that the ultimate and the sacred can be known in ordinary human experience (for example, of contingency, temporality, relativity, freedom, autonomy, and estrangement) and, beyond that, that God is "necessarily affirmed...by all our basic beliefs and understanding."[11] One goal of this theology is to find the universal Logos in existence generally, rather than to wait in faith for it to speak.[12] One presupposition is that sinners have a conception of God that is adequate to enable them to distinguish claims of God's presence in human experience from the presence of the Devil disguised as an angel of light.

The ultimate goal of this phenomenological theology is to demonstrate, presumably to believer and nonbeliever alike, the adequacy of Christian categories for illuminating all experience. Here the purview of faith seems to be ignored, the insights of Wittgenstein concerning language-games are bypassed, and we seem to have returned to a Cartesian objective world. Presumably, if we could prove that there were an Ultimate Unifying Power—or God defined in some other way—more people

---

[11]David Tracy, *Blessed Rage for Order: The New Pluralism in Theology* (New York: Seabury/Crossroad, 1975) 56. See also 44, 47-48, 55. Langdon Gilkey, *Naming the Whirlwind: The Renewal of God-Language* (Indianapolis: Bobbs-Merrill, 1969) 275, 279, 284, 306, 365, 451.

[12]This concern for certainty is as strong as Tillich's, although Tillich spoke out against this approach to attaining it when he opposed the error of deriving God from the world, based on "some characteristics of the world" that "make the conclusion 'God' necessary" (*Systematic Theology* 1:205). That God is not universally available for apprehending is implied in Moses' question to the Hebrews: "Has a people ever heard the voice of God speaking from the midst of the fire, as you have heard, and lived?" (Deut. 4:33).

would find reason to trust It or to try to get into harmony with It. But even people who believe firmly in God do not do either of those things fully. So proof of a divine reality does not seem to be what we need. What we need is "new creation" (2 Cor. 5:17; Gal. 6:15), and that comes from the God Who comes.

Use of Language

Jüngel provides for God to come primarily through metaphorical use of language, through which new insights and new Being may be generated. Metaphor transcends the ordinary definitions of words, thereby providing God, "Himself," with the opportunity to give "His" own meaning to the words used about "Him."

In the terminology of deconstructionism, even though a signifier cannot embrace an objective, transcendent referent without distortion, and even though there may generally not be "transcendental signifieds" that can guarantee the "truth" of a word or text, divine reality is a "transcendental signified" with the power so to impinge on the human mind as to enable particular signifiers to convey—albeit only momentarily—the verity of that ultimacy.

The dynamic reality of God calls for this type of revelation at least as much as active interpersonal relationships require current action on the part of the people involved. As a specific example, if you want to deal with me, you cannot deal merely with what I said in the past. You need me to give those statements the meaning that they have for me in the present.

The need for God's present manifestation is especially great if revelation provides not simply information but a new quality of Being. This understanding of revelation, coupled with an acknowledgement of the pervasiveness of sin, makes it clearer why it is inappropriate to treat God as an object of investigation and why God's unique first-century revelation needs repeated divine illumination. And since, in metaphor, the imagination and experiences of the hearer play an essential part in the success of the communication, the "repeated illumination" will occur always in terms that are most appropriate to each individual.

Effective metaphorical language about God (1) places God in union with transitoriness, (2) provides for God to be more similar to us than dissimilar, at a particular point in time when "speaking" directly to us,[13] and (3) enables us to think and speak properly about God, in the first place. The value of metaphor and of its story form, parable, lies, additionally, in the fact that they make God present but still not fully subject to our comprehension. A language about God that would make stronger claims would be implausible.

Jüngel's distinctive view of metaphor may gain clarity by contrasting it to Ricoeur's view, especially since both men generally agree on the functioning and significance of metaphor in theological discourse. Indeed, Ricoeur makes use of Jüngel in his own work on biblical hermeneutics.[14] They also agree that the meaning of a text expands when the text is read in different contexts, where new horizons of vision extend and illuminate the author's original intention. But Jüngel's dynamic, Heideggerian ontology, his non-Cartesian existentialist view of a nonobjective world, and his belief in a less-than-omnipresent God keep him from sharing Ricoeur's interest in symbol. For Ricoeur, a religious symbol is bound to the universe viewed as sacred and is identified as a sacred symbol when the sacredness of nature reveals itself through it. Ricoeur's symbols are rooted in "the durable constellations of life," whereas Jüngel's metaphors, while bound to the world through its language, are based on our *changing* relations to the world. Ricoeur's symbol presupposes a fixed ontology, with the symbol revealing to us only more of what we already participate in. Such an understanding of symbol would not be a useful vehicle for the God Who makes all things new. Ricoeur implies, moreover, that the depths even of merely human experience cannot come to our attention linguistically, as by means of metaphor, if they have not emerged first as a symbol. "Metaphors are just the linguistic surface of symbols," he says. They merely contribute to the nondescriptive double meaning of the symbol. For Ricoeur, a symbol is a "scripture of an Other," requiring my interpretation and, to that extent, under my

---

[13]Here Jüngel merges Bultmann's contention that we can speak only about human experience of God and Barth's claim that we can speak of God's own Being, because that Being becomes manifest in the human experience of revelation, when revelation is God's Self-interpretation.

[14]Paul Ricoeur, "Biblical Hermeneutics," *Semeia* 4 (1975): 36, 91.

control.[15] The value that Jüngel finds in metaphor is that it can be a vehicle for the presence of the Other directly, outside my control.

While Jüngel counterbalances subjectivity by insisting on knowing the literal or conventional meaning of words, by acknowledging the objective status of the Bible, and by using the historical-critical method, he has no interest in the completely objective and totally closed system of structuralism, which dismisses the historical, redactional stages of texts, limits words to their immanent meaning within a text, shows no interest in additional meaning being derived from the subjectivity of the reader, and disassociates textual content from real life situations. He does not appear to be making a mistake in ignoring that kind of structuralism.

Although practitioners of the New Hermeneutic have been criticized for not letting their interests in language lead them into further investigation of the intricacies of literary and poetic construction,[16] the thrust of my own criticism moves in the opposite direction. It was summarized by Bonhoeffer in a letter written on April 30, 1944, when he said, "The time when people could be told everything by means of words . . . is over."[17] It may even be argued that language as the medium of God's communication with the world (as represented by the Law on Mt. Sinai) has been replaced by human being and action (as represented by Jesus).

While Jüngel claims that when he speaks of "word," he intends to include action as well as speech, the focus of his attention is undeniably skewed toward speech. It is as though he needs to be reminded—even though he knows better—that God's action in the world precedes any talk about it and that God acts often through human action, as in the case of Jesus. Without denying the metaphorical value of biblical language, one cannot overlook the fact that the Hebrew slaves were not freed primarily from figurative bondage. Their religion was founded on actual liberation from physical slavery. Such fundamental categories cannot properly be ignored, therefore, by theologians in the Judeo-Christian tradition.

As reiteration of God's Being, revelation provides God's quality of Being, which, if it is to be communicated, is communicated less well by

[15]Ricoeur, *Interpretation Theory*, 46, 59, 61-64, 69.

[16]Norman Perrin, *Jesus and the Language of the Kingdom: Symbol and Metaphor in New Testament Interpretation* (Philadelphia: Fortress, 1976) 124-25.

[17]Dietrich Bonhoeffer, *Letters and Papers from Prison*, ed. Eberhard Bethge (New York: Macmillan, 1971) 279.

words than simply by repeating it in our own being, just as we cannot teach a person a song by describing it; we must sing it again. Those who receive revelation are empowered (for varying lengths of time) to engage in just such repetition of Being. While Jüngel does not overlook the function of God's *Being* as Word, he fails to acknowledge fully the analogous role of our own beings (including our acts) as "words" or vehicles for communicating God's revelation. We have seen examples of Jüngel's awareness of the close relationship between being and theology. And we have noted his willingness judiciously to bring into his theology elements from outside the Bible. What appears called for is continued movement in that direction; a greater commitment on his part to the "action" dimensions of Being, as a modality of his own discovery of God's present action in the world; and recognition of the catalytic value of action for making God present as event.

Natural Theology

Jüngel's theology leaves the door open to the appropriation of all modes of natural theology for their metaphorical value, while rejecting the belief that any natural theology can say anything about God that is literally true.

In the centuries-old debate between natural and revealed theology, Jüngel at least starts with God's direct revelation as recorded in the Bible before employing concepts, phenomenological analyses, and other examples from outside the Bible, in the process of increasing faith's understanding. Even then, he acknowledges that illumination from outside the Bible is incomplete until God completes it. Natural theology says the same thing, but it has laid its foundations outside God's direct revelation and thereby runs the risk of having established erroneous preconditions that may distort its understanding of any eventual divine illumination.

Perhaps the discussion boils down to the question of whether humanity is in some essential way perverted, so that we are incapable of developing an appropriate straight-line argument to Ultimate Truth, or whether we are simply incomplete and impure, a mixture of good and evil, with the ability to move generally in the right direction when we want to, but without the ability to attain the ultimate Good unassisted.

Even these alternatives may resolve themselves around the question of the degree of divine illumination that is expected. Since both theologies claim that God is outside their grasp, the distinction between them may lie as much at the end of their thought process as it does at the place where they begin. Even though revealed theology begins with God's revelation, it would seem also to provide for God to enter into the midst of its thought process from a ninety-degree angle, that is, from a direction that its thinking would never have considered. Natural theology, on the other hand, develops a logical chain of thought that begins in nature and assumes that God must be just beyond a straight-line extension of that thought process.

Perhaps revealed theology could accept a natural theology that endorses revealed theology's presuppositions about human nature and about God's relation to its theological deliberations. Such a natural theology might well shun forming a theological system (because of the uncertainty of using nature as the foundation for the divine), but it could be a creative force in responding to divine truth in sources outside the Bible and in presenting its insights for incorporation into biblical theology and thus for further illumination by God. Although Jüngel's is a biblically based theology, his work with transitoriness and his interest in overcoming Nothingness indicate that he has begun to explore this type of natural theology. Those interests enable him to speak to the modern mind, and they express, in modern terminology, some of the concerns of the New Testament, as well. For example, the Resurrection surely deals with transitoriness and the Nothingness of literal and figurative death. And God's involvement in transitoriness underlies the freedom with which Jesus interpreted the Law and mingled with outcasts.

A theology that makes use of economic and social analysis could fit into this type of natural theology, too. For instance, a theology that gives serious consideration to the power structures of society might see in Jesus' movement from Galilee to Jerusalem an attack by a "country bumpkin" on the establishment, as Frederick Herzog has suggested. That awareness of social power structures, stimulated by an analysis that originated outside the Bible, might yield the insight that it is God's will that the status quo be challenged, when doing so will result in more perfect justice. Such an insight is congruent with biblical materials, but it might not have occurred as readily, apart from the extrabiblical analysis provided by this type of natural theology.

Other forms of a qualified version of natural theology, as discussed in the preceding two paragraphs, along with other examples of Jüngel's hermeneutical stance, will be evident as we consider Jüngel's concept of God and of God's relation to the world.

God and the World

How Jüngel Grasps God's Being

Our examination of Jüngel's doctrine of God provided indications that a high degree of sophistication can be masked by the use of traditional biblical and theological language. Jüngel also uses nonbiblical categories and devices from time to time, in order to gain insight, in the mundane sphere, into the truth found antecedently in the Bible. Indeed, he even can call the affirmation of Being in the face of nonbeing "the revelation of God," because faith attributes to what is mundanely real more than what meets the eye. He makes it clear that Being is not God, but the fact that Being can be affirmed is itself a manifestation of what he is willing to call "God." But he does not claim that the affirmation of Being is a manifestation of God on the basis of a general, anthropocentrically Western assumption that Being is better than nonbeing and that since God is usually associated with the good, to choose Being is good and therefore is a manifestation of God. Instead, he makes his claim because his insight into another event of Christian faith leads him to the conclusion that God is the unity of death and life for the sake of life. It is for that reason that he can say that when Being (or life) is affirmed, God is revealed. Accordingly, he does not explain that affirmation in terms of human capability, but, speaking from faith, he reverts to metaphor to give God the glory: A person can affirm Being because "God decides between Being and nonbeing." This shifting between conventional and metaphorical language can be very exasperating to the reader who is expecting a purely rational argument in secular terms. It is the consequence of moving between language games (or between worldviews). And it provides evidence for the claim that Jüngel grounds his theology in the Bible, for otherwise he could complete his argument purely in the nonbiblical realm. But his arguments often are just interpretations or paraphrases in nonbiblical categories of biblical narratives or symbols; their ultimate justification rests on faith in the biblical material and in the God to which it points. Ultimately, therefore, he must return to that material. In his "Heidggerian mode," he ventures outside the Bible and takes up issues in the culture that he finds there, using the language of that culture. But since he does not believe that the "answers" lie within the culture and its attendant philosophies, he eventually must revert to his "Barthian mode" and simply assert the Christian *kerygma*.

He reasons that we can think and speak of God only because God "spoke" to us first and continues to speak. His position stands in contrast to those who argue that the word "God" has a theistically demonstrable content that can or should command general acceptance. Accordingly, he bases his Trinitarian doctrine of God on the fact that God enters into relations with humanity, as seen by faith and recorded in the Bible. That fact, along with the human consequence of that fact as embodied in Jesus, causes him to postulate both differentiation and developing relations within God. Then, building on that skeleton, working with the New Testament proclamation that God is love, and understanding love as the event in which God is more similar to us than dissimilar, he justifies a phenomenology of human love that enables him to show that the divine nature must be triune, since love consists simultaneously in relating to oneself and in reaching out, as in the relationship of Holy Spirit between Father and Son. He also implies that we can learn about human love from the nature of God's own love, since the latter indicates that *eros* and *agape* are not mutually exclusive.

God as Coming

"Love never ends." No wonder, then, that Jüngel observes that God's Being, which is the ever new relation of love between the Father and the Son, must always be future and in coming. It is interesting to note that he changes his description of God's internal and eternal movement from "becoming" to "coming"—probably a reflection (1) of his culture's concern with the absence of God, (2) of the entrenchment of his own perspective more firmly "from below," and (3) of a desire to move away from a term that can be mistakenly identified with process theology's concept of a materially changing, "consequential" nature in God. By identifying eternity with God, he invests it with quality and not merely with duration. Moreover, he goes beyond Heidegger and unites Being and time metaphorically in God. He also implies, thereby, that God's movement from origin to goal is not subject to the constraints of time. But that does not mean that God is a static ideal. Indeed, saying that God's reality is in motion, moving from origin to goal, is precisely Jüngel's way of saying that God is not a static ideal. We are urged to recognize God as mystery, rather than to hold God in our minds as an ideal. We who exist in time can only (1) act upon our memory of the God Who came in time and, in faithful trust, (2) be open to the newness that God's next, imminent appearance in time will bring.

Jüngel's reference to God as "coming" does not deal only with time. It, along with the doctrine of the Trinity, asserts that neither the world as we normally experience it nor a particular context of human interaction are the generators of God. The concept of God as "coming" and the doctrine of the immanent Trinity deny that the dynamic interplay of forces within the world can, by itself, generate a divine word of address or evoke God's presence. The word "God" points to a mystery beyond those forces.

Both Jüngel and Moltmann speak of God's coming to the world, and the way in which they do so highlights both Jüngel's strengths and his weaknesses. Jüngel is much more confident of what God will be like when God comes, because he is able to conceive of how God enables Jesus to reflect divine fullness in human form, a fullness that has not changed essentially since Jesus' death. In contrast, Moltmann, in the early part of his career, treated Jesus as having only foreshadowed God's reality, and he claimed that, with Jesus' death, there was a clean break between the historical Jesus and the Jesus whom God declared to be the Son of God eschatologically and who therefore comes to us from an unknown future.[18]

Jüngel's God comes only as Word, whereas Moltmann's comes as *fulfillment* of promises, the universal in concrete form. Jüngel tends to consider his theological efforts to be completed at the point at which God has an impact upon us as individuals; Moltmann looks for that impact to take concrete form in changing society and the world at large. Sin will enter between impact and accomplishment, of course, but since Jüngel can provide for the Universal to be reflected in human form in Jesus, he ought also to be able to provide for divine reality to become manifest in specific human action on at least some other occasions. Indeed, his own concept of God's double relational Being can be understood to mean that the Father's love for the Son is repeated in new circumstances, that is,

---

[18]Jürgen Moltmann, *The Crucified God: The Cross of Christ as the Foundation and Criticism of Christian Theology*, trans. R. A. Wilson and John Bowden (New York: Harper & Row, 1974) 122, 125.

here on earth, so that God can exist or occur "between us," as we love one another.[19]

Implications of Metaphor for God's Being

Since Being, too, is "in" God, God is not conditioned by anything that we do, that is, by our being. Being is in God in the sense of being "within God's Self-relationship" and therefore subject to God's control, not in the sense of being literally within *the* universal Entity, Who is affected by all subordinate beings, as process theology would have it.

The mystery of God requires that language about God be metaphorical. But metaphorical language keeps one from ever being able to give a definitive answer to the question about God and the world. It also makes the point that God is not to be understood objectively, within or outside an objective world, and within the framework of the world's cause and effect relationships. God is portrayed by the dynamics of God's own presence. When *we* speak of God we must speak figuratively, as we do when we speak of "serving God." We serve God by doing God's will, thereby making God's reality present. But God's own Being is not enhanced by our action. Similarly, God is sad in the same way that a picture that conveys an air of sadness is sad. All other adjectives apply to God in the same way. These comments are directed particularly to process theology's alternative to Jüngel, because only when God is understood *literally* as being absolute and in relationship is the concept of a dipolar God appropriate.

Does the traditional bifurcation of uncreated God and created world still hold, or are those just figurative ways of talking about the perfect, essential unity and potential of the world vs. the imperfect, superficial present? To speak metaphorically about God's coming does not help to answer this question, because God could come from another (divine) realm or from the depths of this one. But what are the "depths" of this one? They are just as much a metaphor as "heaven" is a metaphor of the world's "heights" or sublime qualities. Jüngel's response to this quandary is to make the point that God is outside human control. That is the

---

[19]In that way, God, the All, becomes increasingly in all. But just as a drop of water is as complete an instance of water as a tub full of water, so God is All even before being in all.

Bible's claim when it talks about building a temple to house God.[20] God is an extraordinary event. Therefore, while God may be or come from a primal unity of the cosmos or from the depths of human being, there is little value in accepting such hypotheses if our only access to God is when God comes to us. One disservice of these hypotheses is to limit our attention to certain particular spheres of interest, thereby causing us to overlook the possibility of divine presence in other spheres. Another disservice is to cause us to think that by careful study of certain areas we can find God, or piece God's reality together, or encounter God within a particular, unique context. So a psychological (for example, Jungian) theism is to be avoided as much as a metaphysical theism. Moreover, if God be unity, must God not also be necessary for the world? But if we make God necessary, do we not rob God of the excitement that the Hebrews found when the Word spoke, unexpectedly, and "it was done"? Perhaps it is better to think of God as the unity of the world only in potential, only in (and beyond) faith's vision of what should be. We might add that when God comes to the world God affects it and in that way slowly unites it. In that case, God is the future unity of the world made present eschatologically (the ideal actualized), when people function harmoniously within themselves, with their neighbors, in society as a whole, and with nature.

An Intermittent God?

With Being and time in God, God is also not separated from them. Rather, God's reality is freely among them.

Even more radically, although Jüngel takes pains to establish the Being of the *immanent* Trinity, in order not to reduce God to the mundane, he also implies that that Being not only coincides with merely sporadic events experienced in the world but that it does not exist apart from those events. Could he inadvertently be implying that God's Being is merely intermittent? He seems to do this when he refers to God as

• existing in the Word of address,

---

[20]"But will God dwell indeed with man on earth [to say nothing of 'in man' or 'in earth']? Behold heaven and the highest heaven cannot contain thee." 2 Chron. 6:18; 1 Kings 8:27.

- not hidden but abandoned "entirely to the word that he speaks,"[21]
- existing in the act of revelation,
- not existing in the abstract but only in acts that demonstrate that God is "for us,"
- being Mystery only *when* God comes to the world,
- constantly given afresh,
- making "Himself" objective, which could mean that there is no God at all, apart from the moment of our encounter with God, and
- understood *anew*, each time the Holy Spirit interprets the Bible to us.

This possibility of God's discontinuous Being can be construed to be implied also when he speaks of

- the need to think revelation and God's essence simultaneously,[22]
- the word "God" having no objective definition but being tied to the moment of its use,
- our not speaking of God if we are not speaking of an event,
- the Kingdom (which God is) as being not a noun but an occurrence,
- time being in God, which could mean that God, in order not to be controlled by time, is the sheer instant of occurrence, and
- truth as occurrence.

He does seem to oppose the notion of God as a continuous entity or reality. Consider the following statements:

- There is not a separate transcendence apart from an immanent Word-event.
- There is no revelation of God apart from *faith's* combining the natural and the supernatural. Here Jüngel does not invoke a separate supernatural entity.
- The word "God" is a *very formal* designation of the cause of—or the mystery surrounding—one's believing.

If, by emphasizing the event-nature of God, Jüngel does indeed intend to assert that God's Being is not continuous, there is a model that he could follow that would make the point quite clearly. It is a model based on music or on speech. Its contrasting alternative, the one that provides for continuous existence, is a visual model, exemplified by a pic-

---

[21]GMW, 177 (trans. modified). GGW, 238. See also GMW, 75: "The divine being is to be understood as a sequence of events." (It is not clear whether Jüngel is here expressing his own ideas or whether he is paraphrasing Hegel.)
[22]GMW, 104; GGW, 137.

ture or a painting.[23] The contrast becomes evident by comparing a picture with music. A picture is static and permanent, with time having no essential effect on it, once it is created. Music, on the other hand, is dynamic and constantly changing. Time is essential to music, since it comes to us over time, one note—or one group of notes—at a time, with each note existing only at the time it is being played. Another important contrast pertains to the control we have over the process of looking at a picture, compared with the process of listening to music. In looking at a picture, we are essentially active. We take the initiative to focus our attention on different features of the picture. When we listen to music, however, we are essentially passive. We are forced to wait for the notes to come to us. These two artistic modes represent very different forms of reality; yet each is genuinely real.

The anthropocentric religious language that the Western world has inherited follows the picture-model. We simply assume that our heavenly Father is a continuous entity and that His divinity lies, in part, in His ability to outlast us. But if Jüngel's notion of God as event is on the right track, the model of musical note is more appropriate for God. Perhaps divine reality consists of many split-second, discontinuous "lives," rather than one of infinite duration.

The music-model is not without its problems, but it would serve to simplify Jüngel's concept of "double relational Being." The music-model does not require that an ideal note be described apart from the instance of its sound in the world to which it is "relating" (that is, there is no need to describe the Trinity as relating internally to itself and also externally beyond itself). That instance of sound can be understood as the ideal or idea (Father) actualized (Son) in some mysterious way (Holy Spirit). As in the traditional doctrine of the Trinity, one Person cannot be present without the others, nor can one be separated from the others. They all are required for a note to sound. God "*in se*" would *simultaneously* be for us and would be showing that orientation in the only way that reality can exist, namely, in action.

---

[23]These contrasts are described in Thorlief Boman, *Hebrew Thought Compared with Greek*, trans. Jules L. Moreau (Philadelphia: Westminster, 1960). They are explored further in William H. Poteat, *Polanyian Meditations: In Search of a Post-Critical Logic* (Durham NC: Duke University, 1985) chap. 7.

It would be in accordance with Jüngel's teaching to say that divine Being is a worldly occurrence of the extraordinary, following the model of a musical note. In this understanding, such an occurrence is not fully accounted for by the world as human beings understand it, since the occurrence includes the *extra*ordinary, which is another designation for the mysterious "dimension" of the world.

However fully this speculation may conform to Jüngel's own thinking, it does seem that Jüngel urges one to regard God not as a constant but only as an ever new possibility, Who is real only at the moment of encounter with humanity (while not being totally unlike earlier Self-revelations). Or does he speak of God's being in "coming" precisely to avoid limiting God's reality to unpredictable moments and for the purpose of ensuring duration in God? Possibly so, and if so, his metaphor is an ingenious way of combining the static and the dynamic. For even in the "static" duration of the process of coming, God is in motion, both in our direction and internally (or essentially).

Although God's Being may not be limited to moments of encounter with human beings, those encounters and what we learn in them provide all the knowledge of God that we are able to have, in any case. Jüngel peppers his readers with metaphors at every crucial juncture precisely to make the point that God cannot be reduced to a more durable and more universal, humanly devised metaphysical construct.[24]

Implications for the Future

What do Jüngel's concepts of God and his method of doing theology portend for the future?

Some significant shifts in theological sensitivity have taken place during the past few decades. Some of those shifts have occurred because the action of the economically and politically disenfranchised has brought God to the attention of many in a new way. As a result, a mutation has taken place in theology. Indeed, some theologians have so rallied to the cries of the oppressed that they fail to consider a Word from any other

---

[24]Consequently, he does not fully resolve the issue of whether God's Being is continuous, in dynamic movement ("becoming"), or intermittent, in appearances and word-events (revelation). To do so would be to take more of a metaphysical stand than he could justify.

source. It is not clear, therefore, whether the mutant will survive in its present form. Meanwhile, others have returned to the delights of natural theology, where the security of human control also produces a reluctance to consider a Word from any other Source. From another perspective, deconstructionism would seem to urge that such a Source, if there be one, is neither permanently accessible nor metaphysically supernatural.

Into this matrix Jüngel brings a theology which, itself, may be moving in new directions. That such movement is likely to occur is due to the significance of his work thus far in resolving many of the disputes that have arisen within German Protestant theology during the past half-century. Movement does not require abandonment of a present position, however, but only extension and development. For despite its present limitations, Jüngel's work offers at least four conditions that would provide a hospitable environment for fruitful evolution of Christian theology.

First, Jesus Christ is God's unique—though not yet fully understood—revelation and the only foundation for Christian theology; and the Bible, when interpreted with the aid of the Holy Spirit, is the sole human criterion of divine truth.

Second, phenomena outside the Bible and the Church can serve as catalysts for gaining insight into divine reality, when those phenomena are interpreted in the light of the Bible and its Lord.

Third, God's reality can and does speak for itself. We cannot describe God adequately, nor do we have to. We are better advised to expect surprises when dealing with God and to be ready to respond.

Accordingly, God is known as and through event. God's Word does not exist in addition to God, but God is properly designated "Word." Consequently, God is not to be found in permanent form in either human beings or the world.

Another corollary of the third condition is that God is not to be reduced to a principle, or to anything literal, or to anything incomplete.

Fourth, acknowledging theological language as metaphorical can breathe new life into many theological modes and can save from error those who think of God in literal terms. At the same time, Jüngel and others can be reminded not to overlook the literal meaning of biblical accounts, especially as they deal with God's concrete will in a physical world.

It is likely that several forms of theology will be able to develop in this environment. For the fecundity of the theological enterprise, that likelihood is to be applauded. At the same time one can hope that, while evolving, theologians will direct their gaze where God is to be found and that they will glance over their shoulder, occasionally, just in case they are mistaken.

What about Jüngel's own evolution? He has cultivated a fertile environment for sound theological thought in the future. For that reason, his work need not mark only the end of a great era. With proper adaptation in response to God's own movement, it can spawn insight of equally high calibre for decades to come.

Bibliography

A. Jüngel's Works[1]

1961

*"Der Schritt zurück: Eine Auseinandersetzung mit der Heidegger-Deutung Heinrich Otts." *Zeitschrift für Theologie und Kirche* 58 (1961): 104-22.

1962

Paulus und Jesus: Eine Untersuchung zur Präzisierung der Frage nach dem Ursprung der Christologie. Hermeneutische Untersuchungen zur Theologie 2. Tübingen: J. C. B. Mohr (Paul Siebeck), 1962.
*"Die Möglichkeit theologischer Anthropologie auf dem Grunde der Analogie: Eine Untersuchung zum Analogieverständnis Karl Barths." *Evangelische Theologie* 22 (1962): 535-57. Also in *Barth-Studien*, 1982.

1963

"Das Gesetz zwischen Adam und Christus: Eine theologische Studie zu Röm. 5,12-21." *Zeitschrift für Theologie und Kirche* 60 (1963): 42-68. Also in *Unterwegs zur Sache*, 1972.
"Ein paulinischer Chiasmus: Zum Verständnis der Vorstellung vom Gericht nach den Werken in Röm. 2,2-11." *Zeitschrift für Theologie und Kirche* 60 (1963): 69-74. Also in *Unterwegs*, 1972.
Review of *Sein und Existenz*, by Gerhard Noller. *Evangelische Theologie* 23 (1963): 218-23.

1964

Zum Ursprung der Analogie bei Parmenides und Heraklit. Berlin: Walter de Gruyter & Co., 1964. Also in *Entsprechungen*, 1980.
"'Theologische Wissenschaft und Glaube' im Blick auf die Armut Jesu." *Evangelische Theologie* 24 (1964): 419-43. Also in *Unterwegs*, 1972.

---

[1]Works are listed in chronological order, beginning in 1961. An asterisk (*) indicates that the following work is cited or referred to in this study.

1965

Gottes Sein ist im Werden: Verantwortliche Rede vom Sein Gottes bei Karl Barth: Eine Paraphrase. Tübingen: J. C. B. Mohr (Paul Siebeck), 1965. ET: *The Doctrine of the Trinity: God's Being Is in Becoming.* Monograph Supplements to the Scottish Journal of Theology. Grand Rapids: Eerdmans, 1976. Translated by Arnoldo Canclini as *La Doctrina de la Trinidad.* Miami: Editorial Caribe, 1980. Translated as *L'essere di Dio e nel divenire: Due studi sulla teologia di Karl Barth.* Casale Monferrato: Marietti, 1986.

1966

"Jesu Wort und Jesus als Wort Gottes: Ein hermeneutischer Beitrag zum christologischen Problem." In *Parrhesia: Karl Barth zum 80. Geburtstag,* edited by E. Busch, J. Fangmeier, and M. Geiger, 82-100. Zurich: EVZ-Verlag, 1965. Also in *Unterwegs,* 1972.

"Das Sakrament—was ist das?" *Evangelische Theologie* 26 (1966): 320-36. Also in *Was ist ein Sakrament?* 1971.

"Der königliche Mensch: Eine christologische Reflexion auf die Würde des Menschen in der Theologie Karl Barths." *Zeichen der Zeit* 20 (May 1966): 186-93. Also in *Barth-Studien,* 1982.

"Erwägungen zur Grundlegung evangelischer Ethik im Anschluss an die Theologie des Paulus: Eine biblische Meditation." *Zeitschrift für Theologie und Kirche* 63 (1966): 379-90. Also in *Unterwegs,* 1972.

*"Vorwärts durch Annäherung?" *Theologische Literaturzeitung* 91 (May 1966) cols. 329-38.

Review of *Einführung in das Studium der evangelischen Theologie,* by Rudolf Bohren. *Theologische Literaturzeitung* 91 (Apr 1966) cols. 257-59.

Review of *Karl Barth,* by B. A. Willems. *Theologische Literaturzeitung* 91 (Apr 1966) cols. 299-300.

Review of *Hermeneutische Probleme der Schriftauslegung,* by James D. Smart. *Theologische Literaturzeitung* 91 (Oct 1966) cols. 791-93.

Review of *Der sterbliche Gott oder Leviathan gegen Behemoth,* by Dietrich Braun. *Theologische Literaturzeitung* 91 (Nov 1966) cols. 857-58.

1967

Die Freiheit der Theologie: Vortrag für den vom Rat der Evangelischen Kirche in Deutschland berufenen theologischen Ausschuss "Schrift und Verkündigung." Theologische Studien 88. Zurich: EVZ-Verlag, 1967. Also in *Entsprechungen,* 1980.

Review of *Augustin und das paulinische Freiheitsproblem,* by Hans Jonas. *Theologische Literaturzeitung* 92 (Jan 1967) cols. 38-40.

*Review of *Der spätere Heidegger und die Theologie* and *Die neue Hermeneutik*, edited by James M. Robinson and John B. Cobb. *Theologische Literaturzeitung* 92 (Apr 1967) cols. 296-300.

Review of *Gott existert*, by Carl Heinz Ratschow. *Theologische Literaturzeitung* 92 (July 1967) cols. 540-43.

1968

Predigten. Munich: Chr. Kaiser Verlag, 1968. Also in *Geistesgegenwart*, 1979.

"Gottes umstrittene Gerechtigkeit: Eine reformatorische Besinnung zum paulinischen Begriff *dikaiosune theou*." In Eberhard Jüngel and M. Geiger, *Zwei Reden zum 450. Geburtstag der Reformation*, 3-26. Theologische Studien 93. Zurich: EVZ-Verlag, 1968. Also in *Unterwegs*, 1972.

Karl Barths Lehre von der Taufe: Ein Hinweis auf ihre Probleme. Theologische Studien 98. Zurich: EVZ-Verlag, 1968. Also in *Barth-Studien*, 1982. Translated as *Il battesimo nel pensiero di Karl Barth*. Piccola collana moderna 20. Torino: Editrice Claudiana, 1971.

"Das Verhältnis der theologischen Disziplinen untereinander." In *Die Praktische Theologie zwischen Wissenschaft und Praxis*, edited by Eberhard Jüngel, Karl Rahner, and Manfred Seitz, 11-45. Studien zur Praktischen Theologie 5. Munich: Chr. Kaiser Verlag, 1968. Also in *Unterwegs*, 1972.

"Bekennen und Bekenntnis." In *Theologie in Geschichte und Kunst: W. Elliger zum 65. Geburtstag*, edited by Siegfried Herrmann and Oskar Söhngen, 94-105. Wittenberg: Luther-Verlag, 1968.

"Predigt über Matth. 2,2-6." In *Wort und Gemeinde: Problem und Aufgaben der praktischen Theologie: Edward Thurneysen zum 80. Geburtstag*, edited by Rudolf Bohren and Max Geiger. Zurich: EVZ-Verlag, 1968.

"Vom Tod des lebendigen Gottes: Ein Plakat." *Zeitschrift für Theologie und Kirche* 65 (1968): 93-116. Also in *Unterwegs*, 1972.

"Freiheitsrechte und Gerechtigkeit." *Evangelische Theologie* 28 (1968): 486-95. Also in *Unterwegs*, 1972.

Review of *Jesus Christus Wende der Welt*, by Friedrich Gogarten. *Theologische Literaturzeitung* 93 (Mar 1968) cols. 213-17.

Review of *Geschichtlichkeit und Vollendung des Wissens Christi*, by Helmut Riedlinger. *Theologische Literaturzeitung* 93 (Mar 1968) cols. 372-73.

Review of *Eschatologie und Geschichte in der Theologie des jungen Karl Barth*, by Tjarko Stadtland. *Theologische Literaturzeitung* 93 (June 1968) cols. 453-55.

*"Nicht nur eine geographische Bestimmung." *Evangelische Kommentare* 1 (Aug 1968): 468-69.

Review of *Gott in Menschengestalt*, by Harminus Martinus Kuitert. *Evangelische Theologie* 28 (1968): 612.

1969

"Der Schritt des Glaubens im Rhythmus der Welt." In *Das Problem des Fort-schrittes—heute*, edited by R. W. Meyer, 143-63. Darmstadt: Wissenschaft-liche Buchgesellschaft, 1969. Also in *Unterwegs*, 1972.

"Karl Barth zu Ehren." In *Karl Barth, 1886–1968: Gedenkfier im Basler Mün-ster*, 47-50. Theologische Studien 100. Zurich: EVZ-Verlag, 1969.

*"Gott—als Wort unserer Sprache." *Evangelische Theologie* 29 (Jan 1969): 1-24. ET by Robert T. Osborn as "God—as a Word of Our Language," in *Theolo-gy of the Liberating Word*, edited by Frederick Herzog, 25-45. Nashville: Abingdon, 1971. Also in *Unterwegs*, 1972.

"Offener Brief an Herrn Pfarrer Johannes Weygand." *Evangelische Theologie* 29 (1969): 334-35.

*"Die Welt als Möglichkeit und Wirklichkeit: Zum ontologischen Ansatz der Rechtfertigungslehre." *Evangelische Theologie* 29 (1969): 417-22. Also in *Unterwegs*, 1972, and *Essays*, 1989.

"Karl Barth." *Neue Züricher Zeitung*, 2 March 1969, 51. Also in *Evangelische Theologie* 29 (1969): 621-26; and in *Barth-Studien*, 1982.

Review of *Theologie als Geschichte*, edited by James M. Robinson and John B. Cobb. *Theologische Literaturzeitung* 94 (Mar 1969) cols. 232-33.

"Das dunkle Wort vom 'Tode Gottes'." *Evangelische Kommentare* 2 (Mar and Apr 1969): 133-38, 198-202. Also in *Von Zeit zu Zeit*, 1976.

"Four Preliminary Considerations on the Concept of Authority." *Ecumenical Review* 21 (Apr 1969): 150-52.

1970

"L'autorité du Christ suppliant." In *L'infaillibilité, son aspect philosophique et théologique*, edited by Enrico Castelli, 201-208. Paris: Aubier Montaigne Editions, 1970. Also in *L'infallibilita: Aspetto filosofico e teologico*, 210-208. Padova: CEDAM, 1970. Expanded as "Die Autorität des bittenden Christus: Eine These zur materialen Begründung der Eigenart des Wortes Gottes: Erwägungen zum Problem der Infallibilität der Theologie," in *Unter-wegs*, 1972.

"Die tödliche Blamage: Lukas 24,1-6." *Auferstehung heute gesagt: Osterpredig-ten der Gegenwart*, 69-74. Edited by H. Nitzschuke. Gütersloh: Gütersloher Verlagshaus Mohn, 1970.

Review of *Offene Fragen zur Formgeschichte des Evangeliums*, by Erhardt Gütt-gemanns. *Evangelische Theologie* 30 (1970): 447-48.

Review of *Verantwortung des Glaubens*, by Peter Knauer. *Evangelische Theolo-gie* 30 (1970): 510-12.

Review of *Atheismus in der Christenheit*, by Klaus Bockmühl. *Evangelische Theologie* 30 (1970): 570.

1971

*Tod. Themen der Theologie 8. Berlin and Stuttgart: Kreuz-Verlag, 1971. ET by Iain und Ute Nicol as *Death: The Riddle and the Mystery*. Philadelphia: Westminster, 1974.

**"Womit steht und fällt heute der christliche Glaube? Elementare Verantwortung gegenwärtigen Glaubens." *Experiment: Glaube*, 29-46. Edited by Claus Kemper. Beiheft zur Ökumenischen Rundschau 16. Stuttgart: Evangelischer Missionsverlag, 1971. Also in *Spricht Gott in der Geschichte?*, 154-77. Freiburg: Herder, 1972.

"Zur Kritik des sakramentalen Verständnisses der Taufe." *Zu Karl Barths Lehre von der Taufe*, 25-43. Edited by Joachim Beckmann, et al. Evangelische Kirche der Union, 1971. Also edited by F. Viering for Verlagshaus Mohn in Gütersloh. Also in *Barth-Studien*, 1982.

"Thesen zu Karl Barths Lehre von der Taufe." *Zu Karl Barths Lehre von der Taufe*, 161-64. Edited by Joachim Beckmann, et al. Evangelische Kirche der Union, 1971. Also published by Gütersloher Verlagshaus Mohn. Also in *Barth-Studien*, 1982.

"Annahme oder Abtreibung." 1971. 135-43.

**"Grenzen des Menschseins." *Probleme biblischer Theologie: Gerhard von Rad zum 70. Geburtstag*, 199-205. Edited by Hans Walter Wolff. Munich: Chr. Kaiser Verlag, 1971. Also in *Entsprechungen*, 1980.

" ' . . . keine Menschenlosigkeit Gottes . . . ': Zur Theologie Karl Barths zwischen Theismus und Atheismus." *Evangelische Theologie* 31 (1971): 376-90. Also in *Barth-Studien*, 1982. Translated by Paul Corset as " . . . Pas de Dieu sans l'homme . . . " In *Karl Barth*, 195-215. Edited by Pierre Gisel. Geneva: Labor et Fides, 1987.

"Irren ist menschlich: Zur Kontroverse um Hans Küngs Buch 'Unfehlbar? Eine Anfrage'." *Evangelische Kommentare* 4 (1971): 75-80. Also in *Unterwegs*, 1972.

Review of *Die anthropologische Wende*, by Peter Eicher. *Evangelische Theologie* 31 (1971): 390-92.

With Karl Rahner, *Was ist ein Sakrament? Vorstösse zur Verständigung*. Kleine ökumenische Schriften 6. Freiburg: Herder, 1971.

1972

*Unterwegs zur Sache: Theologische Bemerkungen. Beiträge zur evangelischen Theologie 61. Munich: Chr. Kaiser Verlag, 1972.

"Deus qualem Paulus creavit, dei negatio: Zur Denkbarkeit Gottes bei Ludwig Feuerbach und Friedrich Nietzsche." *Nietzsche Studien: Internationales Jahrbuch für die Nietzsche-Forschung*, 1:286-96. New York and Berlin, 1972.

*Säkularisierung—Theologische Anmerkungen zum Begriff einer weltlichen Welt." *Christliche Freiheit im Dienst am Menschen: Deutungen der kirchlichen Aufgabe heute*, 163-68. Edited by Karl Herbert. Frankfurt-on-Main: Verlag Otto Lembeck, 1972. Also in *Entsprechungen*, 1980.

"Was ist 'das unterscheidend Christliche'?" *Christlich—was heisst das?* Edited by Gerhard Adler. Dusseldorf: Patmos-Verlag, 1972. Also in *Unterwegs*, 1972.

"Quae supra nos, nihil ad nos: Eine Kurzformel der Lehre vom verborgenen Gott—im Anschluss an Luther interpretiert." *Evangelische Theologie* 32 (1972): 197-240. Also in *Entsprechungen*, 1980.

"Der Tod als Verweigung gelebten Lebens: Tod und Zeit—die Hoffnung des Glaubens." *Reformatio* 21 (Apr 1972): 219-23.

1973

Theologie in der Spannung zwischen Wissenschaft und Bekenntnis. Impulse 7. Stuttgart: Evangelische Zentralstelle für Weltanschauungsfragen, 1973. Also in *Entsprechungen*, 1980.

"Gott ist Liebe: Zur Unterscheidung von Glaube und Liebe." *Festschrift für Ernst Fuchs*, 193-202. Edited by Gerhard Ebeling, Eberhard Jüngel, and Gerd Schunack. Tübingen: J. C. B. Mohr (Paul Siebeck), 1973.

"Lob der Grenze." *Attempo* 47/48 (1973): 12-15. Also in *Entsprechungen*, 1980.

Coeditor with Gerhard Ebeling and Gerd Schunack. *Festschrift für Ernst Fuchs*. Tübingen: J. C. B. Mohr (Paul Seibeck), 1973.

1974

Geistesgegenwart: Predigten. Munich: Chr. Kaiser Verlag, 1974. Also in Geistesgegenwart, 1979.

*"Metaphorische Wahrheit: Erwägungen zur theologischen Relevanz der Metapher als Beitrag zur Hermeneutik einer narrativen Theologie." In Paul Ricoeur and Eberhard Jüngel, *Metapher: Zur Hermeneutik religiöser Sprache*, 71-122. Evangelische Theologie: Sonderheft. Munich: Chr. Kaiser Verlag, 1974. Also in *Entsprechungen*, 1980, and *Essays*, 1989. As "Thesen zur theologischen Metaphorologie," also in *Erinnern, um Neues zu sagen*, 52-67. Edited by Jean Pierre van Noppen. Frankfurt-on-Main: Athenäum, 1988.

*"Redlich von Gott reden: Bemerkungen zur Klarheit der Theologie Rudolf Bultmanns." *Evangelische Kommentare* 7 (Aug 1974): 475-77.

1975

"Der Gott entsprechende Mensch: Bemerkungen zur Gottebenbildlichkeit der Menschen als Grundfigur theologischer Anthropologie." *Neue Anthropologie,* 6:342-72. Edited by Hans-Georg Gadamer and Paul Vogler. Stuttgart: Georg Thieme Verlag, 1975. Also in *Entsprechungen,* 1980, and *Essays,* 1989.

*"Der Dilemma der natürlichen Theologie und die Wahrheit ihres Problems: Überlegungen für ein Gespräch mit Wolfhart Pannenberg." *Denken im Schatten des Nihilismus: Festschrift für Wilhelm Weischedel zum 70. Geburtstag,* 419-40. Edited by Alexander Schwan. Darmstadt: Wissenschaftliche Buchgesellschaft, 1975. Also in *Entsprechungen,* 1980.

"Recht auf Leben—Recht auf Sterben: Theologische Bemerkungen." *Vorbereitungsheft zum Thema der Bundestagung 1975 "Recht auf Leben—Recht auf Sterben",* 55-60. Stuttgart: Deutscher Evangelischer Verband für Altenhilfe e. V., 1975. Also in *Entsprechungen,* 1980.

"57 Antworten auf eine Umfrage." *Chance christlicher Ökumene: Papsttum, heute und morgen,* 85-86. Edited by Georg Denzler. Regensburg: Friedrich Pustet, 1975.

"Extra Christum nulla salus—als Grundsatz natürlicher Theologie? Evangelische Erwägungen zur 'Anonymität' des Christenmenschen." *Zeitschrift für Theologie und Kirche* 72 (1975): 337-52. Also in *Christentum innerhalb und ausserhalb der Kirche,* 122-38. Edited by Elmar Klinger. Freiburg: Herder, 1976. Also in *Entsprechungen,* 1980, and *Essays,* 1989.

*"Das Verhältnis von 'ökonomischer' und 'immanenter' Trinität: Erwägungen über eine biblische Begründung der Trinitätslehre—im Anschluss an und in Auseinandersetzung mit Karl Rahners Lehre vom dreifaltigen Gott als transzendentem Urgrund der Heilsgeschichte." *Zeitschrift für Theologie und Kirche* 72 (1975): 353-64. Also in *Entsprechungen,* 1980. Summarized in "The Relationship Between 'Economic' and 'Immanent' Trinity." *Theology Digest* 24 (Summer 1976): 179-84.

*"Gott—um seiner selbst willen interessant: Plädoyer für eine natürlichere Theologie." *Neue Zürcher Zeitung,* 20/21 Sept 1975, 57. Also in *Entsprechungen,* 1980.

1976

Gott—für den ganzen Menschen. Theologische Meditationen 39. Einsiedeln, Zurich, and Cologne: Benziger, 1976.

Gefangenes ich—befreiender Geist: Zwei Tübinger Römerbrief-Auslegungen. Munich: Chr. Kaiser Verlag, 1976.

Von Zeit zu Zeit: Betrachtungen zu den Festzeiten im Kirchenjahr. Kaiser-Traktate 22. Munich: Chr. Kaiser Verlag, 1976.

Anfechtung und Gewissheit des Glaubens oder wie die Kirche wieder zu ihrer Sache kommt: Zwei Vorträge. Kaiser-Traktate 23. Munich: Chr. Kaiser Verlag, 1976. Contents include "Anfechtung und Gewissheit des Glaubens: Auf der Suche nach der Sache der Kirche." *Evangelische Kommentare* 9 (Aug 1976): 454-58. Expansion of "Die Freude am Erzählen wiedergewinnen: Geistliche Konzentration des kirchlichen Lebens." *Evangelische Kommentare* 9 (Sept 1976): 531-34. Translated by T. Badenhosrt as "Aanvegting en versekering van die geloof: Hoe bly die kerk vandag by sy saak." *Theologia Evangelica* 16 (Mar 1983): 4-20.

"Der Tod als Geheimnis des Lebens." *Der Mensch und sein Tod*, 108-25. Edited by Johannes Schwartländer. Kleine Vandenhoek Reihe 1426. Göttingen: Vandenhoeck & Ruprecht, 1976. Expanded in *Grenzerfahrung Tod*, 9-39. Edited by Ansgar Paus. Graz, Vienna, and Cologne: Styria, 1976. Also in *Entsprechungen*, 1980.

"Zukunft und Hoffnung: Zur politischen Funktion christlicher Theologie." *Müssen Christen Sozialisten sein?*, 11-30. Edited by Wolfgang Teichert. Hamburg: Lutherisches Verlagshaus, 1976.

"Warum gleich mit dem Fass geworfen: Über die Kunst mit Roter Tinte umzugehen." *Müssen Christen Sozialisten sein?*, 41-49. Edited by Wolfgang Teichert. Hamburg: Lutherisches Verlagshaus, 1976.

"Wer denkt konkret?" *Müssen Christen Sozialisten Sein?*, 111-17. Edited by Wolfgang Teichert. Hamburg: Lutherisches Verlagshaus, 1976.

*"The Truth of Life: Observations on Truth as the Interruption of the Continuity of Life." *Creation, Christ and Culture: Studies in Honor of T. F. Torrance*, 231-36. Edited by Richard W. A. McKinney. Edinburgh: T. & T. Clark, 1976.

*"Der alte Mensch—als Kriterium der Lebensqualität: Bemerkungen zur Menschenwürde der leistungsunfähigen Person." *Der Wirklichkeitsanspruch von Theologie und Religion: Die sozialethische Herausforderung*, 129-32. Edited by Dieter Henke, Günther Kehrer, and Gunda Schneider-Flume. Tübingen: J. C. B. Mohr (Paul Siebeck), 1976. Also in *epd-Dokumentation* 10 (1976): 51-53. Also in *Entsprechungen*, 1980.

"Gott im Totentanz: Eine theologische Meditation." *Bibel und Kirche* 31 (1976): 79-81.

Coeditor with Hans-Anton Drewes. Karl Barth, *Das christliche Leben: Die kirchliche Dogmatik* IV/4. Karl Barth Gesamtausgabe: Akademische Werke: 1959–1961. Zurich: Theologischer Verlag Zürich, 1976. ET by Geoffrey W. Bromiley as *The Christian Life*. Grand Rapids: Eerdmans, 1981.

1977

*"Vor Gott schweigen? Theologie in der Nachbarschaft des Denkens von Martin Heidegger." *Frankfurter Allgemeine Zeitung*, 25 May 1977, 25. Expanded in "Gott entsprechendes Schweigen? Theologie in der Nachbarschaft des Denkens von Martin Heidegger." *Martin Heidegger: Fragen an sein Werk*, 37-45. Stuttgart: Reclam, 1977.

Gott als Geheimnis der Welt: Zur Begründung der Theologie des Gekreuzigten im Streit zwischen Theismus und Atheismus. Tübingen: J. C. B. Mohr (Paul Siebeck), 1977. ET by Darrell L. Guder as *God as the Mystery of the World: On the Foundation of the Theology of the Crucified One in the Dispute between Theism and Atheism.* Grand Rapids: Eerdmans, 1983. Also translated by Geoffrey Wainwright. Edinburgh: T.&T. Clark, 1984. Translated under the direction of Horst Hombourg as *Dieu, mystère du monde: Fondement de la théologie du Crucifie dans le debat entre theisme et atheisme.* Cogitatio fidei 116 and 117. Paris: Les Editions du Cerf, 1983.

"Vergebung der Schuld: Predigt über Römer 8,26." *Evangelische Kommentare* 10 (July 1977): 432.

*"Gelegentliche Thesen zum Problem der natürlichen Theologie." *Evangelische Theologie* 37 (Sept/Oct 1977): 485-88. Also in *Entsprechungen*, 1980.

Der Wahrheit zum Recht verhilfen. Stuttgart: Kreuz Verlag, 1977.

1978

"Mut zur Angst: Dreizehn Aphorismen zum Jahreswechsl." *Evangelische Kommentare* 11 (Jan 1978): 12-15. Also in *Entsprechungen*, 1980.

"Elefant und Walfisch." *Evangelische Kommentare* 11 (Feb 1978): 113.

Zur Freiheit eines Christenmenschen: Eine Erinnerung an Luthers Schrift. Kaiser-Traktate 30 / Kaiser Taschenbücher 102. Munich: Christian Kaiser Verlag, 1978, 1987, 1991. Also in *Luther*, 1980. ET by Roy A. Harrisville as *The Freedom of a Christian: Luther's Significance for Contemporary Theology.* Minneapolis: Augsburg, 1988.

"Die Wirksamkeit des Entzogenen: Zum Vorgang geschichtlichen Verstehens als Einführung in die Christologie." *Gnosis: Festschrift für Hans Jonas*, 15-32. Edited by Barbara Aland. Göttingen: Vadenhoeck & Ruprecht, 1978. Also in *Essays*, 1989.

"Zur Lehre von den Zeichen der Kirche." *Zukunft aus dem Wort: Helmut Class zum 65. Geburtstag*, 113-17. Edited by Günther Metzger. Stuttgart: Calwer Verlag, 1978.

*"Das Sein Jesu Christi als Ereignis der Versöhnung Gottes mit einer gottlosen Welt: Die Hingabe des Gekreuzigten." *Evangelische Theologie* 38 (Nov/Dec 1978): 510-17. Also in *Entsprechungen*, 1980.

Editor. *Tübinger Theologie im 20. Jahrhundert*. Zeitschrift für Theologie und Kirche Beiheft. Tübingen: J. C. B. Mohr (Paul Siebeck), 1978.

With Ernst Topitsch. "Der Tod Gottes und der Atheismus: Anmerkungen zu einem Buch und eine Replik." *Evangelische Kommentare* 11 (Dec 1978): 722-27.

With Ingolf U. Dalferth. "Sprache als Träger der Sittlichkeit." *Handbuch der christlichen Ethik* 2:454-73. Edited by Anselm Hertz et al. Freiburg: Herder, 1978.

1979

Reden für die Stadt: Zum Verhältnis von Christengemeinde und Bürgergemeinde. Kaiser-Traktate 38. Munich: Chr. Kaiser Verlag, 1979.

Geistesgegenwart: Predigten I und II. Munich: Chr. Kaiser Verlag, 1979.

*"Wertlose Wahrheit: Christlich Wahrheitserfahrung im Streit gegen die 'Tyrannei der Werte'." *Die Tyrannei der Werte*, 45-75. Edited by S. Schelz. Hamburg: Lutherisches Verlagshaus, 1979.

"Die andere Weinachtsgeschichte." *Jesus: Für heute geboren. Politiker, Autoren, Wissenschaftler antworten auf die Frage: Was bedeutet nun die Geburt Jesu?*, 99-106. Tübingen: Katzmann, 1979.

"Aus Freude an Gott." *Warum ich Christ bin*, 207-15. Edited by Walter Jens. Munich: Kindler, 1979.

Response in *Papsttum als ökumenische Frage*. Edited by the Arbeitsgemeinschaft ökumenischer Universitätsinstitut. Munich: Chr. Kaiser Verlag, 1979.

"Am Anfang: Er. Hinweis auf eine geglückte Übersetzung." *Evangelische Kommentare* 12 (May 1979): 284-85.

"Theologie der Gnade," *Evangelische Kommentare* 12 (June 1979): 360.

"Glaube, der Unfreiheit überwindet." *Evangelische Kommentare* 12 (July 1979): 416-17. Also in *Katechetische Blätter* 105 (1980): 10-13.

1980

Entsprechungen: Gott—Wahrheit—Mensch. Theologische Erörterungen. Beiträge zur evangelischen Theologie 88. Munich: Chr. Kaiser Verlag, 1980.

"Barth, Karl." *Theologische Realenzyklopädie* 5:251-68. Edited by Gerhard Krause and Gerhard Müller. Berlin and New York: Walter de Gruyter & Co., 1980. Expanded in *Barth-Studien*, 1982. An expanded version translated by Paul Corset as "La vie et l'oeuvre de Karl Barth." *Karl Barth*, 15-68. Edited by Pierre Gisel. Geneva: Labor et Fides, 1987.

"Anrufung Gottes als Grundethos christlichen Handelns: Einführende Bemerkungen zu den nachgelässenen Fragmenten der Ethik der Versöhnungslehre Karl Barths." *Anspruch der Wirklichkeit und christlicher Glaube: Probleme und Wege theologischer Ethik heute*, 208-24. Edited by H. Weber and D. Mieth.

Dusseldorf: Patmos-Verlag, 1980. Also in *Barth-Studien*, 1982, and *Essays*, 1989.
"Predigt über Num. 13,2-14,5." *Unterwegs zur Einheit: Festschrift für Heinrich Stirnimann*, 923-29. Edited by Johannes Brantschen and Pietro Selvatico. Freiburg: Herder, 1980.
"Zur Bedeutung Luthers für die gegenwärtige Theologie." *Luther und die Theologie der Gegenwart*, 17-79. Edited by Leif Grane and Bernhard Lohse. Göttingen: Vandenhoeck & Ruprecht, 1980.
"Wege zum Frieden: Frieden als Kategorie theologischer Anthropologie." *Dem Staate verpflichtet: Festgabe für Gerhard Schröder*, 21-35. Edited by H. Kunst. Stuttgart: Kreuz Verlag, 1980. Translated as "El camino hacia la paz: La paz como categoria de antropología teológica." *Folio Humanistica* 20/231 (1982): 261-72.
"Freude über Freude." *Evangelische Kommentare* 13 (Dec 1980): 728-29.

1981

"Theologische Zusammenfassung." *Kirche und Sozialismus*, 112-28. Edited by Helmuth Flammer. Gütersloh: Gütersloher Verlagshaus Mohn, 1981.
With Ingolf U. Dalferth. "Person und Gottebenbildlichkeit." *Christlicher Glaube in moderner Gesellschaft* 24:57-99. Edited by F. Böckle, F.-X. Kaufmann, K. Rahner, and B. Welte. Freiburg: Herder, 1981.
Editor. *Das Neue Testament heute: Zur Frage der Revidierbarkeit von Luthers Übersetzung*. Zeitschrift für Theologie und Kirche Supplement 5 (1981).
Coeditor with Ingolf U. Dalferth. Karl Barth, *Fides quaerens intellectum: Anselms Beweis der Existenz Gottes im Zusammenhang seines theologischen Programms*. Karl Barth Gesamtausgabe 2. Zurich: Theologischer Verlag Zürich, 1981.

1982

Barth-Studien. Ökumenische Theologie 9. Gütersloh: Gütersloher Verlagshaus Gerd Mohn; Zurich and Cologne: Benziger Verlag, 1982. ET: selections translated by Garrett E. Paul in *Karl Barth, a Theological Legacy*. Philadelphia: Westminster Press and Edinburgh: Scottish Academic Press, 1986.
"Anthropomorphismus als Grundproblem neuzeitlicher Hermeneutik." *Verifikationen: Festschrift für Gerhard Ebeling zum 70. Geburtstag*, 499-521. Edited by Eberhard Jüngel, Johannes Wallmann, and Wilfred Werbeck. Tübingen: J. C. B. Mohr (Paul Siebeck), 1982. Also in *Essays*, 1989.
"La signification de l'analogie pour la théologie." *Analogie et Dialectique: Essais de théologie fondamentale*, 247-58. Edited by Pierre Gisel and Philibert Secretan. Geneva: Labor et Fides, 1982.
"Bibelarbeit über 2 Timotheus 3,14-17." *Bibel in der Welt* 19 (1982): 93-106.

1983

Zum Wesen des Friedens: Frieden als Kategorie theologischer Anthropologie. Munich: Chr. Kaiser Verlag, 1983.

Schmecken und Sehen: Predigten III. Munich: Chr. Kaiser Verlag, 1983.

"Im Angesicht des Todes." *Luther Kontrovers*, 162-72. Edited by Hans Jürgen Schultz. Stuttgart: Kreuz Verlag, 1983.

"Zur Lehre vom Heiligen Geist: Thesen." *Die Mitte des neuen Testaments: Einheit und Vielfalt neutestamentlicher Theologie*, 97-188. Edited by Ulrich Luz and Hans Weder. Göttingen: Vandenhoeck & Ruprecht, 1983.

"Die Kirche als Sakrament?" *Zeitschrift für Theologie und Kirche* 80 (Nov 1983): 432-57. Also in *Essays*, 1989.

"Das Geheimnis der Stellvertretung: Ein dogmatisches Gespräch mit Heinrich Vogel." *Zeichen der Zeit* 37 (1983): 16-22. Also in *Berliner Theologischer Zeitschrift* 1/1 (1984): 65-80.

"Einheit der Kirche—konkret." *Süddeutsche Zeitung*, 1-2 Oct 1983.

1984

*Mit Frieden Staat zu machen: Politische Existenz nach Barmen V. Munich: Chr. Kaiser Verlag, 1984. ET by D. Bruce Hamill and Alan J. Torrance as *Christ, Justice and Peace: Toward a Theology of the State.* Edinburgh: T.&T. Clark, 1992.

"Einleitung: Die Barmer Theologische Erklärung als Bekenntnis der Kirche." Karl Barth, *Texte zur Barmer Theologischen Erklärung*, ix-xxii. Edited by Martin Rohkrämer. Zurich: Theologischer Verlag Zurich, 1984.

"Die Offenbarung der Verborgenheit Gottes: Ein Beitrag zum evangelischen Verständnis der Verborgenheit des göttlichen Wirkens." *Vor dem Geheimnis Gottes den Menschen verstehen*, 74-104. Edited by Karl Lehmann. Munich: Verlag Schnell & Steiner, 1984.

"'Auch das Schöne muss sterben'—Schönheit im Lichte der Wahrheit: Theologische Bemerkungen zum ästhetischen Verhältnis." *Zeitschrift für Theologie und Kirche* 81 (January 1984): 106-26.

"Pater im Glauben." *Evangelische Kommentare* 17 (May 1984): 237-38.

"Menschwerdung des Menschen." *Evangelische Kommentare* 17 (Aug 1984): 446-48.

With Michael Trowitzsch. "Provozierendes Denken: Bemerkungen zur theologischen Anstössigkeit der Denkwege Martin Heideggers." *Neue Hefte für Philosophie* 23 (1984): 59-74.

Coeditor with Klaus M. Müller. "Rudolf Bultmann," *Theologische Enzyklopädie*. Tübingen: J. C. B. Mohr (Paul Siebeck), 1984.

1985

Glauben und Verstehen: Zum Theologiebegriff Rudolf Bultmanns. Heidelberg: Carl Winter, Universitätsverlag, 1985.

*"Der menschliche Mensch: Die Bedeutung der reformatorischen Unterscheidung der Person von ihren Werken für das Selbstverständnis des neuzeitlichen Menschen." *Zeichen der Zeit* 39 (1985): 35-43. Translated by Leo Freuler and Jean-Philippe Bujard as "Homo Humanus: La signification de la distinction réformatrice entre la personne et ses oeuvres pour la façon dont l'homme moderne se comprend lui-même." *Revue de théologie et de philosophie* 119/1 (1987): 33-50.

1986

"Zum Verhältnis von Kirche und Staat nach Karl Barth." *Zur Theologie Karl Barths: Beiträge aus Anlass seines 100. Geburtstag,* 76-135. Edited by Eberhard Jüngel. Zeitschrift für Theologie und Kirche, Beiheft 6. Tübingen: J. C. B. Mohr (Paul Siebeck), 1986.

"Antwort auf Josef Blank." *Das neue Paradigma von Theologie,* 66-71. Edited by Hans Küng and David W. Tracey. Zurich: Benziger Verlag, 1986.

"Gottes ursprüngliches Anfangen als Schöferische Selbstbegrenzung: Ein Beitrag zum Gespräch mit Hans Jonas über den 'Gottesbegriff nach Auschwitz'." *Gottes Zukunft—Zukunft der Welt: Festschrift für Jürgen Moltmann,* 265-75. Edited by Hermann Denser, Gerhard M. Martin, Konrad Stock, et al. Munich: Chr. Kaiser Verlag, 1986.

"Theologische Existenz: Erinnerung an Karl Barth." *Evangelische Kommentare* 19 (May 1986): 258-60.

"Tro og forståelse: om Rudolf Bultmanns teologibegrep." Translated by S. Hjelde. *Norsk Teologisk Tidsskrift* 87/2 (1986): 81-99.

"Die Bedeutung der Reich-Gottes-Erwartung für das Zeugnis der christlichen Gemeinde." *Berliner Theologische Zeitschrift* 3/4 (1986): 344-53.

"Festpredigt über Gen. 32,23-32." *Theologische Zeitschrift* 42 (July/Aug 1986): 352-60.

With Roman Herzog and Helmut Simon. *Evangelische Christen in unseren Demokratie: Beiträge aus der Synode der EKD.* Gütersloh: Gütersloher Verlagshaus Mohn, 1986.

1988

"Verweigertes Geheimnis? Bemerkungen zu einer unevangelischen Sonderlehre." *Vernunft des Glaubens: Wissenschaftliche Theologie und kirchliche Lehre: Festschrift zum 60. Geburtstag von Wolfhart Pannenberg,* 488-501. Edited by Jan Rohls and Gunther Wenz. Göttingen: Vandenhoeck & Ruprecht, 1988.

"La rilevanza dogmatica del problema del Gesù storico." Translated by G. Russo. *Il "Gesù storico:" problema della modernità*, 161-85. Edited by Giuseppe Pirola and Francesco Coppellotti. Casale Monferrato: Edizioni Piemme, 1988.

"Hat der christliche Glaube eine besondere Affinität zur Demokratie?" *Scriptura* 27 (1988): 1-7.

"Leben aus Gerechtigkeit: Gottes Handeln und menschliches Tun." *Evangelische Kommentare* 21 (Dec 1988): 696-701.

"The Christian Understanding of Suffering." *Journal of Theology for Southern Africa* 65 (Dec 1988): 3-13.

1989

"Empfangene Gerechtigkeit: Gottes Handeln und menschliches Tun." *Evangelische Kommentare* 22 (Jan 1989): 36-38.

"Nihil divinitatis, ubi non fides: Ist christliche Dogmatik in rein theoretischer Perspektiv möglich? Bemerkungen zu einem theologischen Entwurf von Rang." *Zeitschrift für Theologie und Kirche* 86 (Apr 1989): 204-35.

"Thèses dogmatiques sur l'ecclésiologie." Translated by Jean Yves Lacoste. *Foi et Vie* 88 (Apr 1989): 5-11.

"La colère de l'apôtre et le Dieu incomparable: Un sermon sur 2 Corinthiens 4:5-10." Translated by Jean Yves Lacoste. *Foi et Vie* 88 (Apr 1989): 13-22.

"Le salut de paix: Le discours biblique de paix." Translated by Francois Barre. *Foi et Vie* 88 (Apr 1989): 23-31.

"Leben nach dem Tod? Gegen das theologische Schweigen vom ewigen Leben." *Evangelische Kommentare* 22 (June 1989): 31-32. ET: "Life after Death? A Response to Theology's Silence about Eternal Life." *Word and World* 11 (Winter 1991): 5-8.

"Predigt zu Markus 10,17-22." *Creatio ex amore: Beiträge zu einer theologreicher Liebe*, 125-33. Edited by Thomas Franke, Markus Knapp, and Johannes Schmid. Würzburg: Echter Verlag, 1989.

"Zur Lehre vom Bösen und von der Sünde. *Wissenschaft und Kirche: Festschrift für Eduard Lohse*, 177-88. Edited by Kurt Aland and Siegfried Meurer. Bielefeld: Luther-Verlag, 1989.

"Zum Begriff der Offenbarung." *Glaube—Bekenntnis—Kirchenrecht*, 215-21. Edited by Gerhard Besier and Eduard Lohse. Hannover: Lutherisches Verlagshaus, 1989.

*Theological Essays. Translated and edited by J. B. Webster. Edinburgh: T. & T. Clark, 1989.

"What Does It Mean to Say, 'God Is Love'?" *Christ in Our Place: The Humanity of God in Christ for the Reconciliation of the World: Festschrift for J. Torrance*, 294-312. Edited by Trevor A. Hart and Daniel P. Thimell. Princeton Theological Monograph Series 25. Allison Park PA: Pickwick Publications, 1989.

1990

Wertlose Wahrheit: Zur Identität und Relevanz des christlichen Glaubens. Theologische Erörterungen 3. Munich: Chr. Kaiser, 1990.

"The Last Judgment as an Act of Grace." *Louvain Studies* 15/4 (1990): 389-405.

Editor. *Die Heilsbedeutung des Kreuzes für Glaube und Hoffnung des Christen.* Zeitschrift für Theologie und Kirche Supplement 8. 1990.

1991

"Die Bedeutung der Rechtfertigungslehre für das Verständnis des Menschen: Ein Beitrag reformatorischen Denkens für Europa der Zukunft." *Luther* 62/3 (1991): 110-26.

*"Toward the Heart of the Matter." Translated by Paul E. Capetz. *Christian Century* 108 (27 Feb 1991): 228-33.

1993

"Kirsche im Sozialismus—Kirche im Pluralismus: Theologische Rückblicke und Ausblicke." *Evangelische Kommentare* 26 (Jan 1993): 6-13.

B. Reviews of Jüngel's Works

Anfechtung und Gewissheit des Glaubens (1976)
   Smolík, Josef. *Communio Viatorum* 20 (Autumn 1977): 263-64.

Death / Tod (1971)
   Atkinson, James. *Scottish Journal of Theology* 29/3 (1976): 276-78.
   Calbreath, D. F. *Journal of American Scientific Affiliation* 29 (Sept 1977): 132-33.
   Davidson, Glen W. *Journal of Religion* 57 (Apr 1977): 195-97.
   Dirschauer, Klaus. *Deutsches Pfarrer Blatt* 80 (Mar 1980): 149-50.
   Hunter, W. F. *Journal of Psychology and Theology* 4 (Summer 1976): 253-55.
   Neiman, Joseph C. *New Review of Books and Religion* 1 (Sept 1976): 21-22.
   Skar, Ø. *Norsk Teologisk Tidsskrift* 72/4 (1971): 249-50.

The Doctrine of the Trinity / Gottes Sein ist im Werden (1965)
   Berkhof, H. *Nederlands Theologisch Tijdschrift* 33 (Apr 1979): 154-57.
   Brinkman, B. R. *Heythrop Journal* 19 (Apr 1978): 203-204.
   Buri, Fritz. *How Can We Still Speak Responsibly of God?* Translated by Charley D. Hardwick (Philadelphia: Fortress, 1968), 7-9.
   Dahlstrom, E. C. *Covenant Quarterly* 35 (Feb 1977): 40-41.
   Davidson, G. W. *Journal of Religion* 57 (Apr 1977): 195-97.
   Dittberner, J. M. *Theological Studies* 38 (Mar 1977): 185-87.
   Fangmeier, J. *Theologische Zeitschrift* 22 (Mar/Apr 1966): 153-54.
   Farrelly, John. *Theological Studies* 39 (Mar 1978): 161-62.
   Fritzsche, H. G. *Theologische Literaturzeitung* 103 (Dec 1978): 894-97.
   Geyer, Hans-Georg. "Gottes Sein als Thema der Theologie." *Verkündigung und Forschung* 11 (1966): 3-37.
   Hasselmann, K. B. *Lutheran World* 13/2 (1966): 246.
   Jenson, Robert W. *Interpretation* 32 (Jan 1978): 104, 106.
   Kaiser, C. B. *Reformed Review* 31 (Winter 1978): 107-108.
   McKelway, Alexander J. *Religious Studies Review* 6 (July 1980): 219.
   McWilliams, Warren. *Review and Expositor* 75 (Winter 1978): 130- 31.
   Migliore, Daniel L. *Theology Today* 35 (Apr 1978): 95-97.
   Miller, Crawford. *Reformed Theological Review* 37 (Jan-Apr 1978): 19-20.
   Morgan, Robert. *Theology* 81 (May 1978): 211.
   Ott, Heinrich. *Reality and Faith* (Philidelphia: Fortress, 1972), 56-57.
   Rodgers, J. H. *Churchman* 93/1 (1979): 60.
   Subilia, Vittorio. *Protestantesimo* 43/3-4 (1988): 227-28.

Williams, Rowan. *Downside Review* 96 (Oct 1978): 316-18.
Wood, Charles M. *Perkins Journal* 31 (Winter 1978): 46-47.
Zimany, Roland Daniel. *Journal of the American Academy of Religion* 49 (June 1981): 326-27.

Entsprechungen (1980)
Buckley, James J. *Religious Studies Review* 9 (Jan 1983): 57.
Daecke, S. M. "Natürlichere Theologie." *Evangelische Kommentare* 14 (Aug 1981): 474.
Fischer, H. *Theologische Zeitschrift* 108 (Jan 1983): 50-53.
McDermott, J. M. *Theological Studies* 43 (Dec 1982): 714- 16.
Neufeld, K. H. *Gregorianum* 62/4 (1981): 761-62.

The Freedom of a Christian / Zur Freiheit eines Christenmenschen (1978)
Armellada, Bernardino de. *Naturaleza y Gracia* 25 (May-Dec 1978): 406.
Barnes, Robin B. *Lutheran Quarterly* 3 (Winter 1989): 444-46.
Dreier, Mary S. Dehmlow. *Word & World* 10 (Spring 1990): 200-202.
Edelmann, Helmut. *Luther* 63/1 (1992): 44-45.
Fritzsche, H. G. *Theologische Literaturzeitung* 104 (June 1979): 456-57.
Knauer, P. *Theologie und Philosophie* 53/4 (1978): 603.
Kolb, Robert. *Religious Studies Review* 16 (Jan 1990): 58-59.
Marlé, René. *Recherches de Science religieuses* 67 (Jan-Mar 1979): 79-81.
Owen, Michael. *Pacifica* 4 (Feb 1991): 102-105.
Paulson, Steven. *Dialog* 29 (Spring 1990): 152f.
Rochelle, Jay C. *Currents in Theology and Mission* 16 (Aug 1989): 303.
Schild, Maurice E. *Lutheran Theological Journal* 24 (May 1990): 42-44.
Stroble, Paul E. *Critical Review of Books in Religion* (1990): 440-41.
Thomas, Terry C. *Book Newsletter of Augsburg Publishing House* 537 (Winter 1989): 4.
Zachman, Randall C. *Anglican Theological Review* 72 (Winter 1990): 108- 110.
Zimany, Roland Daniel. *Interpretation* 45 (Apr 1991): 206.

Die Freiheit der Theologie (1967)
Gunleiksrud, G. *Theologi og Kirke* 39 (1968): 308.
Quervain, A. de. *Theologische Literaturzeitung* 93 (Nov 1968): 865-66.

Glaube und Verstehen (1985)
Hensen, R. *Nederlands Theologisch Tijdschrift* 41 (July 1987): 258-59.
Hueber, Hans. *Theologische Literaturzeitung* 112 (Apr 1987): 833-36.
Morgan, Robert. *Journal of Theological Studies* 39 (Apr 1988): 332-33.

God as the Mystery of the World / *Gott als Geheimnis der Welt* (1977)

Berkhof, H. *Nederlands Theologisch Tijdschrift* 33 (Apr 1979): 154-57.

Bolt, John. *Calvin Theological Journal* 21 (Nov 1986): 250-55.

Brandenburg, Albert. "Oekumene aus der Tiefe der Schrift: Die Gotteslehre als letzer Orientierungspunkt für ale theologischen Positionen." *Rheinischer Merkur*, 26 May 1978, 29.

Brändle, Rudolf. *Kirchenblatt für die reformierte Schweiz* 134/17 (1978).

Bray, G. *Churchman* 98/2 (1984): 167-169.

Buhofer, Ines. *Neue Zürcher Zeitung* 25-26 Mar 1978.

Clark, N. *Baptist Quarterly* 30 (April 1984): 287-89.

Farrelly, J. *Theological Studies* 45 (Summer 1984): 561-63.

Forde, Gerhard O. *World & World* 4 (Fall 1984): 458-61.

Fries, Heinrich. "*Gott als Geheimnis der Welt*: Zum neuesten Werk von Eberhard Jüngel." *Herder Korrespondenz* 31 (1977): 523-29.

Fritzsche, H. G. *Theologische Literaturzeitung* 103 (Dec 1978): 894-97.

Gaybba, Brian. *Journal of Theology for Southern Africa* (Mar 1985): 70-71.

Gisel, Pierre. *Revue de théologie et de philosophie* 110/2 (1978).

Gounelle, A. *Études théologiques et religieuses* 59/1 (1984): 121-22.

Granier, Jean. "La théologie moderne en quête d'une philosophie." *Revue des Sciences philosophiques et théologiques* 68 (Oct 1984): 577-86.

Green, Garrett. "The Mystery of Eberhard Jüngel: A Review of His Theological Program." *Religious Studies Review* 5 (Jan 1979): 34-40.

Henry, Martin. *Irish Theological Quarterly* 46 (1979): 300-304.

Hinson, E. G. *Christian Century* 100 (Dec 21-28, 1983): 1186.

Kasper, Walter. "Abschied vom Gott der Philosophen." *Evangelische Kommentare* 10 (Oct 1977): 622-23.

Keiser, R. Melvin. *Religious Studies Review* 13 (Jan 1987): 57.

Kettler, Christian D. *TSF Bulletin* 9 (Sept/Oct 1985): 32-33.

Klann, Richard. *Concordia Journal* 15 (Oct 1989): 498-501.

Knauer, P. *Theologie und Philosophie* 53/5 (1978): 285-88.

Krupp, R. A. *Christian Librarian* 28 (Nov 1984): 14-15.

La Cugna, Catherine Mowry. *Religious Studies Review* 13 (Apr 1987): 141-42, 144-46.

Lochman, Jan Milič. *Theologische Zeitschrift* 35 (July/Aug 1979): 254-55.

Louth, Andrew. *Journal of Theological Studies* 30 (Apr 1979): 388-92.

MacKinnon, Donald M. *Journal of Theological Studies* NS 36 (Oct 1985): 543-46.

Marceau, William C. *Journal of Ecumenical Studies* 21 (Fall 1984): 768-70.

Marlé, René. "Dieu 'mystère du mond' selon Eberhard Jüngel." *Recherches de Science religieuses* 67 (July-Sept 1979): 357-72.

Marquard, Reiner. *Deutsches Pfarrer Blatt* 78/5 (1978): 156.

Mildenberger, Friedrich. *Lutherische Monatshefte* 17 (June 1978).

Morrison, John D. *Grace Theological Journal* 7 (Spring 1986): 143-46.

Mueller, D. L. *Perspectives in Religious Studies* 8 (Summer 1981): 154-61.

_____. *Review and Expositor* 78 (Summer 1981): 437-40.

Newlands, George. *Expository Times* 95 (Feb 1984): 152-53.

Nieuwenhuizen, M. van den. *Tijschrift voor Theologie* 17 (Oct-Dec 1977): 428-29.

O'Donnell, John. *Heythrop Journal* 27 (Jan 1986): 78-81.

O'Donovan, Leo J. "The Mystery of God as a History of Love: Eberhard Jüngel's Doctrine of God." *Theological Studies* (June 1981): 251-71.

Oliphant, David. *St. Mark's Review* 123-124 (Sept/Dec 1985): 86-87.

Osterhaven, M. Eugene. *Reformed Review* 39 (Winter 1986): 124.

Owen, J. M. *Reformed Theological Review* 43 (May-August 1984): 55-56.

Pambrun, James R. "Eberhard Jüngel's *Gott als Geheimnis der Welt*: An Interpretation." *Église et Théologie* 15 (Oct 1984): 321-46.

Peters, A. "Gedanken zu Eberhard Jüngels These: Gott als Geheimnis der Welt," in *Wer ist das—Gott? Christliche Gotteserkenntnis in der Herausforderungen der Gegenwart*, 178-89, ed. Helmut Burkhardt (Giessen: Brunnen Verlag, 1982).

Peters, Ted. *Currents in Theology and Mision* 11 (Oct 1984): 312-13.

Rey, B. *Mélanges de Science religieuse* 40 (Sept 1983): 176-79.

Richard, Jean R. "Théologie évangélique et théologie philosophique: à propos d'Eberhard Jüngel." *Science et Esprit* 38 (Jan-Apr 1986): 5-30.

Rohls, J. *Neue Zeitschrift für systematische Theologie und Religionsphilosophie* 22/3 (1980): 282-96.

Rumscheidt, H. Martin. "Theology between Scylla and Chrybdis." *Journal of Religion* 59 (July 1979): 347-51.

Scharlemann, Robert P. *Interpretation* 40 (Jan 1986): 77-79.

Seim, J. *Evangelische Theologie* 38 (May/June 1978): 269-79.

Sheridan, D. P. *Horizons* 11 (Spring 1984): 184-85.

Smolík, Josef. *Communio Viatorum* 24/3 (1981): 193-94.

Stickelberger, Hans. "Unbestechliche Theologie oder 'durch denkende Abstraktion die Konkretheit zu steigern': Marginalien zu Eberhard Jüngels 'Gott als Gehemins der Welt'." *Reformatio* 27 (Oct 1978): 585-91.

Theological Students Fellowship Bulletin 9 (Sept/Oct 1985): 32-33.

Wainwright, Geoffrey. "Recent Foreign Theology: Historical and Systematic." *Expository Times* 89 (Nov 1977): 41.

Webster, John B. *Scottish Journal of Theology* 39/4 (1986): 551-56.

Williams, Rowan. *Downside Review* 96 (Oct 1978): 317.

Karl Barth, a Theological Legacy / *Barth-Studien* (1982)
Adriaanse, H. J. *Norsk Teologisk Tidsskift* 39 (Jan 1985): 68-70.
Barth, U. "Zur Barth-Deutung Eberhard Jüngels." *Theologische Zeitscheift* 40 (1984): 296-320, 394-415.
Blaser, K. *Revue de théologie et de philosophie* 115/3 (1983): 309-10.
Dean, Eric. *Church History* 57 (June 1988): 251.
Fiddes, Paul S. *Journal of Theological Studies* 40 (Oct 1989): 696-99.
Fischer, Hermann. *Theologische Literaturzeitung* 110 (July 1985): 549-52.
Ford, David F. *Scottish Journal of Theology* 43/2 (1990): 287-88.
Goetz, Ronald G. *Journal of Religion* 68 (July 1988): 464-65.
Gounelle, André. *Études théologiques et religieuses* 63/1 (1988): 142-143.
Henry, David Paul. *Interpretation* 42 (July 1988): 324-26.
Hodgson, Peter C. *Religious Studies Review* 13 (Oct 1987): 334-35.
Journal of Psychology and Christianity 6 (Feb 1987): 77.
McKelway, Alexander J. "Karl Barth and Politics." *Perspectives in Religious Studies* 15 (Fall 1988): 269-281.
_____. *Theology Today* 44 (January 1988): 546-49.
Mueller, David L. *Review and Expositor* 85 (Summer 1987): 525-26.
Muller, R. A. *Reformed Journal* 37 (Oct 1987): 28-31.
Nederlands Theologisch Tijdschrift 39 (Jan 1985): 68-70.
Palmer, Russell W. *Theological Studies* 48 (Dec 1987): 792-93.
Placher, William C. *Encounter* 48 (Autumn 1987): 424-25.
Reformed Journal 37 (Oct 1987): 28, 30-31.
Reid, J. K. S. "Jüngel on Barth." *Expository Times* 99 (Dec 1987): 91.
Sanders, Carl. *Criswell Theological Review* 2 (Spring 1988): 451-52.
Schwoebel, Christoph. *Theology* 91 (May 1988): 218-19.
Spykman, Gordon J. *Calvin Theological Journal* 23 (Apr 1988): 80-82.
Stewart, William. *Scottish Journal of Religious Studies* 9 (Autumn 1988): 126.
Stroble, Paul E. *Christian Century* 104 (21 Oct 1987): 920.
Webster, John. *Themelios* 13 (Apr/May 1988): 104-105.
Winzeler, Peter. "'Ökumenische Theologie' ohne Sozialismus? Kritische Anmerkungen zu Eberhard Jüngels *Barth-Studien*." *Evangelische Theologie* 44 (May/June 1984): 306-12.
Wood, Ralph C. *Books and Religion* 16 (Winter 1989): 5, 26, 29-31.
Zimany, Roland Daniel. *Journal of the American Academy of Religion* 57 (Spring 1989): 200-202.

Metapher (1974)
Krückenberg, Eduard. *Theologische Revue* 72/4 (1976): 300-301.

Paulus und Jesus (1962)
Baasland, E. *Theologi og Kirke* 43 (1972): 72.
Bruce, F. F. *Evangelical Quarterly* 35 (Apr 1963): 121-22.
Käsemann, Ernst. *Theologische Literaturzeitung* 90 (Mar 1965): 184-87.
Norsk Teologisk Tidsskrift 84/1 (1993): 26.
Schoeps, H. J. *Zeitschrift für Religions- und Geistesgeschichte* 33/1 (1981): 78-79.
Schwarz, H. *Zeitschrift für Religions- und Geistesgeschichte* 15/4 (1963): 389-92.
Winter, P. *Anglican Theological Review* 47 (Jan 1965): 111- 13.

Die Praktische Theologie zwischen Wissenschaft und Praxis (1968)
Krause, G. *Theologische Literaturzeitung* 94 (Feb 1969): 147-49.
Lavalette, H. de. *Recherches de Science religieuses* 58 (Apr-June 1970): 314-17.

Predigten (1968)
Winkler, E. *Theologische Literaturzeitung* 94 (Oct 1969): 790-91.

Theological Essays (1989)
Bauman, Michael. *Journal of the Evangelical Theological Society* 34 (Dec 1991): 555-57.
Gaybba, Brian. *Journal of Theology for Southern Africa* 77 (Dec 1991): 91-92.
Gunton, Colin. *Expository Times* (Nov 1990): 57.
Hart, Trevor A. *Themelios* 17 (Apr/May 1992): 30.
Mattes, Mark. *Journal of Religion* 71 (July 1991): 444-45.
McKelway, Alexander J. *Princeton Seminary Bulletin* 13/2 (1992): 235-37.
Migliore, Daniel L. *Interpretation* 45 (Jan 1991): 94-96.
Pacifica 4 (Fall 1991): 102-105.
Newlands, George M. *Theology* 93 (July/Aug 1990): 309-10.
Stroble, Paul E. *Critical Review of Books in Religion* (1991): 443-45.
Thompson, John. *Irish Theological Quarterly* 56/1 (1990): 71-72.
Zimany, Roland Daniel. *Dialog* 31 (Winter 1992): 74-75.

Theologische Enzyklopädie (1984)
Alemany, Jose J. *Estudios Eclesiásticos* 61 (Jan-Mar 1986): 114-15.
Cahill, Joseph P. *Religious Studies and Theology* 5 (May 1985): 103.
Études théologiques et religieuses 60/3 (1985): 450-52, 486.
Haerle, Wilfred. *Regulae Benedicti Studia* 13 (1984): 162-64.
Norsk Teologisk Tidsskrift 86/3 (1985): 188-92.

Theologische Quartalschrift 165/1 (1985): 67.

"The Truth of Life" (1976)
Rogers, Jack. *Journal of Religion* 58 (Jan 1978): 71-72.

Tübinger Theologie im 20. Jahrhundert (1978)
Neufeld, K. H. *Gregorianum* 60/2 (1979): 389-90.
Rasmussen, T. *Norsk Teologisk Tidsskrift* 81/1 (1980): 60- 63.
Scharlemann, Robert P. *Religious Studies Review* 6 (Apr 1980): 132.

Verifikationen (1982)
Christoffersen, S. A. *Norsk Theologisk Tidsskrift* 85/1 (1984): 64-67.
Fritzsche, H. G. *Theologische Literaturzeitung* 108 (Apr 1983): 38-39.
Klein, J. L. *Études théologiques et religieuses* 60/2 (1985): 341-43.
Neufeld, K. H. *Gregorianum* 64/3 (1983): 576-77.
Perlitt, F. *Theologische Rundschau* 49/1 (1984): 91-104.
Schmitt, H. C. *Zeitschrift für die alttestamentliche Wissenschaft* 95/3 (1983): 474.

Der Wahrheit zum Recht Verhilfen (1977)
Lohse, Eduard. "Abbau der Berührungsangst." *Lutherische Monatshefte* 17 (Apr 1978): 223-24.

Was ist ein Sakrament? (1971)
Kiesling, Christopher. *Journal of Ecumenical Studies* 12 (Winter 1975): 96.
Kühn, U. *Theologische Literaturzeitung* 99 (March 1974): 223-25.

Wertlose Wahrheit (1990)
Wainwright, Geoffrey. *Expository Times* 102 (Aug 1991): 335.

C. Other Sources

Aristotle. *The Works of Aristotle.* Edited by W. D. Ross. Vol. 11. Oxford: Clarendon Press, 1924.

Austin, J. L. *How to Do Things with Words.* New York: Oxford, 1962.

Barth, Karl. *Church Dogmatics.* I/1. Translated by G. T. Thomson. Edinburgh: T.&T. Clark, 1936.

_____. *Church Dogmatics.* I/2. Translated by G. T. Thomson and Harold Knight. New York: Scribner's, 1956.

_____. *Church Dogmatics.* II/1. Translated by T. H. L. Parker, W. B. Johnston, Harold Knight, and J. L. M. Haire. New York: Scribner's, 1957.

_____. *Church Dogmatics.* III/1. Translated by J. W. Edwards, O. Bussey, and Harold Knight. Edinburgh: T.&T. Clark, 1958.

_____. *Church Dogmatics.* III/3. Translated by G. W. Bromiley and R. J. Ehrlich. Edinburgh: T.&T. Clark, 1960.

_____. *Church Dogmatics.* IV/3. Translated by G. W. Bromiley. Edinburgh: T.&T. Clark, 1961.

_____. *The Epistle to the Romans.* Translated by Edwyn C. Hoskyns. London: Oxford, 1933.

_____. *How I Changed My Mind.* Introduction and Epilogue by John D. Godsey. Edinburgh: Saint Andrew Press, 1969.

_____. "No!" In *Natural Theology.* Edited by John Baillie. London: Geoffrey Bles, 1946.

Bartsch, Hans Werner, ed. *Kerygma and Mythos.* Hamburg-Volksdorf: Herbert Reich, 1952. *Kerygma and Myth: A Theological Debate.* Translated by Reginald H. Fuller. Harper Torchbooks 80. New York: Harper & Row, 1961.

Boman, Thorlief. *Hebrew Thought Compared with Greek.* Translated by Jules L. Moreau. Library of History and Doctrine. Philadelphia: Westminster, 1960.

Bonhoeffer, Dietrich. *Letters and Papers from Prison.* Edited by Eberhard Bethge. New York: Macmillan, 1971.

Bultmann, Rudolf. *Essays: Philosophical and Theological.* Translated by C. G. Greig. New York: Macmillan, 1955.

_____. *Existence and Faith: Shorter Writings of Rudolf Bultmann.* Translated and edited by Schubert M. Ogden. Meridian Books / Living Age Books. Cleveland and New York: World Publishing, 1960.

_____. *History and Eschatology.* Edinburgh: University Press, 1957.

_____. *Jesus and the Word.* Translated by Louise Pettibone Smith and Erminie Huntress Lantero. New York: Scribner's, 1958.

_____. *Jesus Christ and Mythology.* New York: Scribner's, 1958.

_____. *Theology of the New Testament*. Translated by Kendrick Grobel. Two volumes. New York: Scribner's, 1951 and 1955.

Dupré, Louis. Review of *The Self-Embodiment of God*, by Thomas J. J. Altizer. *Cross Currents* 27 (Winter 1977-78): 468-69.

Ebeling, Gerhard. *Introduction to a Theological Theory of Language*. Translated by R. A. Wilson. London: Collins, 1973.

_____. *The Nature of Faith*. Translated by Ronald Gregor Smith. Philadelphia: Fortress, 1961.

_____. *Word and Faith*. Translated by James W. Leitch. Philadelphia: Fortress, 1963.

Fuchs, Ernst. *Hermeneutik*. Fourth edition. Tübingen: J. C. B. Mohr (Paul Siebeck), 1970.

_____. *Studies of the Historical Jesus*. Translated by Andrew Scobie. Studies in Biblical Theology 42. London: SCM; Naperville IL: Alec R. Allenson, 1964.

_____. *Zum hermeneutischen Problem in der Theologie: Die existentiale Interpretation*. Gesammelte Aufsätze. Volume 1. Second edition, revised. Tübingen: J. C. B. Mohr (Paul Siebeck), 1965.

Funk, Robert W. *Language, Hermeneutic, and Word of God: The Problem of Language in the New Testament and Contemporary Theology*. New York: Harper & Row, 1966.

Gertz, Bernhard. *Glaubenswelt als Analogie: Die theologische Analogie-Lehre Erich Przywaras und ihr Ort in der Auseinandersetzung um die analogia - fidei*. Düsseldorf: Patmos-Verlag, 1969.

Gilkey, Langdon. *Naming the Whirlwind: The Renewal of God-Language*. Indianapolis: Bobbs-Merrill, 1969.

Green, Garrett. "The Mystery of Eberhard Jüngel: A Review of His Theological Program." *Religious Studies Review* 5 (January 1979): 34-40.

Heidegger, Martin. *Being and Time*. Translated by John Macquarrie and Edward Robinson. New York: Harper & Row, 1962.

_____. *Existence and Being*. Edited by Werner Brock. London: Vision Press, 1949.

_____. *Holzwege*. Frankfurt-on-Main: Vittorio Klostermann, 1950.

_____. "Nur noch ein Gott kann uns retten." *Spiegel*, 31 May 1976, 193ff.

_____. *Phänomenologie und Theologie*. Frankfurt-on-Main: Vittorio Klostermann, 1970.

_____. *The Piety of Thinking: Essays by Martin Heidegger*. Translated and edited by James G. Hart and John C. Maraldo. Bloomington: Indiana University Press, 1976.

_____. *Platons Lehre von der Wahrheit. Mit einem Brief über den "Humanismus."* Bern: Verlag A. Francke, 1947. Translated in part by Edgar Lohner

as "Letter on Humanism" in *Philosophy in the Twentieth Century*. Volume 2. Edited by William Barrett and H. D. Aiken. New York: Random, 1962.
_____. *Vorträge und Aufsätze*. Pfullingen: Günther Neske, 1954.
_____. *Was ist Metaphysik?* Eleventh edition. Frankfurt-on-Main: Vittorio Klostermann, 1975. ET: original lecture (1929) and postscript (1943) translated by R. F. C. Hull and Alan Crick as "What Is Metaphysics?" in *Existence and Being*. Introduction (1949) translated by Walter Kaufmann as "The Way Back into the Ground of Metaphysics" in his *Existentialism from Dostoevsky to Sartre*. New York: Meridian Books, 1956.
_____. *What Is Philosophy?* Translated by William Kluback and Jean T. Wilde. New York: Twayne, 1958.
Hordern, William E. *A Layman's Guide to Protestant Theology*. Revised edition. New York: Macmillan, 1968.
Jenson, Robert. *God after God: The God of the Past and the God of the Future, Seen in the Work of Karl Barth*. New York: Bobbs-Merrill, 1969.
Kasper, Walter. "Abschied vom Gott der Philosophen." *Evangelische Kommentare* 10 (October 1977): 622-23.
Kaufman, Gordon D. *An Essay on Theological Method*. American Academy of Religion Studies in Religion 11. Missoula MT: Scholars Press, 1975.
Livingston, James C. *Modern Christian Thought: From the Enlightenment to Vatican II*. New York: Macmillan, 1971.
Macquarrie, John. *Thinking About God*. New York: Harper & Row, 1975.
Moltmann, Jürgen. *The Crucified God: The Cross of Christ as the Foundation and Criticism of Christian Theology*. Translated by R. A. Wilson and John Bowden. New York: Harper & Row, 1974.
Pannenberg, Wolfhart. *Theology and the Philosophy of Science*. Translated by Francis McDonagh. Philadelphia: Westminster, 1976.
Perrin, Norman. *Jesus and the Language of the Kingdom: Symbol and Metaphor in New Testament Interpretation*. Philadelphia: Fortress, 1976.
Plass, Ewald M., editor. *What Luther Says*. St. Louis: Concordia Publishing House, 1959.
Poteat, William H. *Polanyian Meditations: In Search of a Post-Critical Logic*. Durham NC: Duke University Press, 1985.
Rahner, Karl. *Nature and Grace*. Translated by Dinah Wharton. London: Sheed and Ward, 1963.
_____. *The Trinity*. Translated by Joseph Donceel. New York: Herder and Herder, 1970.
Richardson, William J. *Heidegger: Through Phenomenology to Thought*. The Hague: Martinus Nijhoff, 1963.
Ricoeur, Paul. "Biblical Hermeneutics," *Semeia* 4 (1975): 29-148.

_____. *Interpretation Theory: Discourse and the Surplus of Meaning.* Fort Worth: Texas Christian University Press, 1976.

_____. "Naming God." Translated by David Pellauer. *Union Seminary Quarterly Review* 34 (Summer 1979): 215-27.

Robinson, James M., and John B. Cobb, Jr., eds. *The Later Heidegger and Theology.* New Frontiers in Theology 1. New York: Harper & Row, 1963.

_____. *The New Hermeneutic.* New Frontiers in Theology 2. New York: Harper & Row, 1964.

Schweitzer, Albert. *The Quest of the Historical Jesus: A Critical Study of Its Progress from Reimarus to Wrede.* Translated by William Montgomery. Pbk. repr. New York: Macmillan, 1961 (=London: Macmillan, 1910).

Smart, James D. *The Divided Mind of Modern Theology: Karl Barth and Rudolf Bultmann, 1908–1933.* Philadelphia: Westminster, 1967.

Tillich, Paul. *Systematic Theology.* Volumes 1 and 2. Chicago: University of Chicago Press, 1951 and 1957.

Tracy, David. *Blessed Rage for Order: The New Pluralism in Theology.* A Crossroad Book. New York: Seabury, 1975.

Wainwright, Geoffrey. "Today's Word for Today: Eberhard Jüngel," *Expository Times* 92 (Feb 1981): 131-35.

Wittgenstein, Ludwig. *Philosophical Investigations.* Translated by G. E. M. Anscombe. Third edition. New York: Macmillan, 1958.

Zimany, Roland Daniel. "Human Love and the Trinity: Jüngel's Perception." *Dialog* 21 (Summer 1982): 220-23.

Index

DATE DUE
